NAWAWĪ AL-JĀWĪ'S

TĪJĀN AL-DARĀRĪ

NAWAWĪ AL-JĀWĪ'S TĪJĀN AL-DARĀRĪ

A Commentary on al-Bājūrī's Treatise on Monotheism

Shaykh Muḥammad Nawawī al-Jāwī

Translation with notes by
MUSA FURBER

ISBN   978-1-944904-26-5 (paper)

Published by:
Islamosaic
islamosaic.com
publications@islamosaic.com

All praise is to Allah alone, the Lord of the Worlds
And may He send His benedictions upon
our master Muḥammad, his Kin
and his Companions
and grant them
peace

TRANSLITERATION KEY

ء   ' (A distinctive glottal stop made at the bottom of the throat.)

ا   ā, a

ب   b

ت   t

ث   th (Pronounced like the *th* in *think*.)

ج   j

ح   ḥ (A hard *h* sound made at the Adam's apple in the middle of the throat.)

خ   kh (Pronounced like *ch* in Scottish *loch*.)

د   d

ذ   dh (Pronounced like *th* in *this*.)

ر   r (A slightly trilled *r* made behind the upper front teeth.)

ز   z

س   s

ش   sh

ص   ṣ (An emphatic *s* pronounced behind the upper front teeth.)

ض   ḍ (An emphatic *d*-like sound made by pressing the entire tongue against the upper palate.)

ط   ṭ (An emphatic *t* sound produced behind the front teeth.)

ظ   ẓ (An emphatic *th* sound, like the *th* in *this*, made behind the front teeth.)

ع   ' (A distinctive Semitic sound made in the middle of the throat and sounding to a Western ear more like a vowel than a consonant.)

غ   gh (A guttural sound made at the top of the throat, resembling the untrilled German and French *r*.)

ف   f

ق   q (A hard *k* sound produced at the back of the palate.)

ك   k

ل   l

م   m

ن   n

ه   h (This sound is like the English *h* but has more body. It is made at the very bottom of the throat and pronounced at the beginning, middle, and ends of words.)

و   ū, u

ي   ī, i, y

ﷺ   A supplication made after mention of the Prophet Muḥammad, translated as "May Allah bless him and grant him peace."

CONTENTS

الْمُحْتَوَيَاتُ

TRANSLATOR'S PREFACE

[مُقَدِّمَةُ المُتَرجِمِ]

In the name of Allah the Most Merciful and Compassionate

This book presents Shaykh Muḥammad Nawawī al-Jāwī al-Bantanī's *Tījān al-darārī*, a commentary on Imam Ibrāhīm al-Bājūrī's (1198–1276 AH/1787–1861 CE) *Risālah fi-t-tawḥīd*, which provides an introduction to the creed that is essential for all responsible Muslims to know, along with their rational proofs. It is more advanced than his *Al-Nahjah al-jayyidah li-ḥall alfāẓ Nuqāwat al-ʿaqīdah* (published as *The Correct Approach to Unpacking "The Select Creed"*) in that it includes rational proofs. However, our book has a narrower focus in that it concentrates on matters related to the Divine and to the Prophets (may Allah bless them and give them peace) and does not include much of the supplementary materials included in *The Correct Approach*.

ABOUT THE AUTHOR

The author of the commentary is Shaykh Abū ʿAbd al-Muʿṭī Muḥammad Nawawī bin ʿUmar bin ʿArabi bin ʿAlī al-Bantanī al-Jāwī. The last two words in his name refer to him originating from Banten, the westernmost province of the island of Java, in Indonesia. He was born in 1230 AH/1813 CE, in the Tanara district located on the central north coast of Banten, in present day Indonesia. He was a descendent of Sharif Hedayat Allāh, also known as Sunan Gunungjati and one of the "Wali Songo": the nine *awliyāʾ*, or friends of Allah, who were influential in spreading Islam in the Malay world. Through Sharif Hedayat Allāh, the Shaykh is a descendent of the Prophet (may Allah bless him and give him peace).

The Shaykh's father and several of his ancestors were also scholars. The Shaykh began his religious studies with his father and then studied with other shaykhs in his region. He performed Ḥajj at the age of fifteen. Afterwards, he remained in Mecca an additional three years to study with its scholars. He then returned to Banten. Due to the state of affairs under Dutch colonialism, he soon returned to Mecca where he spent the rest of his life studying, teaching, and writing.

The Shaykh authored approximately forty works in various subjects, including creed (*'aqīdah*), theology (*kalām*), Qu'ranic exegesis (*tafsīr*), jurisprudence (*fiqh*), principles of jurisprudence (*uṣūl al-fiqh*), and spiritual purification and excellence (*tazkiyah, iḥsān,* and *taṣawwuf*). Several of his books spanned multiple subjects, namely creed, jurisprudence, and spiritual purification and excellence. Many of his books were published during his lifetime; others remain unpublished. His books were praised by *'ulamā'* in the west as well as in the east.

He is perhaps best known outside the Malay world for *Murāḥ labīb*, an exegesis of the Qu'ran; *Qūt al-ḥabīb al-gharīb*, a meta-commentary on Ibn Qāsim al-Ghazzī's *Fatḥ al-qarīb*, itself a commentary on Abū Shujā''s conspectus on Shāfi'ī jurisprudence *Ghāyat al-taqrīb*; *Marāqī al-'ubūdiyyah*, a commentary on Imām al-Ghazālī's *Bidāyat al-hidāyah*; and *Nūr al-ẓalām*, a commentary on Shaykh Aḥmad al-Marzūqī al-Mālikī's versification of creed *'Aqīdat al-'awwām*.

The Shaykh passed away in his home in Mecca, in 1314 AH/1896/97 CE.

ABOUT THE AUTHOR

The title of our book is *Tījān al-darārī*, or *The Stellar Crowns*. The text is approximately 8,850 words long, with 960 being Imam al-Bājūrī's text. Shaykh Muḥammad Nawawī finished our book in 1297 AH. It was first published within his lifetime in 1301 AH.

Al-Bājūrī's risālah is a concise creedal primer organised around fifty points of doctrine. Forty-one concern Allah (Exalted is He):

twenty necessary attributes — one essential, five negative, seven entitative, and seven qualitative — their twenty impossible contraries, and one point of rational possibility. Nine concern the Messengers: four necessary attributes (truthfulness, trustworthiness, conveyance, and acuity), their four contraries, and one point of possibility. Each attribute is stated with its contrary and a brief proof. The risālah closes with the Prophet's lineage, the Basin and the Greatest Intercession, the twenty-five prophets named in the Qur'ān, the superiority of the first three generations, and the Prophet's children.

Shaykh Muḥammad Nawawī al-Jāwī's commentary expands this into a full doctrinal manual. He supplies technical definitions the matn takes for granted — the three rational categories, decisive knowledge, and general versus detailed proofs. He unpacks each attribute with extended discussion: the ten scenarios negated by dissimilarity, the five quantities negated by unicity, the proofs of mutual hindrance and coincidence, the fourfold classification of causation, and the seven linkages of capability. He distinguishes will from command, approval, and knowledge, and clarifies pre-eternal versus uttered speech. In the prophetic section, he differentiates rational from legislative proofs, details what is and is not possible for the Messengers, and reproduces the full intercession narration. The concluding pages expand on the hierarchy of the Companions, the caliphate, and the Prophet's household.

ABOUT THE TRANSLATION

The initial translation was completed on 29 Jumādā al-Thānī 1444 AH/22 Jan 2023 CE in approximately 16,000 words of English.

I referenced several editions while translating this book, including the Muṣṭafā al-Bābī al-Ḥalabī wa Awlāduhi edition published in Cairo in 1342 AH; the Maktabah al-Hāshimiyyah edition published in Turkey in Istanbul in 2013 CE; the Maktabah At-Turmusy Littarots edition published in Jawa Barat, Indonesia, in 1442 AH/2021 CE; and an undated edition published by Pondok Pesantren al-Birr Pandaan Pasuruan of East Java, Indonesia.

Much of Shaykh Muḥammad Nawawī's commentary matches what is in Imām al-Bājūrī's *Tuḥfat al-murīd* and *Taḥqīq al-maqām*. Most also matches what he has in *Fatḥ al-majīd,* his commentary on Shaykh Aḥmad al-Naḥrāwī's *Al-Durr al-farīd.* I have provided cross-references to *Tuḥfat al-murīd* and *Fatḥ al-majīd* where I have found them. I sometimes also provide reference to Imām al-Bājūrī's *Taḥqīq al-maqām,* and to Shaykh Muḥammad Nawawī's other books.

Something to note is that when referencing *Tuḥfat al-murīd,* I give the relevant verse number from Imām al-Laqqānī's *Jawharat al-tawḥīd* as well as the paragraph number in Shaykh Ali Gomaa's edition of *Tuḥfat al-murīd* (Dār al-Salām) since its paragraph numbers allow for a more precise referencing than a page number, and a verse number facilitates locating the material in other editions of *Tuḥfat al-murīd* and in other commentaries on the *Jawharah.*

I have also given references for hadiths mentioned explicitly or alluded to in the book. Indexes and online search make it relatively easy to locate hadith texts, so I often limit my referencing to the major hadith collections containing that hadith or to a meta-compendium, such as Imām al-Suyūṭī's *Jāmiʿ al-aḥādīth.*

* * *

I am very thankful for the individuals who supported this project. I would like to thank Anaz, Asif, and Sumayah for assisting with the finishing touches.

May Allah bless the author of our text Shaykh Muḥammad Nawawī, those mentioned in the text or footnotes, those who contributed in any way to bringing it to English readers, and their fellow readers. And may He forgive the translator and protect readers from his copious shortcomings.

MUSA FURBER
CYBERJAYA, MALAYSIA
1447 AH/2026 CE

IMĀM IBRĀHĪM AL-BĀJŪRĪ'S
TREATISE ON MONOTHEISM

Risālah fi-t-tawḥīd

بِسْمِ اللَّهِ الرَّحْمَنِ الرَّحِيْمِ

In the name of Allah, the All-Merciful, the Most Merciful

الْحَمْدُ لِلَّهِ رَبِّ الْعَالَمِيْنَ، وَالصَّلَاةُ وَالسَّلَامُ عَلَى رَسُوْلِ اللَّهِ ﷺ.

Praise be to Allah, Lord of the worlds. May blessings and peace be upon the Messenger of Allah (may Allah bless him and give him peace).

وَبَعْـدَ: فَيَقُـوْلُ فَقِيْـرُ رَحْمَـةِ رَبِّـهِ الْخَبِيْـرِ الْبَصِيْـرِ إِبْرَاهِيْمُ الْبَاجُـوْرِيُّ ذُوْ التَّقْصِيْرِ: طَلَبَ مِنِّي بَعْضُ الْإِخْوَانِ – أَصْلَحَ اللَّهُ لِي وَلَهُمْ الْحَالَ وَالشَّأْنَ – أَنْ أَكْتُبَ لَهُ رِسَـالَةً لَطِيْفَةً تَشْـتَمِلُ عَلَى صِفَاتِ الْمَوْلَى وَأَضْدَادِهَا، وَمَا يَجُـوْزُ فِي حَقِّهِ تَعَالَى، وَعَلَى مَا يَجِبُ فِي حَقِّ الرُّسُـلِ وَمَا يَسْـتَحِيْلُ فِي حَقِّهِم وَمَا يَجُوْزُ، فَأَجَبْتُهُ إِلَى ذَلِكَ فَقُلْتُ وَبِاللَّهِ التَّوْفِيْقُ:

To proceed: The one in need of the mercy of his Lord, the All-Aware, the All-Seeing – Ibrāhīm al-Bājūrī, the one given to falling short – says: Some of the brethren – may Allah mend our state and affair – requested that I write for him a light monograph containing the attributes of the Lord, their contraries, and what is possible for Him (Exalted is He); what is necessary for the Messengers, what is impossible for them, and what is possible.

So I granted his request to do this and said – and by Allah is success –:

يَجِـبُ عَلَـى كُلِّ مُكَلَّـفٍ أَنْ يَعْرِفَ مَـا يَجِـبُ فِي حَقِّهِ تَعَالَـى وَمَا يَسْتَحِيْلُ وَمَا يَجُوْزُ.

It is required of every legally responsible person to be cognisant of what is necessary for Allah (Exalted is He), what is impossible, and what is possible.

فَيَجِبُ فِي حَقِّهِ تَعَالَى الْوُجُوْدُ وَضِدُّهُ الْعَدَمُ. وَالدَّلِيْلُ عَلَى ذَلِكَ وُجُوْدُ هَذِهِ الْمَخْلُوْقَاتِ.

Existence (*wujūd*) is necessary for Allah (Exalted is He). Its contrary is nonexistence (*'adam*). The proof of this is the existence of created things (*makhlūqāt*).

وَيَجِبُ فِي حَقِّهِ تَعَالَى الْقِدَمُ، وَمَعْنَاهُ أَنَّهُ تَعَالَى لَا أَوَّلَ لَهُ. وَضِدُّهُ الْحُدُوْثُ. وَالدَّلِيْلُ عَلَى ذَلِكَ أَنَّهُ لَوْ كَانَ حَادِثًا لَاحْتَاجَ إِلَى مُحْدِثٍ، وَهُوَ مُحَالٌ.

Pre-eternity (*qidam*) is necessary for Allah (Exalted is He). Its meaning is that He has no beginning. Its contrary is origination. The proof of this is that if He had been originated, He would require an originator (*muḥdith*). But that is impossible.

وَيَجِبُ فِي حَقِّهِ تَعَالَى الْبَقَاءُ، وَمَعْنَاهُ أَنَّهُ تَعَالَى لَا آخِرَ لَهُ. وَالدَّلِيْلُ عَلَى ذَلِكَ: أَنَّهُ لَوْ كَانَ فَانِيًا لَكَانَ حَادِثًا، وَهُوَ مُحَالٌ.

Everlastingness (*baqā'*) is necessary for Allah (Exalted is He). Its meaning is that He (Exalted is He) has no end. The proof of this is that if He were transient, He would be originated. But that is impossible.

وَيَجِبُ فِي حَقِّهِ تَعَالَى الْمُخَالَفَةُ لِلْحَوَادِثِ. وَمَعْنَاهُ أَنَّهُ تَعَالَى لَيْسَ مُمَاثِلًا لِلْحَوَادِثِ فَلَيْسَ لَهُ يَدٌ وَلَا عَيْنٌ وَلَا أُذُنٌ وَلَا غَيْرُ ذَلِكَ مِنْ صِفَاتِ الْحَوَادِثِ. وَضِدُّهَا الْمُمَاثِلَةُ. وَالدَّلِيْلُ عَلَى ذَلِكَ أَنَّهُ لَوْ كَانَ مُمَاثِلًا لِلْحَوَادِثِ لَكَانَ حَادِثًا، وَهُوَ مُحَالٌ.

Dissimilarity to originated things (*mukhālafah li-l-ḥawādith*) is necessary for Allah (Exalted is He). Its meaning is that Allah (Exalted is He) is not similar to them. He does not have a hand, eye, ear, or anything else among the attributes of originated things. Its contrary is likeness to originated things (*mumāthalah li-l-ḥawādith*). The proof of this is that if He were similar to originated things, He would be originated. But that is impossible.

وَيَجِبُ فِي حَقِّهِ تَعَالَى الْقِيَامُ بِالنَّفْسِ، وَمَعْنَاهُ أَنَّهُ تَعَالَى لَا يَفْتَقِرُ إِلَى مَحَلٍّ وَلَا إِلَى مُخَصِّصٍ. وَضِدُّهُ الِاحْتِيَاجُ إِلَى الْمَحَلِّ وَالْمُخَصِّصِ. وَالدَّلِيلُ عَلَى ذَلِكَ أَنَّهُ لَوِ احْتَاجَ إِلَى مَحَلٍّ لَكَانَ صِفَةً وَكَوْنُهُ صِفَةً مُحَالٌ وَلَوِ احْتَاجَ إِلَى مُخَصِّصٍ لَكَانَ حَادِثًا، وَكَوْنُهُ حَادِثًا مُحَالٌ.

Self-subsistence (*qiyām bi-l-nafs*) is necessary for Allah (Exalted is He). Its meaning is that Allah (Exalted is He) does not need a substrate or a specifier. Its contrary is needing a substrate and a specifier. The proof of this is that if He needed a substrate (*maḥall*) He would be an attribute. But His being an attribute is impossible. And if He needed a specifier (*mukhaṣṣiṣ*) He would be originated. But His being originated is impossible.

وَيَجِبُ فِي حَقِّهِ تَعَالَى الْوَحْدَانِيَّةُ فِي الذَّاتِ وَفِي الصِّفَاتِ وَفِي الْأَفْعَالِ، وَمَعْنَى الْوَحْدَانِيَّةِ فِي الذَّاتِ أَنَّهَا لَيْسَتْ مُرَكَّبَةً مِنْ أَجْزَاءٍ مُتَعَدِّدَةٍ، وَمَعْنَى الْوَحْدَانِيَّةِ فِي الصِّفَاتِ أَنَّهُ لَيْسَ لَهُ صِفَتَانِ فَأَكْثَرُ مِنْ جِنْسٍ وَاحِدٍ كَقُدْرَتَيْنِ، وهكذا، وَلَيْسَ لِغَيْرِهِ صِفَة تشابه صفته تَعَالَى، وَمَعْنَى الْوَحْدَانِيَّة فِي الْأَفْعَالِ أَنَّهُ لَيْسَ لِغَيْرِهِ فِعْلٌ مِنَ الْأَفْعَالِ. وَضِدُّهَا التَّعَدُّدُ. وَالدَّلِيلُ عَلَى ذَلِكَ أَنَّهُ لَوْ كَانَ مُتَعَدِّدًا لَمْ يُوجَدْ شَيْءٌ مِنْ هَذِهِ الْمَخْلُوقَاتِ.

Unicity (*waḥdāniyyah*) in His entity, His attributes, and His actions is necessary for Allah (Exalted is He). The meaning of unicity in entity is that it is not composed of multiple elements. The meaning of unicity in attributes is that He does not have two or more attributes of the same kind, such as two capabilities, and so on. And none other than Him (Exalted is He) has an attribute resembling His attribute. The meaning of unicity in actions is that no one else performs any action. Its contrary is plurality (*taʿaddud*). The proof of this is that if He were multiple none of these created things would exist.

وَيَجِبُ فِي حَقِّهِ تَعَالَى الْقُدْرَةُ، وَهِيَ صِفَةٌ قَدِيمَةٌ قَائِمَةٌ بِذَاتِهِ تَعَالَى يُوجِدُ بِهَا وَيُعْدِمُ. وَضِدُّهَا الْعَجْزُ. وَالدَّلِيلُ عَلَى ذَلِكَ أَنَّهُ لَوْ كَانَ عَاجِزًا لَمْ يُوجَدْ شَيْءٌ مِنْ هَذِهِ الْمَخْلُوقَاتِ.

Capability (*qudrah*) is necessary for Allah (Exalted is He). It is a pre-eternal attribute subsistent in His essence through which He brings into existence and annihilates. Its contrary is incapacity (*'ajz*). The proof of this is that if He were incapable, none of these created things would exist.

وَيَجِبُ فِي حَقِّهِ تَعَالَى الْإِرَادَةُ، وَهِيَ صِفَةٌ قَدِيمَةٌ قَائِمَةٌ بِذَاتِهِ تَعَالَى يُخَصِّصُ بِهَا الْمُمْكِنَ بِالْوُجُودِ أَوْ بِالْعَدَمِ أَوْ بِالْغِنَى أَوْ بِالْفَقْرِ أَوْ بِالْعِلْمِ أَوْ بِالْجَهْلِ إِلَى غَيْرِ ذَلِكَ. وَضِدُّهَا الْكَرَاهَةُ. وَالدَّلِيلُ عَلَى ذَلِكَ أَنَّهُ لَوْ كَانَ كَارِهًا لَكَانَ عَاجِزًا، وَكَوْنُهُ عَاجِزًا مُحَالٌ.

Will (*irādah*) is necessary for Allah (Exalted is He). It is a pre-eternal attribute subsistent in His divine essence (Exalted is He) through which He specifies contingent things with existence or nonexistence, with wealth or poverty, with knowledge or ignorance, and so forth. Its contrary is aversion (*karāhah*). The proof of this is that if He were averse He would be incapable (*'ājiz*). But His being incapable is impossible.

وَيَجِبُ فِي حَقِّهِ تَعَالَى الْعِلْمُ، وَهِيَ صِفَةٌ قَدِيمَةٌ قَائِمَةٌ بِذَاتِهِ تَعَالَى، يَعْلَمُ بِهَا الْأَشْيَاءَ. وَضِدُّهَا الْجَهْلُ. وَالدَّلِيلُ عَلَى ذَلِكَ أَنَّهُ لَوْ كَانَ جَاهِلًا لَمْ يَكُنْ مُرِيدًا، وَهُوَ مُحَالٌ.

Knowledge (*'ilm*) is necessary for Allah (Exalted is He). It is a pre-eternal attribute subsistent in Allah's divine essence (Exalted is He) through which He knows things. Its contrary is ignorance (*jahl*).

The proof of this is that if He were ignorant, He would not be willing. But that is impossible.

وَيَجِبُ فِي حَقِّهِ تَعَالَى الْحَيَاةُ، وَهِيَ صِفَةٌ وُجُودِيَّة قَدِيمَةٌ قَائِمَةٌ بِذَاتِهِ تَعَالَى، لَهُ أَنْ يَتَّصَفَ بِالعِلْمِ وَغَيْرِهِ مِنَ الصِّفَاتِ. وَضِدُّهَا: المَوْتُ. وَالدَّلِيلُ عَلَى ذَلِكَ أَنَّهُ لَوْ كَانَ مَيِّتًا لَمْ يَكُنْ قَادِرًا وَلَا مُرِيدًا وَلَا عَالِمًا، وَهُوَ مُحَالٌ.

Life (*ḥayāh*) is necessary for Allah (Exalted is He). It is a pre-eternal, existential attribute subsistent in Allah's divine essence (Exalted is He). It makes it possible for Him to be attributed with knowledge and other attributes. Its contrary is death (*mawt*). The proof of this is that if He were dead, He would not be capable, willing, or knowing. But that is impossible.

وَيَجِبُ فِي حَقِّهِ تَعَالَى السَّمْعُ وَالبَصَرُ، وَهُمَا صِفَتَانِ قَدِيمَتَانِ قَائِمَتَانِ بِذَاتِهِ تَعَالَى يَنْكَشِفُ بِهَا المَوْجُودُ. وَضِدُّهُمَا الصَّمَمُ وَالعَمَى. وَالدَّلِيلُ عَلَى ذَلِكَ قَوْلُهُ تَعَالَى: ﴿وَهُوَ السَّمِيعُ الْبَصِيرُ﴾ [الشورى: ١١]

Hearing and sight (*samʿ* and *baṣar*) are necessary for Allah (Exalted is He). They are pre-eternal attributes subsistent in Allah's divine essence (Exalted is He), through which what exists is disclosed. Their contraries are deafness and blindness (*ṣamam* and *ʿamā*). The proof of this is His statement (Exalted is He), "He is the Hearer, the Seer."[1]

وَيَجِبُ فِي حَقِّهِ تَعَالَى الكَلَامُ، وَهُوَ صِفَةٌ قَدِيمَةٌ قَائِمَةٌ بِذَاتِهِ تَعَالَى، لَيْسَتْ بِحَرْفٍ وَلَا صَوْتٍ. وَضِدُّهَا البَكَمُ، وَهُوَ الخَرَسُ. وَالدَّلِيلُ عَلَى ذَلِكَ قَوْلُهُ تَعَالَى: ﴿وَكَلَّمَ اللَّهُ مُوسَىٰ تَكْلِيمًا﴾ [النساء، ١٦٤]

Speech (*kalām*) is necessary for Allah (Exalted is He). It is a pre-eternal attribute subsistent in Allah's divine essence (Exalted is He) and is not composed of letters or sounds. Its contrary is mute-

---

1   Qur'an, 42:11.

ness (*bakam*), which is inarticulacy (*kharas*). The proof of this is His statement (Exalted is He), "And Allah spoke directly to Mūsā."[2]

وَيَجِـبُ فِي حَقِّهِ تَعَالَى كَوْنُهُ قَادِرًا. وَضِدُّهُ كَوْنُهُ عَاجِزًا. وَالدَّلِيلُ عَلَى ذَلِكَ دَلِيلُ القُدْرَةِ.

Being capable (*kawnuhu qādiran*) is necessary for Allah (Exalted is He). Its contrary is being incapable (*kawnuhu 'ājizan*). The proof of this is the proof of capability.

وَيَجِـبُ فِي حَقِّـهِ تَعَالَى كَوْنُهُ مُرِيْدًا. وَضِدُّهُ كَوْنُهُ كَارِهًا. وَالدَّلِيلُ عَلَى ذَلِكَ دَلِيلُ الإِرَادَةِ.

Being willing (*kawnuhu murīdan*) is necessary for Allah (Exalted is He). Its contrary is being averse (*kawnuhu kārihan*). The proof of this is the proof of will.

وَيَجِبُ فِي حَقِّهِ تَعَالَى كَوْنُهُ عَالِمًا. وَضِدُّهُ كَوْنُهُ جَاهِلًا. وَالدَّلِيلُ عَلَى ذَلِكَ دَلِيلُ العِلْمِ.

Being knowing (*kawnuhu 'āliman*) is necessary for Allah (Exalted is He). Its contrary is being ignorant (*kawnuhu jāhilan*). The proof of this is the proof of knowledge.

وَيَجِبُ فِي حَقِّهِ تَعَالَى كَوْنُهُ حَيًّا. وَضِدُّهُ كَوْنُهُ مَيِّتًا. وَالدَّلِيلُ عَلَى ذَلِكَ دَلِيلُ الحَيَاةِ.

Being living (*kawnuhu ḥayyan*) is necessary for Allah (Exalted is He). Its contrary is being dead (*kawnuhu mayyitan*). The proof of this is the proof of life.

وَيَجِبُ فِي حَقِّهِ تَعَالَى كَوْنُهُ سَمِيْعًا بَصِيرًا. وَضِدُّهُمَا كَوْنُهُ أَصَمُّ وَكَوْنُهُ أَعْمَى. وَالدَّلِيلُ عَلَى ذَلِكَ دَلِيلُ السَّمْعِ وَدَلِيلُ البَصَرِ.

---

2   Qur'an, 4:164.

Being hearing and being seeing (*kawnuhu samīʿan baṣīran*) are necessary for Allah (Exalted is He). Their contraries are being deaf and blind (*kawnuhu aṣamm* and *kawnuhu aʿmā*). The proof of this is the proof of hearing and the proof of sight.

وَيَجِبُ فِي حَقِّهِ تَعَالَى كَوْنُهُ مُتَكَلِّمًا. وَضِدُّهُ كَوْنُهُ أَبْكَمُ. وَالدَّلِيْلُ عَلَى ذَلِكَ دَلِيْلُ الكَلَامِ.

Being speaking (*kawnuhu mutakalliman*) is necessary for Allah (Exalted is He). Its contrary is being mute (*kawnuhu abkam*). The proof of this is the proof of speech.

وَالجَائِزُ فِي حَقِّهِ تَعَالَى فِعْلُ كُلِّ مُمْكِنٍ أَوْ تَرْكِهِ. وَالدَّلِيْلُ عَلَى ذَلِكَ أَنَّهُ لَوْ وَجَبَ عَلَيْهِ سُبْحَانَهُ وَتَعَالَى فِعْلُ شَيْءٍ أَوْ تَرْكُهُ لَصَارَ الجَائِزُ وَاجِبًا أَوْ مُسْتَحِيْلًا، وَهُوَ مُحَالٌ.

What is possible for Allah (Exalted is He) is performing or forgoing every contingent thing. The proof of this is that if it was necessary for Him (Sublime and Exalted is He) to perform or forgo something, then what is possible would become either necessary or impossible. But that is impossible.

وَيَجِبُ فِي حَقِّ الرُّسُلِ عَلَيْهِمُ الصَّلَاةُ وَالسَّلَامُ الصِّدْقُ وَضِدُّهُ الْكِذْبُ. وَالدَّلِيْلُ عَلَى ذَلِكَ أَنَّهُمْ لَوْ كَذَبُوْا لَكَانَ خَبَرُ اللهِ سُبْحَانَهُ وَتَعَالَى كَاذِبًا وَهُوَ مُحَالٌ.

Truthfulness (*ṣidq*) is necessary for the Messengers (blessings and peace be upon them). Its contrary is lying (*kidhb*). The proof of this is that if they were to lie, then Allah's declaration (Sublime and Exalted is He) would itself be a lie. But that is impossible.

وَيَجِبُ فِي حَقِّهِمْ عَلَيْهِمُ الصَّلَاةُ وَالسَّلَامُ الْأَمَانَةُ وَضِدُّهَا الْخِيَانَةُ. وَالدَّلِيلُ عَلَى ذَلِكَ أَنَّهُمْ لَوْ خَانُوْا بِفِعْلٍ مُحَرَّمٍ، أَوْ مَكْرُوهٍ لَكُنَّا مَأْمُورِينَ بِمِثْلِ ذَلِكَ وَلَا يَصِحُّ أَنْ نُؤْمَرَ بِمُحَرَّمٍ أَوْ مَكْرُوهٍ.

Trustworthiness (*amānah*) is necessary for the Messengers (blessings and peace be upon them). Its contrary is treachery (*khiyānah*). The proof of this is that if they were to commit treachery by performing something unlawful or detested, then we would have been commanded to do the same. Furthermore, it is not valid that we would be commanded to perform something unlawful or detested.

وَيَجِبُ فِي حَقِّهِمْ عَلَيْهِمُ الصَّلَاةُ وَالسَّلَامُ تَبْلِيْغُ مَا أُمِرُوْا بِتَبْلِيْغِهِ لِلْخَلْقِ. وَضِدُّهُ كِتْمَانُ ذَلِكَ. الدَّلِيْلُ عَلَى ذَلِكَ أَنَّهُمْ لَوْ كَتَمُوْا شَيْئًا مِمَّا أُمِرُوْا بِتَبْلِيْغِهِ لَكُنَّا مَأْمُورِيْنَ بِكِتْمَانِ الْعِلْمِ وَلَا يَصِحُّ أَنْ نُؤْمَرَ بِهِ لِأَنَّ كَاتِمَ الْعِلْمِ مَلْعُونٌ.

Conveyance of what they were commanded to convey to the creation (*tablīgh*) is necessary for the Messengers (blessings and peace be upon them). Its contrary is concealing this (*kitmān*). The proof of this is that if they concealed anything of what they were ordered to convey, then we would have been commanded to conceal knowledge. Furthermore, it is not valid that we would be commanded with this since the one who conceals knowledge is cursed.

وَيَجِبُ فِي حَقِّهِمْ عَلَيْهِمُ الصَّلَاةُ وَالسَّلَامُ الْفَطَانَةُ وَضِدُّهَا الْبَلَادَةُ. وَالدَّلِيْلُ عَلَى ذَلِكَ أَنَّهُ لَوِ انْتَفَتْ عَنْهُمُ الْفَطَانَةُ لَمَا قَدَرُوْا أَنْ يُقِيْمُوْا حُجَّةً عَلَى الْخَصْمِ وَهُوَ مُحَالٌ؛ لِأَنَّ الْقُرْآنَ دَلَّ فِي مَوَاضِعَ كَثِيْرَةٍ عَلَى إِقَامَتِهِمُ الْحُجَّةَ عَلَى الْخَصْمِ.

Acuity (*faṭānah*) is necessary for the Messengers (blessings and peace be upon them). Its contrary is dullness (*balādah*). The proof of this is that if acuity were absent from them, they would be unable to establish arguments against their opponents. But that is impossible, because the Qur'an repeatedly affirms that they established arguments against their opponents.

وَالجَائِزُ فِي حَقِّهِمْ عَلَيْهِمُ الصَّلَاةُ وَالسَّلَامُ الْأَعْرَاضُ الْبَشَرِيَّةُ الَّتِي لَا تُؤَدِّي إِلَى نَقْصٍ فِي مَرَاتِبِهِمُ الْعَلِيَّةِ كَالْمَرَضِ وَنَحْوِهِ. وَالدَّلِيلُ عَلَى ذَلِكَ مَشَاهِدُهَا بِهِمْ عَلَيْهِمُ الصَّلَاةُ وَالسَّلَامُ.

What is possible for the Messengers (blessings and peace be upon them) are human conditions that do not detract from their lofty stations, such as illness and the like. The proof (*dalīl*) for this is their observable occurrence in the case of the Messengers (peace and blessings be upon them).

يَجِبُ عَلَى الشَّخْصِ أَنْ يَعْرِفَ نَسَبَهُ ﷺ مِنْ جِهَةِ أَبِيهِ، وَمِنْ جِهَةِ أُمِّهِ.

Individuals are required to know the lineage of the Prophet (may Allah bless him and give him peace) from his father's side and his mother's side.

فَأَمَّا نَسَبُهُ ﷺ مِنْ جِهَةِ أَبِيهِ فَهُوَ سَيِّدُنَا مُحَمَّدُ بْنُ عَبْدِ اللَّهِ بْنُ عَبْدِ الْمُطَّلِبِ بْنِ هَاشِمِ بْنِ عَبْدِ مَنَافِ بْنِ قُصَيٍّ بْنِ كِلَابِ بْنِ مُرَّةَ بْنِ كَعْبِ بْنِ لُؤَيٍّ بْنِ غَالِبِ بْنِ فِهْرِ بْنِ مَالِكِ بْنُ النَّضْرِ بْنِ كِنَانَةَ بْنِ خُزَيْمَةَ بْنِ مُدْرِكَةَ بْنِ إِلْيَاسَ بْنِ مُضَرَ بْنِ نِزَارِ بْنِ مَعْدِ بْنِ عَدْنَانَ. وَلَيْسَ فِيمَا بَعْدَهُ إِلَى آدَمَ عَلَيْهِ الصَّلَاةُ وَالسَّلَامُ طَرِيقٌ صَحِيحٌ فِيمَا يُنْقَلُ.

The lineage of the Prophet (may Allah bless him and give him peace) from his father's side, is as follows: Our Master Muḥammad son of ʿAbd Allāh son of ʿAbd al-Muṭṭalib, son of Hāshim, son of ʿAbd Manāf, son of Quṣayy, son of Kilāb, son of Murrah, son of Kaʿb, son of Luʾayy, son of Ghālib, son of Fihr, son of Mālik, son of al-Naḍr, son of Kinānah, son of Khuzaymah, son of Mudrikah, son of Ilyās, son of Muḍar, son of Nizār, son of Maʿd, son of ʿAdnān. Beyond him extending back to Ādam (peace and blessings be upon him), no authentic lineage has been transmitted.

وَأَمَّا نَسَبُهُ ﷺ مِنْ جِهَةِ أُمِّهِ فَهُوَ سَيِّدُنَا مُحَمَّدُ بْنُ آمِنَةَ بِنْتِ وَهْبِ بْنِ عَبْدِ مَنَافِ ابْنِ زُهْرَةَ بْنِ كِلَابٍ، فَتَجْتَمِعُ مَعَهُ فِي جَدِّهِ كِلَابٌ.

The lineage of the Prophet (may Allah bless him and give him peace) from his mother's side is as follows: Our Master Muḥammad (may Allah bless him and give him peace), son of Āminah, daughter of Wahb, son of ʿAbd Manāf, son of Zuhrah, son of Kilāb – she meets him [(may Allah bless him and give him peace)] at his grandfather Kilāb.

وَمِمَّا يَجِبُ أَيْضًا أَنْ يَعْلَمَ أَنَّ لَهُ حَوْضًا، وَأَنَّهُ يَشْفَعُ فِي فَصْلِ الْقَضَاءِ وَهَذِهِ الشَّفَاعَةُ مُخْتَصَّةٌ بِهِ ﷺ.

It is also required to know that he has a Basin (ḥawḍ) and that he (may Allah bless him and give him peace) will intercede in rendering judgement; this intercession is unique to him (may Allah bless him and give him peace).

وَمِمَّا يَجِبُ أَيْضًا أَنْ يَعْرِفَ الرُّسُلَ الْمَذْكُورِينَ فِي الْقُرْآنِ تَفْصِيلًا. وَأَمَّا غَيْرُهُمْ مِنَ الرُّسُلِ وَالْأَنْبِيَاءِ فَيَجِبُ عَلَيْهِ أَنْ يَعْرِفَهُمْ إِجْمَالًا. وَقَدْ نَظَمَ بَعْضُهُمُ الْأَنْبِيَاءَ الَّتِي تَجِبُ مَعْرِفَتُهُمْ تَفْصِيلًا فَقَالَ:

حَتْـمٌ عَلَى كُلِّ ذِي التَّكْلِيفِ مَعْرِفَةٌ * بِأَنْبِيَـاءٍ عَلَـى التَّفْصِيـلِ قَـدْ عُلِمُوْا
فِـي تِلْـكَ حُجَّتُنَـا مِنْهُـمْ ثَمَانِـى * مِـنْ بَعْدَ عَشَـرٍ وَيَبْقَى سَـبْعَةٌ وَهُمْ
إِدْرِيـسُ هُوْدٌ شَعْـبٌ صَالِـحٌ وَكَذَا * ذُو الْكِفْـلِ آدَمُ بِالْمُخْتَارِ قَدْ خَتَمُوْا

It is also obligatory to know, in detail, the Messengers explicitly mentioned in the Qurʾān. As for messengers (rusul) and prophets (anbiyāʾ) other than those explicitly mentioned in the Qurʾān, it is obligatory for them to know them in a general sense.

Some scholars have composed verses listing the prophets whose detailed recognition is obligatory, saying:

Incumbent (*ḥatm*) upon every legally responsible individual is
knowing (*maʿrifah*) In detail those prophets who are known.
In "That is Our argument"[3] are eight of them after ten. Seven
remain; they are:
Idrīs, Hūd, Shuʿayb, Ṣāliḥ, and also Dhu al-Kifl, Ādam, with
the Chosen One (*mukhtār*) they were sealed

وَمِمَّا يَجِبُ اعْتِقَادُهُ أَيْضًا أَنَّ قَرْنَهُ أَفْضَلُ الْقُرُونِ، ثُمَّ الْقَرْنُ الَّذِي بَعْدَهُ،
ثُمَّ الْقَرْنُ الَّذِي بَعْدَهُ.

It is also obligatory to believe that the Prophet's generation is the
best generation, followed by the one succeeding it, and then the one
succeeding that.

وَيَنْبَغِي لِلشَّخْصِ أَنْ يَعْرِفَ أَوْلَادَهُ ﷺ وَهُمْ سَبْعَةٌ عَلَى الصَّحِيحِ:
سَيِّدُنَا الْقَاسِمُ، وَسَيِّدَتُنَا زَيْنَبُ، وَسِيِّدَتُنَا رُقْيَةُ، وَسَيِّدَتُنَا فَاطِمَةُ، وَسَيِّدَتُنَا أُمُّ
كَلْثُومٍ، وَسَيِّدُنَا عَبْدُ اللَّهِ وَهُوَ الْمُلَقَّبُ بِـ «الطَّيِّبِ» وَ «الطَّاهِرِ»، وَسَيِّدُنَا
إِبْرَاهِيمُ، وَكُلُّهُمْ مِنْ سَيِّدَتِنَا خَدِيجَةَ الْكُبْرَى إِلَّا إِبْرَاهِيمَ فَمِنْ مَارِيَةَ الْقِبْطِيَّةِ.

It is appropriate for an individual to know the children of the
Prophet (may Allah bless him and give him peace). They are seven
according to the sound opinion: our master al-Qāsim, our lady Zaynab, our lady Ruqayyah, our lady Fāṭimah, our lady Umm Kulthūm,
our master ʿAbd Allāh (nicknamed "Al-Ṭayyib" and "Al-Ṭāhir"), and
our master Ibrāhīm. All of them are from our lady Khadījah al-Kubrā
except for our master Ibrāhīm, who was from Māriyah the Copt.

وَهَـذَا آخِـرُ مَا يَسَّـرَهُ اللَّهُ مِنْ فَضْلِهِ وَكَرَمِهِ، وَالْحَمْـدُ لِلَّهِ رَبِّ الْعَالَمِينَ.
وَصَلَّى اللَّهُ عَلَى سَيِّدِنَا مُحَمَّدٍ وَعَلَى آلِهِ وَصَحْبِهِ وَسَلَّمَ.

This is the last of what Allah has facilitated from His bounty and
generosity. All praise belongs to Allah, Lord of the worlds. May Allah

---

3   Qur'an, 6:83–86.

bless our master Muḥammad, his family, and companions, and grant them peace. ❧

THE STELLAR CROWNS

Tījān al-Darārī
Shaykh Muḥammad Nawawī al-Jāwī's
Commentary on
Imām Ibrāhīm al-Bājūrī's
Treatise on Monotheism

INTRODUCTION

[مُقَدِّمَةُ المُؤَلِّفِ]

بِسْمِ اللَّهِ الرَّحْمَنِ الرَّحِيمِ

In the name of Allah, the All-Merciful, the Most Merciful

الحَمْدُ لِلَّهِ المُنَزَّهِ عَنْ سِمَاتِ الحُدُوْثِ وَالأَلْوَانِ وَالكَيْفِيَّاتِ، وَأَشْهَدُ أَنْ لَا إِلَهَ إِلَّا اللَّهُ الغَنِيُّ عَنْ كُلِّ مَا سِوَاهُ، وَالمُفْتَقِرُ إِلَيْهِ كُلُّ شَيْءٍ فِي سَائِرِ الأَوْقَاتِ، وَأَشْهَدُ أَنَّ سَيِّدَنَا مُحَمَّدًا سَيِّدُ المَخْلُوْقَاتِ، وَالصَّلَاةُ وَالسَّلَامُ عَلَى رَسُوْلِ اللَّهِ صَاحِبِ الحَوْضِ وَالشَّفَاعَاتِ، وَعَلَى آلِهِ المُفَضَّلِيْنَ عَلَى سَائِرِ الأُمَمِ، وَأَصْحَابِهِ الفَائِزِيْنَ بِأَنْوَاعِ الخَيْرَاتِ وَالنِّعَمِ.

Praise be to Allah, [the One who is] transcendent above the attributes of origination, colours, and modes of being. I testify that there is no deity except Allah: the one absolutely free of all need, while all things remain in absolute dependence upon Him at every moment. I testify that our master Muḥammad is the chief of creation. May blessings and peace be upon the Messenger of Allah, the possessor of the Basin and intercessions, and upon his household – [who were] chosen above all other nations – and upon his companions, [who were] granted all manner of divine graces and blessings.

أَمَّا بَعْدُ، فَهَذَا شَرْحٌ عَلَى رِسَالَةِ العَلَّامَةِ البَاجُوْرِيِّ فِي التَّوْحِيْدِ سَمَّيْتُهُ: «تِيْجَانُ الدَّرَارِي فِي شَرْحِ رِسَالَةِ البَاجُوْرِيِّ». وَقَدْ سُئِلْتُ فِيْهِ، فَأَنَا أَشْرَعُ

راجِيًّا الاِنْتِفَـاعَ بِهِ، وَعَوْدَ البَرَكَةِ مِنْ ذَلِكَ الشَّـيْخِ لِي وَلِكُلِّ قَارِئٍ وَسَـامِعٍ وَمُطَالِعٍ.

To proceed: This is a commentary on the monograph (*risālah*) of the illustrious scholar (*ʿallāmah*[4]) [Shaykh Ibrāhīm] al-Bājūrī, concerning divine unity (*tawḥīd*). I have named it *Tījān al-Darārī fī Sharḥ Risālat al-Bājūrī* (*The Radiant Pearlescent Crowns in Commentary on al-Bājūrī's Monograph*). It was requested of me, and so I now begin, hoping for its benefit and [for] the blessings of that Shaykh to [extend to] me and to every reader, listener, and student.

(بِسْمِ اللَّهِ الرَّحْمَنِ الرَّحِيْمِ)

‹In the name of Allah, the All-Merciful, the Most Merciful›

فَاسْمُ الجَلَالَةِ: دَلَّ عَلَى الـذَّاتِ الجَامِعَةِ لِصِفَاتِ الإِلَهِيَّةِ كُلِّهَا، وَ «الرَّحْمَـنِ»: هُـوَ كَثِيْرُ الرَّحْمَةِ لِعِبَادِهِ بِالسَّـتْرِ فِي الدُّنْيَـا، وَ «الرَّحِيْمِ»: هُوَ كَثِيْرُ الرَّحْمَةِ لَهُمْ بِالغُفْرَانِ فِي العُقْبَى، فَلِلعَبْدِ أَنْ يُلَاحِظَ مِنْ «اللَّهِ» قُدْرَتَهُ، وَمِنْ «الرَّحْمَنِ» نِعْمَتَهُ، وَمِنْ «الرَّحِيْمِ» عِصْمَتَهُ مِنَ الذُّنُوْبِ وَمَغْفِرَتَهُ.

The divine name "Allah" denotes the essence that encompasses all divine attributes.

"The All-Merciful" (*al-Raḥmān*) refers to His abundant mercy toward His servants by concealing [sins] in this world.

"The Most Merciful" (*al-Raḥīm*) refers to His abundant mercy toward them by granting forgiveness in the Hereafter.

Thus, the servant should discern in the name "Allah" His capability (*qudrah*), in al-Raḥmān His beneficence (*niʿmah*), and in al-Raḥīm His safeguarding (*ʿiṣmah*) from sins and His forgiveness (*maghfirah*).[5]

---

4   An *ʿallāmah* is an *ʿālim* who is a master of disciplines based upon reason and transmitted knowledge.

5   Shaykh al-Islam Zakariyā al-Anṣārī says the same in his explanation of the divine names *Tuḥfat al-ʿulamāʾ bi sharḥ asmāʾ rabbi l-ʿālamīn*.

(الحَمْـدُ لِلَّـهِ رَبِّ العَالَمِيْـنَ) أَيْ : مَالِكِ السَّـمَوَاتِ وَالأَرْضِ وَمَعْبُوْدِ مَنْ فِيْهِـما (وَالصَّلَاةُ وَالسَّلَامُ عَلَى رَسُوْلِ اللَّهِ ﷺ) وَ«رَسُوْلُ اللَّهِ» هُنَا هُوَ سَـيِّدُنَا مُحَمَّدٌ ﷺ، فَإِنَّهُ صَارَ عَلَمًا بِالغَلَبَةِ عَلَى تِلْكَ الذَّاتِ الشَّرِيْفَةِ. (وَبَعْدَ) أَيْ : بَعْدَ البَسْمَلَةِ وَالحَمْدَلَةِ وَالصَّلَاةِ عَلَى رَسُوْلِ اللَّهِ. (ت٢٠)

‹**Praise be to Allah, Lord of the worlds**› meaning sovereign of the heavens and the earth, and the one worshipped by all within them‹.›

‹**May blessings and peace be upon the Messenger of Allah (may Allah bless him and give him peace).**› Here, "Messenger of Allah," refers to our master Muḥammad (may Allah bless him and give him peace). It became a proper noun for that noble essence due to its widespread use.

‹**To proceed**› meaning after the *Basmalah, Ḥamdalah,* and prayers upon the Messenger of Allah‹:›

(فَيَقُـوْلُ فَقِيـرُ رَحْمَةِ رَبِّهِ الخَبِيْرِ) أَيْ : العَلِيْمِ بِبَوَاطِنِ الأُمُوْرِ (البَصِيْرِ) أَيْ : الَّـذِي يُبْصِـرُ مَا تَحْتَ الثَّرَى وَمُدْرِك المُبْصَرَاتِ حَالَ وُجُوْدِهَا (إِبْرَاهِيْمُ) بْنُ مُحَمَّـدٍ (البَاجُـوْرِيُّ) نِسْـبَةً إِلَى «بَاجُوْر» بَلْدَةٍ مِـنْ بِلَادِ مِصْرَ (ذُو التَّقْصِيْرِ) وَهُوَ شَيْخُ العُلَمَاءِ فِي الأَزْهَرِ، سَقَى اللَّهُ قَبْرَهُ بِالرَّحْمَةِ وَالرِّضْوَانِ.

‹**The one in need of the mercy of his Lord, the All-Aware**› meaning the One who knows all hidden matters ‹**the All-Seeing**› meaning the One who perceives what lies beneath the earth and comprehends all visible things as they exist ‹**Ibrāhīm**› bin Muḥammad ‹**al-Bājūrī**› attributed to Bājūr, a town in Egypt ‹**the one possessed of shortcomings**› was the shaykh of the scholars (*ʿulamā*) at Azhar. May Allah pour His mercy and pleasure upon his grave[6] ‹**says:**›

---

6   Shaykh Muḥammad Nawawī wrote this commentary some twenty years after Shaykh Ibrāhīm al-Bājūrī had passed. (May Allah pour his mercy and pleasure upon them both.)

(طَلَبَ مِنِّي بَعْضُ الإِخْوَانِ - أَصْلَحَ اللَّهُ لِـي وَلَهُمْ الحَالَ وَالـشَّأْنَ - أَنْ أَكْتُـبَ لَهُ رِسَـالَةً) أَي: كِتَابًا صَغِيـرًا (لَطِيْفَةً) أَي: ظَرِيفَـةً، فَالضَّمِيْرُ الأَوَّلُ رَاجِـعٌ لِلمُضَافِ إِلَيْهِ، وَالثَّانِي لِلمُضَـافِ، وَجَمَعَ المُصَنِّفُ الضَّمِيرَ الأَوَّلِ لِتَعْمِيْـمِ الدُّعَـاءِ، وَأَيْضًـا الضَّمِيْرُ رَاجِعٌ لِلمُضَافِ إِلَّا إِذَا كَانَ لَفْظُ «كُلٍّ» أَوْ «بَعْـض» فَيَرْجِعُ لِلمُضَافِ إِلَيْهِ كَمَا هُنَا، وَأَفْرَدَ ثَانِيًا لِتَخْصِيْصِ الطَّالِبِ (تَشْتَمِلُ) أَي: الرِّسَالَةُ (عَلَى صِفَاتِ المَوْلَى) أَي: الثَّابِتَةِ لَهُ وَالسَّالِبَةِ عَنْهُ مَا لَا يَلِيْـقُ بِهِ (وَأَضْدَادِهَـا) أَي: مَنَافِيهَا (وَمَا يَجُوْزُ فِي حَقِّـهِ⁷ تَعَالَى، وَعَلَى مَا يَجِبُ فِي حَقِّ الرُّسُلِ وَمَا يَسْتَحِيْلُ فِي حَقِّهِم وَمَا يَجُوْزُ)

‹Some of the brethren – may Allah mend our state and affair – requested that I write for him a light› meaning refined **‹monograph›** meaning a small book.

The first pronoun refers to the second noun of the genitive construction and the second to the first.[8] The author used the plural of the first pronoun to generalise the supplication. Additionally, the pronoun generally refers to the first noun of a genitive construction, except when the phrase contains "every" or "some" – in which case it refers to the second noun, as it does here. The singular form of the second pronoun is used due to the specificity of the one asking.

‹It› meaning the monograph **‹contains the attributes of the Lord;›** meaning those affirmed for Him and those negated from Him as unbefitting **‹their contraries›** meaning their contradictories**‹; what is possible for Him (Exalted is He); what is necessary for the Messengers; what is impossible for them; and what is possible.[9]›**

---

7   Throughout the translation, I have translated this phrase as "for" instead of "with respect to."

8   The first pronoun in "for them" ("*lahum*") refers to the second noun "brethren" ("*al-ikhwān*") of the genitive construction, and the second pronoun, in "for him" ("*lahu*") refers to the first noun of the genitive construction, "some of" ("*ba'ḍ*").

9   The next paragraph clarifies that the author here refers to rational judgments, i.e. what is rationally necessary, what is rationally impossible, and what is rationally possible.

فَالْوَاجِبُ: هُوَ الَّذِي لَا يُمْكِنُ عَدَمُـهُ، وَذَلِكَ كَذَاتِهِ تَعَالَـى وَالتَّحَيُّزِ لِلْجِرْمِ، أَيْ: مُمَانعته عَلَى القَدْرِ المَأْخُوذِ مِنْ الفَرَاغِ، أَيْ: مَنْعُكَ الغَيْرَ مِنْ أَنْ يَحِلَّ فِي مَكَانِكَ، وَكَاتِّصَافِ الجُرْمِ بِأَحَدِ الحَرَكَةِ وَالسُّكُوْنِ.

The *necessary* (*wājib*) is that which cannot be negated.

This includes His essence (Exalted is He); the spatial occupation of a body (*jirm*), meaning its imposition upon the portion of void it takes – that is, preventing another from occupying the same space, and a body being characterised by either motion or stillness.[10]

وَالمُسْتَحِيْلُ: هُوَ الَّذِي لَا يُمْكِنُ وُجُوْدُهُ، كَالشَّـرِيْكِ لَهُ، وَخُلُوِّ الجُرْمِ عَنْ الحَرَكَةِ وَالسُّكُوْنِ مَعًا.

The *impossible* (*mustaḥīl*) is that which cannot be affirmed.

This includes Him having a partner (*sharīk*); and a body being free of motion and stillness together.[11]

The definitions here match what the author explains in his *Fatḥ al-majīd*, and the words (*wujūduhu*) and (*'adamuhu*) are translated according to his explanations. See Muḥammad Nawawī *Fatḥ al-majīd*, edited by 'Alawī Abū Bakr Muḥammad al-Saqqāf (Jakarta: Dār al-Kutub al-Islāmiyyah, 1429 AH/2008 CE), 8–9.

He offers a simpler presentation in *Al-Nahajat al-jayyidah*: Necessary (*wājib*) is what does not accept being negated; impossible (*mustaḥīl*) is what does not accept being affirmed; and possible (*jā'iz*) is what accepts being affirmed sometimes and negated at others. See *The Correct Approach to Unpacking 'The Select Creed,'* (n.p., Islamosaic, 2022), 11.

For other definitions, see Imām al-Bājūrī's commentaries on al-Laqqānī, *Jawharat al-tawḥīd* (printed within *Tuḥfat al-murīd*), line 5; al-Bājūrī, *Tuḥfat al-murīd* (Cairo: Dār al-Salām, 2002/1422), paragraphs 78–79.

For the sake of brevity, further references to *Tuḥfat al-murīd* will include the line number in *Al-Jawharah* to facilitate cross-referencing against other editions and commentaries, and will be shortened to "*Al-Jawharah*" followed by a line number, and "*Tuḥfat*" followed by a paragraph number, e.g. *Al-Jawharah*, 5; *Tuḥfat*, 78.

See also Ibrāhīm al-Bājūrī, *Taḥqīq al-maqām 'alā Kifāyat al-'awām fī 'ilm al-kalām* (Beirut: Dār al-Kutub al-'Ilmiyyah, 2007), 45–51.

10   *Fatḥ al-majīd*, 8–9.

11   *Fatḥ al-majīd*, 9.

وَالجَائِـزُ: هُوَ الَّذِي يُمْكِنُ وُجُـوْدُهُ وَعَدَمُهُ، كَتَعْذِيْبِ المُطِيْع الَّذِي لَمْ يَعْصِ اللَّهَ تَعَالَى طَرْفَةَ عَيْنٍ، وَكَاتِّصَافِ الجُرْمِ بَعَيْنِ أَحَدِ الحَرَكَةِ وَالسُّكُوْنِ.

The *possible* (*jāʾiz*) is that which may be affirmed [at times] and negated [at others].

This includes tormenting the obedient individual who has never disobeyed Allah (Exalted is He) for the blink of an eye; and a body being characterised by a specific instance of motion or stillness.[12]

(فَأَجَبْتُـهُ) أَي: بَعْـضَ الإِخْوَانِ (إِلَى ذَلِكَ) أَي: كَتْبِ الرِّسَـالَةِ (فَقُلْتُ وَبِاللَّهِ التَّوْفِيْقُ) أَي: خَلْقُ الطَّاعَةِ.

‹So I granted his request› meaning some of the brethren ‹to do this› meaning to write this monograph ‹and said – and by Allah is success –› meaning the creation of obedience‹:›

---

12   *Fatḥ al-majīd*, 9.

KNOWING ALLAH

(يَجِبُ عَلَى كُلِّ مُكَلَّفٍ) مِنْ ذَكَرٍ وَأُنْثَى وَلَوْ مِنَ العَوَامِّ وَالعَبِيدِ وَالخَدَمِ، وُجُوبًا عَيْنِيًّا (أَنْ يَعْرِفَ مَا يَجِبُ فِي حَقِّهِ تَعَالَى وَمَا يَسْتَحِيْلُ وَمَا يَجُوْزُ) قَالَ اللَّهُ تَعَالَى: ﴿فَاعْلَمْ أَنَّهُ لا إِلَهَ إِلَّا اللَّهُ﴾ [مُحَمَّد، ١٩].

‹**It is required of every legally responsible person**[13]› whether male or female, even for the laity, slaves and servants – as a personal obligation (*fard 'ayn*) ‹**to be cognisant of what is necessary for Allah (Exalted is He), what is impossible, and what is possible.**›

Allah (most High is He) says, "Know that there is no deity except Allah."[14]

وَ«المَعْرِفَةُ»: هُوَ: إِدْرَاكٌ جَازِمٌ بَحْتٌ لَيْسَ مَعَهُ تَرَدُّدٌ مُوَافِقٌ لِمَا فِي الوَاقِعِ نَاشِيءٌ عَنْ دَلِيْلٍ.

"Knowledge" (*ma'rifah*) is a purely decisive perception (*idrāk jāzim baht*), free of doubt, accords with reality and arises from proof.[15]

وَ«يَجِبُ شَرْعًا» عَلَى مَنْ ذُكِرَ وُجُوبًا عَيْنِيًّا مَعْرِفَةُ كُلِّ عَقِيْدَةٍ بِدَلِيْلِهَا الإِجْمَالِيِّ، وَأَمَّا مَعْرِفَتُهَا بِدَلِيْلِهَا التَّفْصِيْلِيِّ فَفَرْضُ كِفَايَةٍ.

It is a personal legal obligation (*fard 'ayn*) for those mentioned to know every doctrinal tenet with its general proof (*dalīl ijmālī*). As for

---

13   A legally responsible human being is one who is physically mature, possesses reason, has been reached by the call to Islam, and possesses sound senses. Cf. *Fath al-majīd*, 9; *Jawharah*, 9; *Tuhfah*, 69.

14   Qur'an, 47:19. Cf. *Jawharah*, 5; *Tuhfah*, 51; *Fath al-majīd*, 9.

15   The word "knowledge" (*ma'rifah*) here refers to conviction that matches reality and is based upon proof. Cf. *Al-Jawharah*, 9; *Tuhfat*, 76; *Fath al-majīd*, 7.

knowing them with detailed proofs (*dalīl tafṣīlī*), that is a communal obligation (*farḍ kifāyah*).[16]

فَيَجِبُ عَلَى أَهْلِ كُلِّ نَاحِيَةٍ يَشُقُّ الْوُصُولُ مِنْهَا إِلَى غَيْرِهَا أَنْ يَكُونَ فِيهِمْ مَنْ يُعَرِّفُهَا بِالدَّلِيلِ التَّفْصِيلِيِّ، لِأَنَّهُ رُبَّمَا طَرَأَتْ فِيهِمْ شُبْهَةٌ فَيَدْفَعُهَا.

It is obligatory for the inhabitants of any region that is difficult to access to have among them someone who is able to explain these tenets with detailed proofs, since a spurious claim may arise among them, requiring its refutation.[17]

وَالدَّلِيلُ الْإِجْمَالِيُّ هُوَ: الْمَعْجُوزُ عَنْ تَفْسِيرِهِ وَدَفْعِ شُبَهِهِ. فَإِذَا قِيلَ لَكَ: «مَا الدَّلِيلُ عَلَى وُجُودِهِ تَعَالَى؟» فَقُلْتَ: «الْعَالَمُ» وَلَمْ تَعْرِفْ جِهَةَ الدَّلَالَةِ هَلْ هِيَ حُدُوثُهُ أَوْ إِمْكَانِهِ أَوْ هُمَا أَوْ عَرَفْتَهَا وَلَمْ تَقْدِرْ عَلَى فَكِّ الشُّبْهَةِ فَهُوَ دَلِيلٌ إِجْمَالِيٌّ. وَأَمَّا إِذَا عَرَفْتَ جِهَةَ الدَّلَالَةِ وَقَدِرْتَ عَلَى رَدِّ الشُّبْهَةِ فَهُوَ دَلِيلٌ تَفْصِيلِيٌّ، كَمَا إِذَا قِيلَ لَكَ: «مَا الدَّلِيلُ عَلَى وُجُودِهِ تَعَالَى؟» فَقُلْتَ: «الْعَالَمُ» وَقَدِرْتَ عَلَى تَصْوِيرِ هَـذَا الدَّلِيلِ وَعَرَفْتَ جِهَةَ الدَّلَالَةِ فِيهِ وَقَدِرْتَ عَلَى فَكِّ شُبَهِهِ.

A general proof (*dalīl ijmālī*) is that which one is unable to explicate or defend against objections. For instance, if someone asks, "What is the proof of His existence (Exalted is He)?" and one answers, "The world," but does not know whether the evidentiary basis is its origination (*ḥudūth*), its contingency (*imkān*), or both – or even if one knows but cannot refute objections – then this is a general proof.[18]

A detailed proof (*dalīl tafṣīlī*), however, requires knowing the evidentiary basis and being able to counter objections. For example, if someone asks, "What is the proof of His existence (Exalted is He)?" and one answers, "The world," while being able to conceptualise this

---

16   *Al-Jawharah*, 5; *Tuḥfat*, 51; *Fatḥ al-majīd*, 7.
17   *Al-Jawharah*, 5; *Tuḥfat*, 51; *Fatḥ al-majīd*, 7.
18   *Al-Jawharah*, 5; *Tuḥfat*, 51; *Fatḥ al-majīd*, 7.

proof, identify the evidentiary basis, and refute objections, then this is a detailed proof.[19]

وَيَقُوْمُ مَقَامَ مَعْرِفَتِهِ العَقَائِدُ بِالدَّلِيْلِ مَعْرِفَتُهَا بِالْكَشْفِ.

Knowing doctrinal tenets through unveiling (*kashf*) takes the place of knowing them through rational proof.[20]

اِعْلَمْ أَنَّهُ يَجِبُ شَـرْعًا عَلَى كُلِّ مُكَلَّفٍ أَنْ يَعْرِفَ جَمِيْعَ مَا يَجِبُ فِي حَقِّهِ تَعَالَى، وَجَمِيْعَ مَا يَسْـتَحِيْلُ عَلَيْهِ تَعَالَى، وَجَمِيْعَ مَا يَجُوْزُ فِي حَقِّهِ تَعَالَى، فَمَا قَامَتْ الأَدِلَّةُ العَقْلِيَّةُ أَوْ النَّقْلِيَّةُ عَلَيْهِ إِجْمَـالًا - وَهُوَ وُجُوْبُ اِتِّصَافِهِ تَعَالَى بِسَائِرِ الكَمَالَاتِ وَوُجُوْبُ تَنْزُّهِهِ عَنْ سَائِرِ النَقَائِصِ - وَجَبَتْ مَعْرِفَتُهُ إِجْمَالًا، فَيَجِبُ عَلَيْنَا أَنْ نَعْتَقِدَ أَنَّ لَهُ تَعَالَى كَمَالَاتٌ لَا نِهَايَةَ لَهَا مِنْ جِهَةِ العَدَدِ فِي نَفْسِ الأَمْرِ، قال اللّه تعالى: ﴿وَلَا يُحِيطُونَ بِهِ عِلْمًا﴾ [طـه، ١١٠]، وَمَا قَامَتْ الأَدِلَّةُ العَقْلِيَّةُ أَوْ النَّقْلِيَّةُ عَلَيْهِ تَفْصِيْلًا تَجِبُ مَعْرِفَتُهُ تَفْصِيْلًا، وَهُوَ العِشْرُوْنَ صِفَةً وَأَضْدَادُهَا.

Know that it is legally obligatory for every legally responsible person to know all that is necessary for Allah (Exalted is He); all that is impossible for Him; and all that is possible for Him.[21]

What rational or transmitted proofs establish as a whole – namely, that it is necessary to attribute Allah (Exalted is He) with every perfection and necessary to negate from Him every imperfection – must be known as a whole.[22]

---

19 *Al-Jawharah*, 5; *Tuḥfat*, 51; *Fatḥ al-majīd*, 7.

20 *Al-Jawharah*, 5; *Tuḥfat*, 51. *Fatḥ al-majīd*, 67.

21 *Fatḥ al-majīd*, 7.

22 Muḥammad Nawawī al-Bantanī al-Jāwī, *Dharīat al-Yaqīn 'Alā Umm al-Barāhīn* (Cairo: Al-Maṭba'ah al-'Uthmāniyyah, 1303), 8; *Fatḥ al-majīd*, 9.

Thus, it is obligatory to believe that He (Exalted is He) possesses perfections without limit in number, as Allah (Exalted is He) says: "They cannot encompass Him in knowledge."[23]

What rational or transmitted proofs establish in detail must be known in detail – and this refers to the twenty attributes (*ṣifāt 'ishrūn*) and their contraries.

ALLAH'S NECESSARY ATTRIBUTES IN DETAIL

EXISTENCE

(فَيَجِبُ فِي حَقِّهِ تَعَالَى الْوُجُوْدُ) الذَّاتِيُّ الَّذِي لَا يَقْبَلُ العَدَمَ أَزَلًّا وَلَا أَبَدًا، وَهُوَ صِفَةٌ نَفْسِيَّةٌ، أَيْ: ثُبُوْتِيَّةٌ، يَدُلُّ الوَصْفُ بِهَا عَلَى نَفْسِ الذَّاتِ دُوْنَ مَعْنًى زَائِدٍ عَلَيْهِ. وَيَكْفِي المُكَلَّفَ أَنْ يَعْرِفَ أَنَّهُ تَعَالَى مَوْجُوْدٌ وُجُوْدًا وَاجِبًا، وَلَا يَجِبُ عَلَيْهِ أَنْ يَعْرِفَ أَنَّ وُجُوْدَهُ تَعَالَى عَيْنُ ذَاتِهِ أَوْ غَيْرُ ذَاتِهِ، لِأَنَّ ذَلِكَ مِنْ غَوَامِضَ عِلْمِ الكَلَامِ.

‹**Existence (*wujūd*) is necessary for Allah (Exalted is He).**› His existence is an intrinsic (*dhātī*) existence[24] not admitting nonexistence – neither in pre-eternity (*azal*) nor in perpetuity (*abad*). It is an essential attribute (*ṣifah nafsiyyah*), meaning an affirmed (*thubūtiyyah*) attribute whose ascription indicates the very essence (*dhāt*) itself, without implying an additional meaning.[25]

It suffices for a legally responsible person (*mukallaf*) to know that He (Exalted is He) is necessarily existent (*wājib al-wujūd*). However, it is not obligatory to know whether His existence is identical to

---

23   Qur'an, 20:110.

24   Al-Bājūri explains that His existence is due to His essence and not due to a cause – meaning something else does not influence His existence (Exalted is He). *Al-Jawharah*, 23; *Tuḥfat*, 140; *Fatḥ al-majīd*, 12.

25   *Al-Jawharah*, 23; *Tuḥfah*, 141; *Fatḥ al-majīd*, 67.

His essence or distinct from it, since this falls among the abstruse discussions of theology (*'ilm al-kalām*).[26]

(وَضِدُّهُ العَدَمُ)

‹**Its contrary is nonexistence (*'adam*).**[27]›

(وَالدَّلِيْلُ عَلَى ذَلِكَ) أَيْ: وُجُوْد اللَّهِ تَعَالَى (وُجُوْدُ هَـذِهِ المَخْلُوْقَاتِ) وَكَيْفِيَّةُ تَرْتِيْبِ إِقَامَةِ الدَّلِيْلِ عَلَى وُجُوْبِ وُجُوْدِهِ تَعَالَى أَنْ تَقُوْلَ: العَالَمُ - مِنْ العَرْشِ إِلَى الفَرْشِ - حَادِثٌ، أَيْ: مَوْجُوْدٌ بَعْدَ عَدَمٍ، وَكُلُّ حَادِثٍ لَهُ صَانِعٌ وَاجِبُ الوُجُوْدِ، فَالعَالَمُ لَهُ صَانِعٌ، ثُمَّ كَوْنُ الصَّانِعِ هُوَ اللَّهُ تَعَالَى مُسْتَفَادٌ مِنْ دَلِيْلِ الوَحْدَانِيَّةِ، وَحَيْثُ وَجَبَ لَهُ تَعَالَى الوُجُوْدُ اِسْتَحَالَ عَلَيْهِ ضِدُّهُ.

‹**The proof of this**› meaning the existence of Allah (Exalted is He) ‹**is the existence of created things (*makhlūqāt*).**› The formulation of this proof is that the world (*'ālam*) – from the Throne to the earth – is originated (*ḥādith*), meaning it exists after previously not existing. Every originated thing has a maker who is necessarily existent. Thus, the world has a maker. The determination that this maker is Allah (Exalted is He) is established through the proof of unicity (*dalīl al-waḥdāniyyah*).[28] Since existence is necessary for Allah (Exalted is He), its contrary is impossible for Him.[29]

---

26   Al-Bājūrī attributes this statement to Muḥammad al-Ṣaghīr (d. 1155 AH). *Al-Jawharah*, 23; *Tuḥfat*, 141.

     Our author repeats this phrase without attributing it to its source in *Fatḥ al-majīd*, 12; *al-Thimār al-yāniʿ* (Beirut: Dār al-Kutub al-ʿIlmiyyah, 1434/2013), 9.

27   *Al-Jawharah*, 43; *Tuḥfat*, 283; *Fatḥ al-majīd*, 16.

28   In *Tuḥfat al-murīd*, al-Bājūrī explains that this proof indicates the existence of a maker but does not indicate whether that maker is named "Allah" or something else. In *Fatḥ al-majīd*, our author gives the same proof of the existence of a maker and then explains that the identity of this maker is not taken from that proof, but rather from the Messengers (peace and blessings be upon them). See al-Bājūrī, *Taḥqīq al-maqām*, 67; *Fatḥ al-majīd*, 14–15; Cf. *Al-Jawharah*, 23; *Tuḥfat*, 139.

29   Cf. *Al-Jawharah*, 18, 29; *Tuḥfat*, 110, 139; *Fatḥ al-majīd*, 13.

PRE-ETERNITY

(وَيَجِـبُ فِـي حَقِّهِ تَعَالَـى الْقِدَمُ، وَمَعْنَاهُ أَنَّهُ تَعَالَى لَا أَوَّلَ لَهُ) أَيْ: لَـمْ يَسْـبِقْ وُجُوْدَهُ تَعَالَى عَدَمٌ.

‹Pre-eternity (*qidam*) is necessary for Allah (Exalted is He). Its meaning is that He has no beginning› meaning His existence (Exalted is He) is not preceded by nonexistence‹.›

(وَضِدُّهُ الْحُدُوْثُ) أَيْ: الْوُجُوْدُ بَعْدَ عَدَمٍ.

‹Its contrary is origination› meaning existence after nonexistence.[30]

(وَالدَّلِيْـلُ عَلَـى ذَلِكَ) أَيْ: وَكَيْفِيَّـةُ إِقَامَةِ الدَّلِيْلِ عَلَى وُجُوْبِ الْقِدَم لَهُ تَعَالَـى أَنْ تَقُـوْلَ: لَوْ لَمْ يَكُنْ قَدِيْمًا لَكَانَ حَادِثًا؛ إِذْ لَا وَاسِطَةَ بَيْنَهُمَا، لَكِنَّ كَوْنَهُ حَادِثَةً مُحَالٌ لـ (أَنَّهُ لَوْ كَانَ حَادِثًا لَاحْتَاجَ إِلَى مُحْدِثٍ) لِأَنَّ كُلَّ حَـادِثٍ لَا بُـدَّ لَهُ مِنْ مُحْدِثٍ، وَلَوْ حَدَثَ بِنَفْسِهِ لَزِمَ اِجْتِمَاعُ النَّقِيْضَيْنِ، وَهُمَا الْمُسَاوَاةُ وَالرُّجْحَانُ (وَ) لَكِنْ (هُوَ) أَيْ: اِحْتِيَاجُهُ تَعَالَى إِلَى مُحْدِثٍ (مُحَـالٌ)؛ إِذْ لَـوِ احْتَاجَ إِلَـى مُحْدِثٍ لَاحْتَاجَ مُحْدِثُهُ إِلَـى مُحْدِثٍ أَيْضًا، فَلَزِمَ الدَّوْرُ أَوِ التَّسَلْسَلُ، وَهُمَا مُحَالَانِ، أَيْ: لَا يُمْكِنُ وُجُودهمَا، وَحَيْثُ وَجَبَ لَهُ تَعَالَى الْقِدَمُ إِسْتَحَالَ عَلَيْهِ ضِدُّهُ.

‹The proof of this› meaning the way to establish the proof for the necessity of pre-eternity ‹is that› if He were not pre-eternal, He would be originated, since there is no intermediate state between them.[31] However, His being originated is impossible (*muḥāl*), because ‹if He had been originated, He would require an originator (*muḥdith*)›, since every originated thing must have an originator. If He had come

---

30   *Al-Jawharah*, 43; *Tuḥfat*, 283; *Fatḥ al-majīd*, 22.

31   There is no intermediary between being pre-eternal and originated. al-Bājūrī, *Taḥqīq al-maqām*, 80; *Fatḥ al-majīd*, 20.

into existence on His own, it would necessitate the conjunction of two contradictories (*naqīḍān*) – namely equivalence (*musāwah*) and preponderance (*rujḥān*) – which is impossible.[32]

‹**And**› yet ‹**it**› meaning His (Exalted is He) need for an originator ‹**is impossible.**[33]› Since if He needed an originator, then His originator would also need an originator – and that would lead to either circularity (*dawr*)[34] or infinite regress (*tasalsul*).[35] Both are impossible – that is, they cannot exist. Since pre-eternity is necessary for Him (Exalted is He), its contrary is impossible for Him.[36]

EVERLASTINGNESS

(وَيَجِـبُ فِـي حَقِّهِ تَعَالَى الْبَقَـاءُ، وَمَعْنَاهُ أَنَّهُ تَعَالَى لَا آخِرَلَـهُ) أَيْ: لَا يَلْحَقُ
وُجُوْدَهَ عَدَمٌ.[37]

‹**Everlastingness (*baqā'*) is necessary for Allah (Exalted is He). Its meaning is that He (Exalted is He) has no end**› meaning His existence is not overtaken by nonexistence‹.[38]›

(وَالدَّلِيْـلُ عَلَـى ذَلِكَ: أَنَّهُ لَوْ) لَمْ يَجِبْ لَهُ الْبَقَاءُ لَأَمْكَنَ أَنْ يَكُوْنَ فَانِيًا،
لَكِـنْ إِمْكَانُ الْفَنَاءِ لَـهُ مُحَالٌ؛ إِذْ لَوْ (كَانَ فَانِيًا) لَكَانَ جَائِرَ الْوُجُوْدِ، لَكِنْ

---

32   And the conjunction of two contradictories is impossible.

33   Al-Bājūrī, *Taḥqīq al-maqām*, 72. Cf. *Al-Jawharah*, 23; *Tuḥfat*, 142.

      Among the textual evidence for this attribute is that Allah (Exalted is He) says, "He is the First and the Last, and the Outward and the Inward; and He is Knower of all things." [Qur'an,, 57:3]

34   Circularity occurs when one thing depends upon another, which also depends upon that prior thing. *Fatḥ al-majīd*, 20–21.

35   An infinite regress occurs when there is an endless chain of consecutive events. *Fatḥ al-majīd*, 20.

36   Cf. *Al-Jawharah*, 23; *Tuḥfat*, 143; *Fatḥ al-majīd*, 20.

37   Some editions then have (وضده الفناء) – meaning its contrary is annihilation [*al-fanā'*]. But many do not have it, and it is not found in the manuscripts.

38   *Al-Jawharah*, 23; *Tuḥfat*, 143, 146; Cf. *Taḥqīq al-maqām*, 84–85; *Fatḥ al-majīd*, 22.

كَوْنُهُ جَائِرَ الوُجُودِ مُحَالٌ؛ إِذْ لَوْ كَانَ جَائِرَ الوُجُودِ **(لَكَانَ حَادِثًا وَ)** لَكِنْ

(هُوَ) أَيْ: كَوْنُهُ حَادِثًا **(مُحَالٌ)**؛ إِذْ لَوْ كَانَ حَادِثًا لَانْتَفَى عَنْهُ القِدَمُ، لَكِنْ

اِنْتِفَاءُ القِدَمِ عَنْهُ مُحَالٌ لِأَنَّهُ قَدْ قَامَ الدَّلِيلُ عَلَى وُجُوبِ القِدَمِ لَهُ تَعَالَى،

وَحَيْثُ وَجَبَ البَقَاءُ لِلَّهِ تَعَالَى اِسْتَحَالَ عَلَيْهِ ضِدُّهُ.

‹**The proof of this is that if** everlastingness were not necessary for Him, then it would be possible for Him to be subject to annihilation (*fanī*). However, the possibility of annihilation is impossible, because if ‹**He were transient,**› He would be merely possible in existence. But His being possible in existence is impossible, because if He were possible in existence, ‹**He would be originated. And**› yet ‹**it**› His being originated ‹**is impossible[39]**› because if He were originated, pre-eternity would be negated from Him. But negating pre-eternity from Him is impossible because the proof has been established for the necessity of His pre-eternity (Exalted is He).[40] And since everlastingness is necessary for Him (Exalted is He), its contrary is impossible for Him.[41]

DISSIMILARITY TO ORIGINATED THINGS

(وَيَجِبُ فِي حَقِّهِ تَعَالَى المُخَالَفَةُ لِلحَوَادِثِ) فَالمُخَالَفَةُ لِلمَخْلُوقَاتِ عِبَارَةٌ

عَنْ سَلْبِ الجِرْمِيَّةِ وَالعَرَضِيَّةِ وَالكُلِّيَّةِ وَالجُزْئِيَّةِ وَلَوَازِمِهَا عَنْهُ تَعَالَى. فَلَازِمُ

الجِرْمِيَّةِ: التَّحَيُّزُ، وَلَازِمُ العَرَضِيَّةِ: القِيَامُ بِالغَيْرِ، وَلَازِمُ الكُلِّيَّةِ: الكِبَرُ، وَلَازِمُ

الجُزْئِيَّةِ: الصِّغَرُ، إِلَى غَيْرِ ذَلِكَ.

‹**Dissimilarity to originated things (*mukhālifah li-l-ḥawādith*) is necessary for Allah (Exalted is He).**›

---

39   Among the textual evidence for this attribute is that Allah (Exalted is He) says, "Everyone that is thereon will pass away; There remaineth but the Countenance of thy Lord of Might and Glory" [Al-Raḥmān, 55:26–27]

40   Cf. *Al-Jawharah*, 23; *Tuḥfat*, 143; *Taḥqīq al-maqām*, 84–85; *Fatḥ al-majīd*, 22.

41   *Taḥqīq al-maqām*, 85–86; *Fatḥ al-majīd*, 22.

Dissimilarity to created things refers to negating from Him (Exalted is He) physicality (*jirmiyyah*), accidentiality (*'araḍiyyah*), wholeness (*kulliyyah*) or partness (*juz'iyyah*), and their necessary entailments. The necessary entailment of physicality is occupying space, the necessary entailment of accidentiality is subsisting in something else, the necessary entailment of wholeness is largeness, and the necessary entailment of partness is smallness – and so forth.[42]

(وَمَعْنَاهُ) أَيْ: الْمُخَالَفَةُ لِمَا ذُكِرَ (أَنَّهُ تَعَالَى لَيْسَ مُمَاثِلًا لِلْحَوَادِثِ) فَإِذَا أَلْقَى الشَّيْطَانُ فِي ذِهْنِكَ أَنَّهُ تَعَالَى إِذَا لَمْ يَكُنْ جِرْمًا وَلَا عَرَضًا وَلَا كُلًّا وَلَا جُزْءاً فَمَا حَقِيقَتُهُ؟! فَقُلْ فِي رَدِّ ذَلِكَ: لَا يَعْلَمُ اللَّهَ إِلَّا اللَّهُ، ﴿لَيْسَ كَمِثْلِهِ شَيْءٌ وَهُوَ السَّمِيعُ الْبَصِيرُ﴾ [الشورى: ١١]. فَهُوَ تَعَالَى لَيْسَ بِجِسْمٍ مُصَوَّرٍ، وَلَا بِجَوْهَرٍ مَحْدُودٍ مُقَدَّرٍ.

‹Its meaning› that is, dissimilarity to what was mentioned ‹is that Allah (Exalted is He) is not similar to them.›

Thus, if Shayṭān casts into your mind the thought: "If He (Exalted is He) is not a body, an accident, a whole, or a part, then what is His true reality?" – then repel it by saying: "No one knows Allah except Allah. 'There is nothing like unto Him, and He is the hearing, the seeing.'"[43]

Thus, He (Exalted is He) is neither a formed body nor a limited and measured substance.

(فَلَيْسَ لَهُ يَدٌ وَلَا عَيْنٌ وَلَا أُذُنٌ وَلَا غَيْرُ ذَلِكَ مِنْ صِفَاتِ الْحَوَادِثِ) لِأَنَّهُ لَا يُمَاثِلُ الْأَجْسَامَ، لَا فِي التَّقْدِيرِ وَلَا فِي قَبُولِ الِانْقِسَامِ، وَلَا تَحِلُّهُ الْجَوَاهِرُ، وَلَيْسَ بِعَرَضٍ وَلَا تَحِلُّهُ الْأَعْرَاضُ، بَلْ لَا يُمَاثِلُ مَوْجُودًا وَلَا يُمَاثِلُهُ مَوْجُودٌ، وَلَا يَحُدُّهُ الْمِقْدَارُ وَلَا تَحْوِيهِ الْأَقْطَارُ، وَلَا تُحِيطُ بِهِ الْجِهَاتُ، وَلَا تَكْتَنِفُهُ

---

42   *Al-Jawharah*, 24; *Tuḥfat*, 147; *Fatḥ al-majīd*, 23.

43   Qur'an, 42:11. *Al-Jawharah*, 24; *Tuḥfat*, 147. I have not found this paragraph in the author's other works.

الْأَرَضُوْنَ وَالسَّمَوَاتُ، رَفِيْعُ الدَّرَجَاتِ عَلَى كُلِّ شَيْءٍ، وَمَعَ ذَلِكَ هُوَ أَقْرَبُ
إِلَى الْعَبْدِ مِنْ حَبْلِ الْوَرِيْدِ، وَهُوَ عَلَى كُلِّ شَيْءٍ شَهِيْدٌ، لَا يُمَاثِلُ قُرْبُهُ قُرْبَ
الْأَجْسَامِ، تَعَالَى عَنْ أَنْ يَحْوِيَهُ مَكَانٌ، كَمَا تُقَدَّسُ عَنْ أَنْ يَحُدَّهُ زَمَانٌ،
كَانَ قَبْلَ أَنْ يَخْلُقَ الزَّمَانَ وَالمَكَانَ، وَهُوَ الآنَ عَلَى مَا عَلَيْهِ كَانَ.

‹He does not have a hand, eye, ear, or anything else among the attributes of originated things› because He is not similar to bodies – not in measurability, nor in admitting division‹.› Substances do not inhere in Him. He is not an accident, nor do accidental qualities subsist in Him. He does not resemble any existent, nor does any existent resemble Him. He is not limited by quantities, enwrapped by regions, nor encompassed by directions. The heavens and the earths do not contain Him. He is exalted above all things, yet, despite that, He is closer to the servant than his jugular vein and is a witness over everything. His nearness does not resemble the nearness of bodies, nor is He subject to spatial limitations. He is transcendent beyond being contained by place, just as He is sanctified from being limited by time. He existed before creating time and space, and He is now just as He was.

(وَضِدُّهَا الْمُمَاثَلَةُ)

‹Its contrary is likeness to originated things (*mumāthilah li-l-ḥawādith*).›[44]

(وَالدَّلِيْلُ عَلَى ذَلِكَ) أَيْ: مُخَالَفَتُهُ تَعَالَى لِلْمَخْلُوْقَاتِ (أَنَّهُ) أَيْ: اللَّهَ
لَوْ لَمْ يَكُنْ مُخَالَفَةٌ لِلْمَخْلُوْقَاتِ لَكَانَ مُمَاثِلًا لَهَا، لَكِنْ مُمَاثِلَتُهُ بَاطِلَةٌ؛
إِذْ (لَوْ كَانَ مُمَاثِلًا لِلْحَوَادِثِ لَكَانَ حَادِثًا) مِثْلَهَا؛ لِأَنَّ جَمِيْعَ مَا ثَبَتَ لِأَحَدِ
الْمِثْلَيْنِ يَثْبُتُ لِلْآخَرِ، (وَ) لَكِنْ (هُوَ) أَيْ: كَوْنُهُ حَادِثًا (مُحَالٌ)؛ لِأَنَّهُ قَدْ قَامَ

---

44   *Al-Jawharah*, 43; *Tuḥfat*, 283; *Fatḥ al-majīd*, 26.

الدَّلِيلُ عَلَى وُجُوبِ القِدَمِ لَهُ تَعَالَى، وَحَيْثُ وَجَبَتْ لَهُ المُخَالَفَةُ لِلحَوَادِثِ إِسْتَحَالَ عَلَيْهِ ضِدُّهَا.

‹The proof of this› meaning His dissimilarity to created things (Exalted is He) ‹is that› if Allah were not dissimilar to created things, He would be similar to them. However, His similarity to them is invalid because ‹if He were similar to originated things, He would be originated› like them, since everything that is affirmed for one of two similars is affirmed for the other‹. And› yet ‹it› meaning His being originated ‹is impossible[45]› because the proof of pre-eternity being necessary for Him (Exalted is He) has been established‹.› Since dissimilarity to originated things is necessary for Him (Exalted is He), its contrary is impossible for Him.[46]

وَصُوَرُ المُمَاثِلَة عَشَرَةٌ:

١. أَنْ يَكُونَ اللَّهُ جِرْمًا، سَوَاءٌ كَانَ مُرَكَّبًا وَيُسَمَّى حَيْنَئِذٍ جِسْمًا، أَوْ غَيْرَ مُرَكَّبٍ وَيُسَمَّى حَيْنَئِذٍ جَوْهَرًا فَرْدًا.

٢. أَوْ يَكُونَ عَرَضًا يَقُومُ بِالجِرْمِ.

٣. أَوْ يَكُونَ فِي جِهَةٍ لِلجِرْمِ، فَلَيْسَ فَوْقَ العَرْشِ وَلَا تَحْتَهُ وَلَا يَمِينَهُ وَلَا نَحْوَ ذَلِكَ مِنْ بَقِيَّةِ الجِهَاتِ.

The scenarios for similarity are ten:[47]
1. Allah being a body (*jirm*), whether it is composite, in which case, it is called a *corporeal body* (*jism*); or not a composite, in which case, it is called an *indivisible substance* (*jawhar fard*)[48].

---

45   Allah (Exalted is He) says, "There is nothing like unto Him, and He is the All-Hearing, the All-Seeing." [Qur'an, 42:11]

46   *Al-Jawharah*, 24; *Tuḥfat*, 147; *Fatḥ al-majīd*, 25.

47   Reminder: numbers and enumerations are from the translator.

48   The word "*jirm*" covers "*jism*" and "*jawhar fard*." A "*jism*" is what is composed of two or more "*jawhar fard*". A "*jawhar fard*" is that which is indivisible due to its smallness. Both of them are "*jirm*" since they do occupy space even if, from our perspective, it appears to be empty. *Fatḥ al-majīd*, 9.

2. Him being an accident (*'araḍ*) which subsists in a body.

3. Him being in a direction relative to a body – thus, He is neither above the Throne, nor below it, nor to its right, nor in any other direction among the remaining directions.

٤. أَوْ لَهُ تَعَالَى جِهَةٌ، فَلَيْسَ لَهُ فَوْقٌ وَلَا تَحْتٌ وَلَا يَمِينٌ وَلَا شِمَالٌ وَنَحْوُ ذَلِكَ.

٥. أَوْ يَحِلَّ فِي مَكَانٍ.

٦. أَوْ يَتَقَيَّدَ بِزَمَانٍ بِحَيْثُ تَكُونُ حَرَكَةُ الْفَلَكِ مُنْطَبِقَةً عَلَيْهِ.

4. Him (Exalted is He) having a direction. Thus, He does not have a top, bottom, left, right, or anything similar to that.

5. Him indwelling in a place.

6. Him being bound by time, such that the motions of celestial orbits apply to Him.

٧. أَوْ يَكُرَّ عَلَيْهِ الْجَدِيدَانِ اللَّيْلُ وَالنَّهَارُ.

٨. أَوْ تَتَّصَفَ ذَاتُهُ الْعَلِيَّةُ بِالْحَوَادِثِ، كَالْقُدْرَةِ الْحَادِثَةِ وَالْإِرَادَةِ الْحَادِثَةِ وَالْحَرَكَةِ أَوْ السُّكُونِ وَالْبَيَاضِ أَوْ السَّوَادِ وَنَحْوِ ذَلِكَ.

٩. أَوْ تَتَّصَفَ ذَاتُهُ بِالصِّغَرِ أَوْ الْكِبَرِ بِمَعْنَى كَثِيرِ الْأَجْزَاءِ.

7. The recurrence of day and night over Him.

8. His lofty essence being attributed with originated things, such as originated capability, originated will, motion, stillness, whiteness, blackness, and similar things.

9. His essence being attributed with smallness or largeness – in the sense of having many parts.

١٠. أَوْ يَتَّصَفَ بِالْأَغْرَاضِ فِي الْأَفْعَالِ أَوْ الْأَحْكَامِ، فَلَيْسَ فِعْلُهُ كَإِيْجَادِ زَيْدٍ لِغَرْضٍ مِنْ الْأَغْرَاضِ، أَيْ: مَصْلَحَةٍ تَبْعَثُهُ عَلَى ذَلِكَ الْفِعْلِ، فَلَا يُنَافِي أَنَّهُ لِحِكْمَةٍ وَإِلَّا كَانَ عَبَثًا، وَهُوَ مُسْتَحِيلٌ فِي حَقِّهِ تَعَالَى. وَلَيْسَ حُكْمُهُ كَإِيْجَابِ الصَّلَاةِ عَلَيْنَا لِغَرْضٍ مِنْ الْأَغْرَاضِ، أَيْ: مَصْلَحَةٍ

تَبَعُثُهُ عَلَى ذَلِكَ الحُكْمِ كَمَا مَرَّ.

10. Him being attributed with purposes in actions or rulings. Thus, His action – such as bringing Zayd into existence – is not for a purpose – meaning an advantage (*maṣlaḥah*) that prompts Him to perform that action. This does not rule out His acting in accordance with wisdom (*ḥikmah*) – for if there were no wisdom behind His acts at all, they would be frivolous, and that is impossible for Him (Exalted is He).

Likewise, His ruling – such as making prayer obligatory for us – is not for a purpose – meaning an advantage that prompts Him to enact that ruling, as has preceded.

فَكُلٌّ مِنْ هَذِهِ الصُّوَرِ العَشَرِ 49 مُسْتَحِيْلٌ فِي حَقِّهِ تَعَالَى.

All of these ten scenarios are impossible for Him (Exalted is He).[50]

SELF-SUBSISTENCE

(وَيَجِبُ فِي حَقِّهِ تَعَالَى القِيَامُ بِالنَّفْسِ، وَمَعْنَاهُ) مُفَسَّرٌ بِأَمْرَيْنِ. الأَوَّلُ (أَنَّهُ تَعَالَى لَا يَفْتَقِرُ إِلَى مَحَلٍّ) يَقُوْمُ بِهِ. (وَ) الثَّانِيُ: أَنَّهُ تَعَالَى (لَا) يَحْتَاجُ (إِلَى مُخَصِّصٍ) أَيْ: مُوْجِدٍ. وَهَذَا الثَّانِيُ وَإِنْ كَانَ يُسْتَغْنَى عَنْهُ بِالقِدَمِ لَا يَكْفِي فِيْهِ الِاسْتِغْنَاءُ لِأَنَّ خَطَرَ الجَهْلِ فِي هَذَا الفَنِّ عَظِيْمٌ، فَلَا بُدَّ فِيْهِ مِنْ التَّصْرِيْحِ بِالعَقَائِدِ.

‹Self-subsistence (*qiyām bi-l-nafs*) is necessary for Allah (Exalted is He). Its meaning› is explained through two matters.[51] The first ‹is that Allah (Exalted is He) does not need a substrate› to subsist in‹.[52]

---

49   Our book has (العشر), while *Taḥqīq al-maqām* has (العشرة).

50   *Al-Jawharah*, 43; *Tuḥfat*, 283. Cf. *Fatḥ al-majīd*, 24, which does not explicitly mention their number.

51   *Al-Jawharah*, 25; *Tuḥfat*, 150; *Fatḥ al-majīd*, 27.

52   *Al-Jawharah*, 25; *Tuḥfat*, 149; *Fatḥ al-majīd*, 27.

And› the second is that He (Exalted is He) does ‹**not**›need ‹**a specifier**› that is, an existentiator (*mūjid*)‹.›[53]

Even though the second is already entailed by His pre-eternity, that entailment alone is not enough: the stakes of error in this discipline are too high. Doctrinal tenets must be stated explicitly.[54]

(وَضِدُّهُ: الِاحْتِيَاجُ إِلَى المَحَلِّ وَالمُخَصِّصِ).

‹**Its contrary is needing a substrate and a specifier.**›[55]

(وَالدَّلِيـلُ عَلَى ذَلِكَ) أَي: القِيَامِ بِالنَّفْـسِ (أَنَّهُ لَوِ احْتَاجَ إِلَى مَحَلٍّ) أَيْ: ذَاتٍ يَقُـوْمُ بِهَا (لَـكَانَ صِفَـةً) أَيْ: لِأَنَّـهُ لَا يَحْتَاجُ إِلَى مَحَلٍّ يَقُـوْمُ بِهِ إِلَّا الصِّفَةُ؛ إِذِ الذَّاتُ لَا تَحْتَاجُ إِلَى ذَاتٍ تَقُوْمُ بِهَا (وَكَوْنُهُ صِفَةً مُحَالٌ)؛ إِذْ لَوْ كَانَ صِفَةً لَمْ يَتَّصَفْ بِصِفَاتِ المَعَانِي وَلَا المَعْنَوِيَّةِ، وَهِيَ وَاجِبَةُ القِيَامِ بِهِ تَعَالَى لِلأَدِلَّةِ عَلَى ذَلِكَ، فَعَدَمُ اتِّصَافِهِ بِذَلِكَ بَاطِلٌ، فَبَطَلَ مَا أَدَّى إِلَيْهِ، وَهُوَ افْتِقَارُهُ إِلَى المَحَلِّ، وَإِذَا بَطَلَ افْتِقَارُهُ إِلَى المَحَلِّ ثَبَتَ اسْتِغْنَاؤُهُ عَنْهُ وَهُوَ المَطْلُوبُ. (وَلَوِ احْتَاجَ إِلَى مُخَصِّصٍ) أَيْ: مُوْجِدٍ يُوْجِدُهُ (لَكَانَ حَادِثًا) لِأَنَّهُ لَا يَحْتَاجُ إِلَى ذَلِكَ إِلَّا الحَادِثُ؛ إِذِ القَدِيْمُ لَا يَحْتَاجُ لَهُ (وَكَوْنُهُ حَادِثًا مُحَالٌ) لِأَنَّهُ قَدْ سَبَقَ وُجُوْبُ وُجُوْدِهِ وَقِدَمِهِ وَبَقَائِهِ ذَاتًا وَصِفَاتٍ.

‹**The proof of this**› meaning self-subsistence ‹**is that if He needed a substrate (*maḥall*)**› meaning an entity in which to subsist ‹**He would be an attribute,**› since only an attribute requires a substrate, whereas an essence does not. ‹**But His being an attribute is impossible**›: were He an attribute, He could not be characterised by the entitative attrib-

---

53   *Al-Jawharah*, 25; *Tuḥfat*, 150; *Fatḥ al-majīd*, 27.

54   *Al-Jawharah*, 25; *Tuḥfat*, 150.

     I have not found it in our author's works, though the first half is in Imām al-Sanūsī's *Sharḥ al-Ṣughrā*. See: Muḥammad bin Yūsuf bin ʿUmar al-Sanūsī, *Sharḥ Al-ʿAqīdat al-ṣughrā*, edited by Anas Muḥammad ʿAdnān al-Sharfāwī (Damascus: Dār al-Taqwā, 1441/2019), 182.

55   *Al-Jawharah*, 43; *Tuḥfat*, 283; *Fatḥ al-majīd*, 28.

utes (*ṣifāt al-maʿānī*) or the qualitative attributes (*ṣifāt maʿnawiyyah*), despite their necessarily subsisting in Him (Exalted is He), as has been proven‹.› Since denying them of Him is false, what leads to it – His needing a substrate – is also false. And once His need for a substrate is invalidated, His independence from one is established, which is the desired conclusion.[56]

‹**And if He needed a specifier (*mukhaṣṣiṣ*)**› meaning an existentiator to bring Him into existence ‹**He would be originated**› since only an originated being requires that; a pre-eternal being does not‹. **But His being originated is impossible**› since the necessity of His existence, His pre-eternity, and His everlastingness – in both essence and attributes – has already been established‹.[57]›

UNICITY

(وَيَجِبُ فِي حَقِّهِ تَعَالَى الوَحْدَانِيَّةُ فِي الذَّاتِ وَفِي الصِّفَاتِ وَفِي الأَفْعَالِ)

‹**Unicity (*waḥdāniyyah*) in His entity, His attributes, and His actions is necessary for Allah (Exalted is He).**›[58]

(وَمَعْنَى الوَحْدَانِيَّةِ فِي الذَّاتِ أَنَّهَا لَيْسَتْ مُرَكَّبَةً مِنْ أَجْزَاءٍ مُتَعَدِّدَةٍ) وَيُقَالُ لِذَلِكَ: كَمٌّ مُتَّصِلٌ فِي الذَّاتِ، وَأَنَّهُ لَيْسَ هُنَاكَ ذَاتٌ تُشْبِهُ ذَاتَهُ تَعَالَى، وَيُقَالُ لَهُ: كَمٌّ مُنْفَصِلٌ فِي الذَّاتِ، لَكِنِ الوَحْدَةُ فِي الذَّاتِ بِمَعْنَى عَدَمِ التَّرْكِيبِ مِنْ أَجْزَاءٍ عُلِمَتْ مِنَ المُخَالَفَةِ لِلْحَوَادِثِ كَمَا مَرَّ.

‹**The meaning of unicity in entity is that it is not composed of multiple elements.**› This is called a continuous quantity (*kamm muttaṣil*) in the entity.

And that there is no entity resembling His entity (Exalted is He). This is called a discrete quantity (*kamm munfaṣil*) in the entity.

---

56   *Al-Jawharah*, 25; *Tuḥfat*, 150; *Fatḥ al-majīd*, 27–28.

57   *Al-Jawharah*, 25; *Tuḥfat*, 150; *Fatḥ al-majīd*, 27.

58   *Fatḥ al-majīd*, 29.

However, unicity in the entity – in the sense of not being composed of parts – is understood from the attribute of dissimilarity to originated things, as previously mentioned.[59]

(وَمَعْنَى الوَحْدَانِيَّةِ فِي الصِّفَاتِ) هُوَ عَدَمُ تَعَدُّدِهَا، فَلَيْسَ لَهُ تَعَالَى صِفَتَانِ فِي الإِسْمِ وَالمَعْنَى، وَبَيَانُ ذَلِكَ (أَنَّهُ) تَعَالَى (لَيْسَ لَهُ صِفَتَانِ فَأَكْثَر مِنْ جِنْسٍ وَاحِدٍ كَقُدْرَتَيْنِ) فَأَكْثَر وعلمينِ فَأَكْثَر (وهكذا) وَيُقَالُ لَهُ: كَمْ مُتَّصِلٍ فِي الصِّفَاتِ (وَ) عَدَمُ النَّظِيرِ فِيهَا وَهُوَ أَنَّهُ (لَيْسَ لِغَيْرِهِ صِفَة تشابه صفته تَعَالَى) فَلَيْسَ لِغَيْرِهِ تَعَالَى قُدْرَةٌ كَقُدْرَتِهِ تَعَالَى، أَوْ عِلْمٌ كَعِلْمِهِ وَهَكَذَا، وَيُقَالُ لَهُ: كَمٌّ مُنْفَصِلٌ فِي الصِّفَاتِ.

‹The meaning of unicity in attributes› is the absence of plurality. Thus, He (Exalted is He) does not have two attributes with the same name and meaning.

The clarification of this ‹is that He› (Exalted is He) ‹does not have two or more attributes of the same kind, such as two› or more ‹capabilities (*qudratān*)›, or two or more knowledge (*'ilmān*)‹, and so on.[60]› This is called a continuous quantity in the attributes.

‹And› the absence of a peer in them, meaning that ‹none other than Him (Exalted is He) has an attribute resembling His attribute.› Thus, none other than Allah (Exalted is He) has capability like His capability, or knowledge like His knowledge, and so on. This is called a discrete quantity in attributes.[61]

(وَمَعْنَى الوَحْدَانِيَّةِ فِي الأَفْعَالِ أَنَّهُ لَيْسَ لِغَيْرِهِ فِعْلٌ مِنَ الأَفْعَالِ) وَيُقَالُ لَهُ: كَمٌّ مُنْفَصِلٌ فِي الأَفْعَالِ. وَأَمَّا الكَمُّ المُتَّصِلُ فِي الأَفْعَالِ، فَإِنْ صَوَّرْنَاهُ بِتَعَدُّدِ الأَفْعَالِ فَهُوَ ثَابِتٌ لَا يَصِحُّ نَفْيُهُ لِأَنَّ أَفْعَالَهُ تَعَالَى كَثِيرَةٌ مِنْ خَلْقٍ وَرِزْقٍ وَأَحْيَاءٍ وَإِمَاتَةٍ إِلَى غَيْرِ ذَلِكَ، وَإِنْ صَوَّرْنَاهُ بِمُشَارَكَةِ غَيْرِ اللَّهِ لَهُ، فَهُوَ

---

59   *Al-Jawharah*, 25; *Tuḥfat*, 152; Cf. *Fatḥ al-majīd*, 30, 32.
60   *Al-Jawharah*, 25; *Tuḥfat*, 152; *Fatḥ al-majīd*, 30, 32.
61   *Fatḥ al-majīd*, 30, 32. Cf. *Al-Jawharah*, 43; *Tuḥfat*, 283.

مَنْفِــيٌّ أَيْضًــا بِوَحْدَانِيَّةِ الأَفْعَالِ، فَهُوَ تَعَالَى مُنْفَرِدٌ بِالخَلْقِ والِاخْتِرَاعِ مُتَوَحِّدٌ بِالإِيْجَادِ وَالإِبْدَاعِ، خَلَقَ الخَلْقَ وَأَعْمَالَهَمْ، وَقَدَّرَ أَرْزَاقَهُمْ وآجَالَهُمْ.

‹**The meaning of unicity in actions is that no one else performs any action.**› It is called a discrete quantity in actions.[62]

As for a continuous quantity in actions: If we were to conceive of it as a plurality of actions, then it is established, and it is not valid to negate it since His actions (Exalted is He) are many, including creating, providing sustenance, giving life, causing death, and so on.

However, if we conceive of it as something other than Allah cooperating with Him, then it is also negated by the unicity of actions.[63] For He (Exalted is He) is singular in creating and innovating, unique in bringing into existence and originating.

He created creation and their actions, and He determined their sustenance and their lifespans.

وَالحَاصِلُ أَنَّ الوَحْدَانِيَّةَ الشَّامِلَةَ لِوَحْدَةِ الذَّاتِ وَوَحْدَةِ الصِّفَاتِ وَوَحْدَةِ الأَفْعَالِ تَنْفِي كُمُومًا خَمْسَةً:

١. الكَمَّ المُتَّصِلَ فِي الذَّاتِ: وَهُوَ تَرْكِيْبُهُ مِنْ أَجْزَاءٍ.

٢. وَالكَـمُّ المُنْفَصِـلُ فِي الذَّاتِ: وَهُوَ التَّعَدُّدُ بِحَيْثُ يَكُوْنُ هُنَاكَ إِلَهٌ ثَانٍ فَأَكْثَرُ.

فَهَذَانِ الكُمَّانِ مُنْفِيَّانِ بِوَحْدَةِ الذَّاتِ.

In short, unicity – which includes unicity in entity, unicity in attributes, and unicity in actions – negates five quantities:

1. Continuous quantity in the entity – which is its composition from parts.
2. Discrete quantity in the entity – which is plurality, such that there is one or more other gods.

---

62 *Fatḥ al-majīd*, 32.
63 *Al-Jawharah*, 25; *Tuḥfat*, 153; *Fatḥ al-majīd*, 35.

These two quantities are negated by unicity in entity.

٣- وَالكَـمُّ المُتَّصِـلُ فِي الصِّفَـاتِ: وَهُوَ التَّعَدُّدُ فِي صِفَاتِهِ تَعَالَى مِنْ جِنْسٍ وَاحِدٍ، كَقُدْرَتَيْنِ فَأَكْثَرُ.

٤- وَالكَمُّ المُنْفَصِلُ فِيهَا: وَهُوَ أَنْ يَكُوْنَ لِغَيْرِهِ تَعَالَى صِفَةٌ تُشْبِهُ صِفَتَهُ تَعَالَى، كَأَنْ يَكُوْنَ لِزَيْدٍ قُدْرَةٌ يُوْجِدُ بِهَـا وَيُعْدِمُ بِهَا كَقُدْرَتِهِ تَعَالَى أَوْ إِرَادَةٌ تُخَصِّصُ الشَّيْءَ بِبَعْضِ المُمْكِنَاتِ، أَوْ عِلْمٌ مُحِيْطٌ بِجَمِيْعِ الأَشْيَاءِ.

وَهَذَانِ الكَمَّانِ مُنْفِيَّانِ بِوْحَدَةِ الصِّفَاتِ.

3. Continuous quantity in attributes – which is plurality in His attributes (Exalted is He) from a single genus, such as two or more capabilities.

4. Discrete quantity in attributes – which is that something other than Allah (Exalted is He) possesses an attribute resembling His attribute (Exalted is He), such as Zayd possessing a capability through which he brings things into existence and annihilates them, like Allah's capability (Exalted is He), or a will that specifies something with certain contingent things (*mumkināt*),[64] or a knowledge that encompasses all things.

These two quantities are negated by unicity in attributes.

---

64   Throughout this translation, I render *mumkin* as "contingent" and *jāʾiz* as "possible." Many kalām texts – including al-Bājūrī's own *Tuḥfat al-murīd* – treat the two as synonyms. Strictly, however, *mumkin* denotes what equally admits of existence and nonexistence in itself, while *jāʾiz* is broader, covering anything reason does not rule out. The distinction surfaces in this text when both terms appear in the same passage (e.g., "contingent things are possible"). Readers moving on to *Fatḥ al-qarīb al-mujīb*, where the matn explicitly synonymises them, should keep this in mind.

٥- وَالكَـمُّ المُنْفَصِـلُ فِي الأَفْعَالِ: وَهُوَ أَن يَكُـوْنَ لِغَيْرِهِ تَعَالَى فِعْلٌ مِنْ الأَفْعَـالِ عَلَى وَجْـهِ الإِيْجَادِ وَإِنَّمَا يَنْسِـبُ الفِعْـلُ لِذَلِكَ الغَيْرِ عَلَى وَجْهِ الكَسْبِ والاِخْتِيَارِ.

وَهَذَا الكَمُّ مَنْفِيٌّ بِوَحْدَانِيَّةِ الأَفْعَالِ.

5. Discrete quantity in actions – which is that something other than Allah (Exalted is He) possesses an action in the manner of bringing things into existence. Rather, the action is attributed to that other entity only in the manner of acquisition (*kasb*) and choice (*ikhtiyār*).

This quantity is negated by the unicity in actions.[65]

(وَضِدُّهَا) أَي: الوَحْدَانِيَّةِ (التَّعَدُّدُ)

‹Its contrary› meaning [the contrary] of unicity ‹is plurality (*ta'addud*)[66].›

وَدَلِيْلُ الوَحْدَانِيَّةِ فِي الـذَّاتِ - بِمَعْنَى عَدَمِ الكَمِّ المُتَّصِلِ فِيْهَا - هُوَ دَلِيْلُ المُخَالَفَةِ لِلحَوَادِثِ المُتَقَدَّمُ، وَدَلِيْلُ الوَحْدَانِيَّةِ فِي الصِّفَاتِ - بِمَعْنَى عَدَمِ الكَمِّ المُتَّصِلِ فِيْهَا - أَنَّ التَّعَدُّدَ لَا يَقْتَضِيهِ مَعْقُوْلٌ وَلَا مَنْقُوْلٌ.

The proof of unicity in the entity – meaning the absence of a continuous quantity in it – is the preceding proof of dissimilarity to originated things.

The proof of unicity in attributes – meaning the absence of a continuous quantity in them – is that plurality is neither necessitated by reason nor by transmitted texts.

65　This summary, starting from "In short…": *Al-Jawharah*, 25; *Tuḥfat*, 153; *Fatḥ al-majīd*, 32.

66　*Al-Jawharah*, 43; *Tuḥfat*, 283; *Fatḥ al-majīd*, 37.

(وَالدَّلِيـلُ عَلَى ذَلِـكَ) أَيْ: الوَحْدَانِيَّةِ - بِمَعْنَى عَدَمِ النَّظِيرِ فِي الذَّاتِ وَالصِّفَاتِ - (أَنَّهُ) تَعَالَى (لَوْ كَانَ مُتَعَدِّدًا) كَأَنْ يَكُونَ هُنَاكَ إِلَهَانِ (لَمْ يُوجَدْ شَيْءٌ) أَيْ: بَعْضٌ (مِنْ هَذِهِ المَخْلُوقَاتِ) لَكِنْ عَدَمُ وُجُودِ ذَلِكَ بَاطِلٌ لِأَنَّهُ مَوْجُودٌ بِالمُشَاهَدَةِ، فَمَا أَدَّى إِلَيْهِ - وَهُوَ التَّعَدُّدُ - بَاطِلٌ، وَإِذَا بَطَلَ التَّعَدُّدُ ثَبَتَتْ الوَحْدَانِيَّةُ وَهُوَ المَطْلُوبُ.

‹The proof of this› meaning unicity in the sense of the absence of a peer in the entity and attributes ‹is that if He› (Exalted is He) ‹were multiple› such that there were two gods ‹none of these created things would exist[67].› However, the nonexistence of created things is invalid, because they exist as is observed. Thus, what leads to that – which is plurality – is invalid. And if plurality is invalidated, unicity is established – and that is the sought conclusion.[68]

وَإِنَّمَـا لَـزِمَ مِـنْ التَّعَدُّدِ عَدَمُ وُجُودِ شَـيْءٍ مِنْ العَالَمِ لِأَنَّهُ لَوْ كَانَ هُنَاكَ إِلَهَانِ .. فَإِمَّا أَنْ يَتَّفِقَا وَإِمَّا أَنْ يَخْتَلِفَا.

Plurality entails the nonexistence of anything in the world, because if there were two gods, then they would either agree or disagree.

فَإِنَّ اتَّفَقَا:

١. فَلَا جَائِزَ أَنْ يُوجِدَاهُ مَعًا لِئَلَّا يَلْزِمَ اجْتِمَاعُ مُؤَثِّرَيْنِ عَلَى وَاحِدٍ.

٢. وَلَا جَائِزَ أَنْ يُوجِدَاهُ مُرَتَّبًا بِأَنْ يُوجِدَهُ أَحَدُهُمَا ثُمَّ يُوجِدَهُ الآخَرُ لِئَلَّا يَلْزِمَ تَحْصِيلُ الحَاصِلِ.

٣. وَلَا جَائِزَ أَنْ يَشْتَرِكَا فِي الإِيجَادِ بِأَنْ يُوجِدَ أَحَدُهُمَا البَعْضَ وَالآخَرُ البَعْضَ الآخَرَ لِلُزُومِ عَجْزِهَا حَيْنِئِذٍ لِأَنَّهُ لَمَّا تَعَلَّقَتْ قُدْرَةُ أَحَدِهِمَا

---

67   Allah (Exalted is He) says, "Had there been gods in them other than Allah, both would have fallen into ruin." [Qur'an, 21:22]

68   *Al-Jawharah*, 25; *Tuḥfat*, 153; *Fatḥ al-majīd*, 36.

بِالْبَعْضِ سُدَّ عَلَى الآخَرِ طَرِيْقُ تَعَلُّقِ قُدْرَتِهِ بِهِ فَلَا يَقْدِرُ عَلَى مُخَالَفَتِهِ، وَهَذَا عَجْزٌ.

وَهَذَا يُسَمَّى بُرْهَانُ التَّوَارُدِ لِمَا فِيهِ مِنْ تَوَارُدِهِمَا عَلَى شَيْءٍ وَاحِدٍ.

If they both agree, then it is not possible that they:

1. Bring it into existence together, lest that entail two effectors acting upon a single thing.
2. Bring it into existence sequentially – by one bringing it into existence, followed by the other – lest that entail achieving what has already been achieved.
3. Share in bringing it into existence – by one bringing part of it into existence, and the other bringing the other part – because this would entail their incapacity. This is because when the capability of one of them is linked to part of it, the other's capability is blocked from linking to it, thus making him incapable of opposing the first – and this is incapacity.

This is called "The Proof of Coincidence" (*burhān al-tawārud*), because of their coinciding upon a single thing.[69]

وَإِنْ اِخْتَلَفَا بِأَنْ يُرِيْدَ أَحَدُهُمَا إِيْجَادَ شَيْءٍ مِنْ الْعَالَمِ وَالآخَرُ إِعْدَامَهُ:

١. فَلَا جَائِزَ أَنْ يُنَفَّذَ مُرَادُهُمَا لِئَلَّا يَلْزِمَ عَلَيْهِ اِجْتِمَاعُ النَّقِيْضَيْنِ.

٢. وَلَا جَائِزَ أَنْ لَا يُنَفَّذَ مُرَادُهُمَا مَعًا لِلُزُوْمِ عَجْزِهِمَا.

٣. وَلَا جَائِزَ أَن يُنَفَّذَ مُرَادُ أَحَدِهِمَا دُوْنَ الآخَرِ لِلُزُوْمِ عَجْزِ مَنْ يُنَفَّذُ مُرَادُهُ وَالآخَرُ مِثْلُهُ لِاِنْعِقَادِ الْمُمَاثَلَةِ بَيْنَهُمَا.

وَهَذَا يُسَمَّى بُرْهَانُ التَّمَانُعِ لِتَمَانِعِهِمَا وَتَخَالِفِهِمَا.

If they disagree – by one of them willing to bring something in the world into existence and the other willing its nonexistence – then it is not possible that:

---

69   *Al-Jawharah*, 25; *Tuḥfat*, 153; *Fatḥ al-majīd*, 36.

1. Both of their wills are carried out, lest that entail the conjunction of two contradictories.

2. Neither of their wills is carried out, for that would entail their incapacity.

3. The will of one is carried out while the other is not, for that would entail the incapacity of the one whose will is not carried out – while the other is just like him, since similarity is established between them.

This is called "The Argument of Mutual Hindrance" (*burhān al-tamānu'*) due to their mutual hindrance and opposition to one another.[70]

وَأَمَّا دَلِيلُ الْوَحْدَانِيَّةِ فِي الْأَفْعَالِ بِمَعْنَى عَدَمِ الْكُمِّ الْمُتَّصِلِ فِيهَا - وَهُوَ عَدَمُ مُشَارَكَةِ الْغَيْرِ لَهُ تَعَالَى فِي فِعْلٍ - فَهُوَ بَعْضُ مَا مَرَّ فِي بُرْهَانِ التَّوَارُدِ.

As for the proof of unicity in actions – meaning the absence of a continuous quantity in them, which is the absence of another cooperating with Him (Exalted is He) in an act – it is part of what has preceded in "The Proof of Coincidence" (*burhān al-tawārud*).

وَأَمَّا دَلِيلُ وَحْدَةِ الْأَفْعَالِ بِمَعْنَى عَدَمِ الْكُمِّ الْمُنْفَصِلِ فِيهَا بِأَنْ يَكُونَ لِغَيْرِهِ تَعَالَى تَأْثِيرٌ فِي فِعْلٍ مِنْ الْأَفْعَالِ عَلَى انْفِرَادِهِ:

١. فَإِنْ قَدَّرْتَ الشَّيْءَ مُؤثِّرًا بِطَبْعِهِ لَزِمَ أَنْ يَسْتَغْنِي ذَلِكَ الْأَثَرُ عَنْ مَوْلَانَا جَلَّ وَعَزَّ كَيْفَ وَهُوَ الَّذِي يَفْتَقِرُ إِلَيْهِ كُلُّ مَا سِوَاهُ.

٢. وَإِنْ قَدَّرْتَهُ مُؤثِّرًا بِقُوَّةٍ جَعَلَهَا اللَّهُ فِيهَا كَمَا يَزْعُمُهُ كَثِيرٌ مِنْ عَوَامِّ الْمُؤْمِنِينَ فَإِنَّهُمْ يَعْتَقِدُونَ أَنَّ الْأَسْبَابَ الْعَادِيَّةَ مُؤَثِّرَةً بِقُوَّةٍ جَعَلَهَا اللَّهُ فِيهَا وَلَوْ نَزَعَهَا مِنْهَا لَا تُؤَثِّرُ - كَزَعْمِهِمْ أَنَّ الْأَكْلَ يُؤَثِّرُ فِي وُجُودِ الشَّبَعِ، وَأَنَّ الشُّرْبَ يُؤَثِّرُ فِي وُجُودِ الرَّيِّ، وَأَنَّ النَّارَ تُؤَثِّرُ فِي وُجُودِ الْإِحْرَاقِ، وَأَنَّ السِّكِّينَ تُؤَثِّرُ فِي وُجُودِ الْقَطْعِ بِقُوَّةٍ جَعَلَهَا اللَّهُ فِي جَمِيعِهَا - فَذَلِكَ

---

70   *Al-Jawharah*, 25; *Tuḥfat*, 154; *Fatḥ al-majīd*, 35.

بَاطِلٌ أَيْضًا لِأَنَّهُ يُصَيِّرُ مَوْلَانَا جَلَّ وَعَزَّ حَيْنَئِذٍ مُفْتَقِرًا فِي إِيْجَادِهِ بَعْضَ الْأَفْعَالِ إِلَى وَاسِطَةٍ، وَالْحَالُ أَنَّهُ تَعَالَى لَهُ الْغِنَى الْمُطْلَقُ عَنْ كُلِّ مَا سِوَاهُ، وَصَاحِبُ هَذَا الِاعْتِقَادِ لَيْسَ كَافِرًا بَلْ فَاسِقٌ، وَيَقْرُبُ مِنْ هَذَا اعْتِقَادُ الْمُعْتَزِلَةِ أَنَّ الْعَبْدَ يَخْلُقُ أَفْعَالَ نَفْسِهِ الِاخْتِيَارِيَّةَ بِقُوَّةٍ جَعَلَهَا اللَّهُ فِيْهِ، فَهَؤُلَاءِ فَسَقَةٌ.

As for the proof of unicity in actions – meaning the absence of a discrete quantity in them, by something other than Him (Exalted is He) having an effect in any action on its own:

1. If you consider the thing to exert an influence by its nature, then that necessitates that the effect is independent of our Lord (Mighty and Majestic is He). How can this be, when He is the One upon whom everything else depends?

2. If you consider the thing to exert an influence by a power Allah has placed within it – as many lay Muslims claim, believing that customary causes (*asbāb ʿādiyyah*) have efficacy by a power Allah has created in them, and that if He were to remove it, they would lose their efficacy – then this is also invalid.

   For example, their claim that eating causes satiety, drinking causes quenching, fire causes burning, and a knife causes cutting – all by a power Allah has placed in them.

   This belief is also invalid because it would necessitate that our Lord (Mighty and Majestic is He) is dependent upon an intermediary to bring some actions into existence.

   Yet, the reality is that He (Exalted is He) has absolute independence from everything other than Him.

   Whoever holds this belief is not a disbeliever but is corrupt (*fāsiq*).

   Close to this is the belief of the Muʿtazilah, who say that the servant creates his own voluntary actions by a power Allah has placed in him. These people, too, are corrupt (*fussāq*).[71]

---

71   Cf. *Fatḥ al-majīd*, 34–35.

مِنْ الْحَوَادِثِ، وَذَلِكَ بَاطِلٌ لِمُشَاهَدَةِ وُجُودِهَا، فَبَطَلَ مَا أَدَّى إِلَيْهِ عَدَمُ الْإِيْجَادِ وَهُوَ عَجْزُهُ، وَإِذَا انْتَفَى الْعَجْزُ انْتَفَتْ الْكَرَاهَةُ وَثَبَتَ نَقِيضُهَا، وَهُوَ الْإِرَادَةُ، وَحَيْثُ وَجَبَتْ لَهُ تَعَالَى الْإِرَادَةُ اسْتَحَالَ عَلَيْهِ ضِدُّهَا.

‹**The proof of this**› meaning establishing will for Him (Exalted is He) is the existence of the world. Its formulation ‹**is that if He**› (Exalted is He) ‹**were**› not attributed with will, He would be averse. If He were ‹**averse**› meaning devoid of will, He would not be attributed with capability. However, His not being attributed with capability is impossible, since if He were not attributed with it, ‹**He would be incapable (ʿājiz). And Him being incapable is impossible**›, because if He were incapable, no originated being would exist‹.› This is invalid, as the existence of originated things is observed.

Thus, whatever the absence of bringing into existence leads to is invalidated – which is His incapacity (ʿajz). And if incapacity is negated, aversion is negated, and its contrary is established – which is will. Since will is necessary for Him (Exalted is He), its contrary is impossible for Him.[104]

KNOWLEDGE

(وَيَجِبُ فِي حَقِّهِ تَعَالَى الْعِلْمُ، وَهِيَ صِفَةٌ مَوْجُودَةٌ (قَدِيمَةٌ قَائِمَةٌ بِذَاتِهِ تَعَالَى، يَعْلَمُ بِهَا الْأَشْيَاءَ) مِنْ الْوَاجِبَاتِ وَالْجَائِزَاتِ وَالْمُسْتَحِيلَاتِ عَلَى وَجْهِ الْإِحَاطَةِ عَلَى مَا هِيَ عَلَيْهِ تَفْصِيلًا، فَيَعْلَمُ سُبْحَانَهُ وَتَعَالَى مَا لَا نِهَايَةَ لَهُ تَفْصِيلًا كَكَمَالَاتِهِ وَأَنْفَاسِ أَهْلِ الْجَنَّةِ، فَتَعَلَّقُ الْعِلْمِ وَاحِدٌ تَنْجِيزِيٌّ قَدِيمٌ، فَهُوَ تَعَالَى عَالِمٌ بِجَمِيعِ الْمَعْلُومَاتِ، مُحِيطٌ بِجَمِيعِ مَا يَجْرِي تَحْتَ تُخُومِ الْأَرْضِ إِلَى أَعْلَى السَّمَوَاتِ، لَا يَعْزُبُ عَنْ عِلْمِهِ مِثْقَالُ ذَرَّةٍ فِي الْأَرْضِ وَلَا فِي السَّمَاءِ، بَلْ يَعْلَمُ دَبِيبَ النَّمْلَةِ السَّوْدَاءِ عَلَى الصَّخْرَةِ

---

104 *Fatḥ al-majīd*, 48–49; Cf. *Al-Jawharah*, 27; *Tuḥfat*, 173.

وَالْحَاصِلُ:

١. أَنَّ مَنِ اعْتَقَدَ أَنَّ الْأَسْبَابَ الْعَادِيَّةَ كَالنَّارِ وَالسِّكِّينِ وَالْأَكْلِ وَالشُّرْبِ تُؤَثِّرُ فِي مُسَبَّبَاتِهَا كَالْحَرْقِ وَالْقَطْعِ وَالشِّبْعِ وَالرَّيِّ بِذَاتِهَا فَهُوَ كَافِرٌ بِالْإِجْمَاعِ.

٢. أَوْ بِقُوَّةٍ جَعَلَهَا اللَّهُ فِيهَا فَفِي كُفْرِهِ قَوْلَانِ، وَالْأَصَحُّ أَنَّهُ لَيْسَ بِكَافِرٍ بَلْ فَاسِقٌ مُبْتَدِعٌ، وَمِثْلُ الْقَائِلِينَ بِذَلِكَ الْمُعْتَزِلَةُ الْقَائِلُونَ بِأَنَّ الْعَبْدَ يَخْلُقُ أَفْعَالَ نَفْسِهِ الِاخْتِيَارِيَّةَ بِقُوَّةٍ خَلَقَهَا اللَّهُ فِيهِ، فَالْأَصَحُّ عَدَمُ كُفْرِهِمْ لِإِقْرَارِهِمْ بِأَنَّ قُدْرَةَ الْعَبْدِ عَلَى ذَلِكَ مِنَ اللَّهِ تَعَالَى.

In summary:

1. Whoever believes that customary causes – such as fire, knives, eating, and drinking – exert an influence on their effects, such as burning, cutting, satiety, and quenching thirst, by their very essence, is a disbeliever by consensus.

2. If he believes that they have an effect by a power Allah has placed within them, then there are two opinions regarding whether he has disbelieved.

The soundest opinion is that he is not a disbeliever but rather a corrupt innovator (*fāsiq mubtadi*ʿ).

Similar to those who hold this opinion are the Muʿtazilah, who say that the servant creates his own voluntary actions by a power Allah has placed in him.

The soundest opinion is that they are not disbelievers[72] since they affirm that the servant's power in this regard is from Allah (Exalted is He).[73]

٣. وَمَنِ اعْتَقَدَ أَنَّ الْمُؤَثِّرَ هُوَ اللَّهُ تَعَالَى لَكِنْ جَعَلَ بَيْنَ الْأَسْبَابِ وَمُسَبَّبَاتِهَا تَلَازُمًا عَقْلِيًّا بِحَيْثُ لَا يَصِحُّ تَأَخُّرُهَا - فَمَتَى وَجَدَ الْمُسَبِّبُ فَمَتَى

---

72   *Al-Jawharah*, 45; *Tuḥfat*, 288; *Fatḥ al-majīd*, 34.
73   *Fatḥ al-majīd*, 34–35.

وَجَدَ السَّبَبُ وَجَدَ الْمُسَبِّبُ - فَهُوَ جَاهِلٌ.

٤ . وَمَنِ اِعْتَقَدَ أَنَّ الْمُؤَثِّرَ هُوَ اللَّهُ وَأَنَّ بَيْنَ الْأَسْبَابِ وَمُسَبِّبَاتِهَا تَلَازُمًا عَادِيًّا بِحَيْثُ يَصِحُّ تَأَخُّرُهَا فَهُوَ الْمُؤْمِنُ النَّاجِي إِنْ شَاءَ اللَّهُ تَعَالَى.

فَالْأَقْسَامُ أَرْبَعَةٌ.

3. Whoever believes that the effector is Allah (Exalted is He), but that He has created a rational entailment (*talāzum ʿaqlī*) between causes and their effects – such that it is not valid for the effect to be delayed, so that whenever the cause is present, the effect is necessarily present – is an ignoramus.[74]

4. Whoever believes that the effector is Allah (Exalted is He), and that there is an customary entailment (*talāzum ʿādī*) between causes and their effects – such that it is possible for the effect to be delayed – is a saved believer (*mu'min nājī*), if Allah (Exalted is He) wills.[75]

So the divisions are four.[76]

وَحَيْثُ وَجَبَتْ لَهُ تَعَالَى الْوَحْدَانِيَّةُ اِسْتَحَالَ عَلَيْهِ ضِدُّهَا وَهُوَ التَّعَدُّدُ سَوَاءٌ كَانَ مَعَ الِاتِّصَالِ أَوِ الِانْفِصَالِ.

And since unicity is necessary for Him (Exalted is He), its contrary, plurality, whether the connected or separate kind – is impossible for Him.[77]

وَاعْلَمْ أَنَّ بَحْثَ الْوَحْدَانِيَّةِ أَشْرَفُ مَبَاحِثِ هَذَا الْفَنِّ، وَلِذَلِكَ كَثُرَ التَّنْبِيهُ عَلَيْهِ فِي الْقُرْآنِ الْعَظِيمِ.

---

74 Minus the part between dashes: *Al-Jawharah*, 45; *Tuḥfat*, 289. *Fatḥ al-majīd*, 34–35.

75 *Al-Jawharah*, 45; *Tuḥfat*, 289; *Fatḥ al-majīd*, 34–35.

76 *Al-Jawharah*, 45; *Tuḥfat*, 289 – but with (ففرق في ذلك) instead of (فالأقسام).

77 *Fatḥ al-majīd*, 37.

Know that the study of unicity is the noblest topic of this discipline.[78]

This is why there are numerous admonitions about it in the Mighty Qur'an.[79]

RECAP: ESSENTIAL AND NEGATIVE ATTRIBUTES

وَهَذِهِ الصِّفَاتُ السِّتّ: الأُوْلَى مِنْهَا وَهِيَ الوُجُوْدُ تُسَمَّى ((نَفْسِيَّةٌ)) لِأَنَّهَا لَا تَدُلُّ عَلَى مَعْنَى زَائِدٍ عَلَى نَفْسِ الذَّاتِ. وَالخَمْسَةُ بَعْدَهَا تُسَمَّى ((سَلْبِيَّةٌ)) لِأَنَّهَا دَلَّتْ عَلَى سَلْبِ مَا لَا يَلِيْقُ بِهِ تَعَالَى، وَالصِّفَاتُ السَّلْبِيَّةُ لَا تَنْحَصِرُ عَلَى الصَّحِيْحِ لِأَنَّ النَّقَائِصَ لَا نِهَايَةَ لَهَا وَكُلُّهَا مَنْفِيَّةٌ عَنْهُ تَعَالَى، وَهَذِهِ الخَمْسَةُ أُصُوْلُهَا فَإِنَّ مَا عَدَاهَا مِنْ نَفْيِ الزَّوْجَةِ وَالوَلَدِ وَالمُعِيْنَ وَغَيْرِ ذَلِكَ رَاجِعٌ إِلَيْهَا.

These six attributes: The first of them, which is existence, is called "essential" (*nafsiyyah*) because it does not indicate a meaning added to the essence itself.[80] The five after it are called "negative" (*salbiyyah*) because they indicate the negation of what does not befit Him (Exalted is He).

Negative attributes are not limited, according to the sound opinion, because deficiencies are endless, and all of them are negated from Him (Exalted is He).

These five are their foundations, for whatever else is negated – such as a spouse, a child, an assistant, and other things – returns to them.[81]

---

78   *Al-Jawharah*, 25; *Tuḥfat*, 152; *Fatḥ al-majīd*, 38.
79   Such as Qur'an, 2:163. Cf. *Tuḥfat*, 152; *Fatḥ al-majīd*, 38.
80   *Fatḥ al-majīd*, 67.
81   *Al-Jawharah*, 23; *Tuḥfat*, 142; *Fatḥ al-majīd*, 67.

CAPABILITY

(وَيَجِبُ فِي حَقِّهِ تَعَالَى الْقُدْرَةُ، وَهِيَ صِفَةٌ) وُجُوْدِيَّةٌ (قَدِيْمَةٌ قَائِمَةٌ بِذَاتِهِ تَعَالَى يُوْجِدُ) تَعَالَى (بِهَا وَيُعْدِمُ) كُلَّ مُمْكِنٍ عَلَى وُفْقِ الإِرَادَةِ.

‹**Capability (***qudrah***) is necessary for Allah (Exalted is He). It is a›n existential ‹pre-eternal attribute subsistent in His essence›** (Exalted is He) ‹**through which He›** (Exalted is He) ‹**brings into existence and annihilates›** every contingent thing in accordance with His will (*irādah*)‹.[82]›

وَلَهَا سَبْعُ تَعَلُّقَاتِ:

It has seven linkages (*ta'alluqāt*).[83]

وَاحِـدٌ صُلُوْحِيٌّ قَدِيْمٌ، وَهُوَ صَلَاحِيَّتُهَا فِي الأَزَلِ لِلإِيْجَادِ وَالإِعْدَامِ بِهَا فِي وَقْتِ الإِمْكَانِ.

One is a pre-eternal aptitudinal (*ṣulūḥī*) linkage:[84]

1. capability's aptness (*ṣalāḥiyyah*), from all eternity, to bring into existence or nonexistence[85] when the time comes for that contingency (*imkān*).

وَثَلَاثَةٌ تَنْجِيزِيَّةٌ حَادِثَةٌ وَهِيَ تَعَلُّقُهَا بِإِيْجَادِ الْمُمْكِنِ بَعْدَ عَدَمِهِ السَّـابِقِ وَتَعَلُّقُهَا بِإِعْدَامِهِ بَعْدَ وُجُوْدِهِ وَتَعَلُّقُهَا بِإِيْجَادِهِ لِلْبَعْثِ مِنْ القَبْرِ.

Three are originated executive (*tanjīziyyah ḥādithah*) linkages.[86] They are:

---

82   *Al-Jawharah*, 27; *Tuḥfat*, 169; *Fatḥ al-majīd*, 38.

83   al-Bājūrī in *Tuḥfat al-murīd* mentions that Shaykh al-Faḍālī clarified them in his *Kifāyat al-'āwām. Al-Jawharah*, 27; *Tuḥfat*, 169, 226.

     "Linkages" refer to the relationships that the attributes of capability, will, knowledge, speech, hearing and sight have to actions and changes.

84   *Al-Jawharah*, 27; *Tuḥfat*, 169.

85   *Al-Jawharah*, 33; *Tuḥfat*, 226; *Fatḥ al-majīd*, 30.

86   *Al-Jawharah*, 27; *Tuḥfat*, 169.

2. bringing a contingent thing into existence after its prior nonexistence;

3. bringing it into nonexistence after it has existed;

4. bringing it into existence for the resurrection from the grave.[87]

وَثَلَاثَةٌ تَعَلُّقَاتٌ قَبْضِيَّةٌ: وَهِيَ: وَتَعَلُّقُهَا بِاسْتِمْرَارِ عَـدَمِ المُمْكِنِ وَقْتَ إِمْكَانِ الوُجُودِ قَبْلَ وُجُودِهِ، وَتَعَلُّقُهَا بِاسْتِمْرَارِ وُجُودِهِ بَعْدَ العَدَمِ، وَتَعَلُّقُهَا بِاسْتِمْرَارِ عَدَمِهِ بَعْدَ الوُجُودِ.

فَهَـذِهِ التَّعَلُّقَاتُ الثَّلَاثَةُ يُقَالُ لَهَا: تَعَلُّقَاتٌ قَبْضِيَّةٌ، بِمَعْنَى أَنَّ المُمْكِنَ فِي القَبْضَةِ فَإِنْ شَـاءَ اللَّهُ أَبْقَاهُ عَلَى حَالِهِ مِنَ العَدَمِ أَوِ الوُجُودِ، وَإِنْ شَـاءَ أَبْدَلَهُ بِضِدِّهِ.

Three are linkages of grasping (*ta'alluqāt qabḍiyyah*).[88] They are:

5. sustaining a contingent thing in nonexistence while existence is possible for it, before its existence;

6. sustaining its existence after its nonexistence; and

7. sustaining its nonexistence after its existence.

These three are called "linkages of grasping" because the contingent thing is in the grasp (*qabḍah*) [of Allah]: if He wills, He leaves it as it is – whether existent or non-existent – and if He wills, He replaces it with its contrary.[89]

فَلَا مُمْكِنَ إِلَّا وَهُـوَ حَـادِثٌ بِفِعْلِهِ، وَفَائِضٌ مِنْ عَدْلِهِ عَلَى أَحْسَـنِ الوُجُوهِ وَأَتَمِّهَا وَأَعْدَلِهَا، فَكُلُّ مَا سِوَاهُ مِنْ إِنْسٍ وَجِنٍّ وَمَلَكٍ وَشَيْطَانٍ وَسَمَاءٍ وَأَرْضٍ وَحَيَوَانٍ وَنَبَاتٍ وَجَمَادٍ وَجَوْهَرٍ وَعَرَضٍ وَمُدْرِكٍ وَمَحْسُوسٍ حَادِثٌ

---

87   Our book is more detailed than what is presented in *Tuḥfat al-murīd*, Cf. *Al-Jawharah*, 33; *Tuḥfat*, 226; Cf. *Fatḥ al-majīd*, 29–30.

88   *Al-Jawharah*, 27; *Tuḥfat*, 169; *Taḥqīq al-maqām*, 110–116. Our author does not mention this specific relation in his other works.

89   The and the previous paragraph: *Al-Jawharah*, 27, 33; *Tuḥfat*, 169, 226; Cf. *Fatḥ al-majīd*, 29–30.

أَنْشَأَهُ بِقُدْرَتِهِ إِنْشَاءً بَعْدَ أَنْ لَمْ يَكُنْ شَيْئًا؛ إِذْ كَانَ اللَّهُ فِي الأَزَلِ مَوْجُودًا لَـمْ يَكُنْ مَعَهُ غَيْـرُهُ، فَأَحْدَثَ الخَلْقَ بَعْدَ ذَلِكَ إِظْهَارًا لِقُدْرَتِهِ وَتَحْقِيقًا لِمَا سَبَقَ فِي إِرَادَتِهِ لَا يَشُـذُّ عَنْ قَبْضَتِهِ مِقْدَار وَلَا تَخْرُجُ عَنْ قُدْرَتِهِ تَصَارِيفُ الأُمُورِ، وَلَا تُحْصَى مَقْدُورَاتُهُ تَعَالَى.

No contingent thing exists except that it is originated by His action and emanates from His justice in the most perfect, most complete, and most just manner. Everything other than Him – including humans, jinn, angels, demons, the heavens, the earth, animals, vegetation, inanimate things, substances, accidents, perceivables, and sensibles – is an originated entity that He brought into existence through His capability after it had been nothing.

Allah was existent from all eternity with nothing else existing alongside Him. He originated creation after that – manifesting His capability and actualising what had preceded in His will. No measure eludes His grasp, no arrangement of affairs escapes His capability, and His objects of capability (*maqdūrāt*) are innumerable (Exalted is He).

(وَضِدُّهَا) أَيْ: القُدْرَةِ (العَجْزُ).

‹Its› meaning capability's ‹**contrary is incapacity (*'ajz*).**›[90]

(وَالدَّلِيلُ عَلَى ذَلِكَ) أَيْ: ثُبُوتُ القُدْرَةِ لَهُ تَعَالَى: وُجُودُ العَالَمِ، وَتَرْكِيبُهُ: (أَنَّـهُ لَـوْ) اَنْتَفَتْ عَنْهُ القُدْرَةُ لَكَانَ عَاجِزًا، وَلَوْ (كَانَ عَاجِزًا لَمْ يُوجَدْ شَيْءٌ) أَيْ: بَعْـضُ (مِـنْ هَـذِهِ المَخْلُوْقَـاتِ)، وَعَدَمُ وُجُودِ شَيْءٍ مِنْهَا مُحَالٌ لِمَا يُخَالِفُهُ الحِسُّ وَالعِيَانُ، فَبَطَلَ مَا أَدَّى إِلَيْهِ وَهُوَ اتِّصَافُهُ تَعَالَى بِالعَجْزِ، فَثَبَتَ نَقِيضُهُ، وَهُوَ اتِّصَافُهُ تَعَالَى بِالقُدْرَةِ، وَحَيْثُ وَجَبَتْ لَهُ القُدْرَةُ اسْتَحَالَ عَلَيْهِ ضِدُّهَا.

---

90   *Al-Jawharah*, 43; *Tuḥfat*, 283; *Fatḥ al-majīd*, 43.

‹The proof of this› meaning establishing capability for Him (Exalted is He) ‹is› the existence of the world (*ʿālam*). Its formulation is ‹that if› capability were to be negated from Him, He would be incapable. And if ‹He were incapable, none›meaning no part ‹of these created things would exist.[91]› The nonexistence of all of them is impossible since sense perception and direct observation contradict it. Thus, what leads to it – namely His being attributed with incapacity – is invalidated. Consequently, its contrary – His being attributed with capability – is established. Since capability is necessary for Him (Exalted is He), its contrary is impossible for Him.[92]

WILL

(وَيَجِبُ فِي حَقِّهِ تَعَالَى الإِرَادَةُ) وَيُرَادِفُهَا الْمَشِيئَةُ (وَهِيَ صِفَةٌ) مَوْجُودَةٌ (قَدِيمَةٌ قَائِمَةٌ بِذَاتِهِ تَعَالَى يُخَصِّصُ بِهَا الْمُمْكِنَ) بِبَعْضِ مَا يَجُوزُ عَلَيْهِ، إِمَّا (بِالْوُجُودِ أَوْ بِالْعَدَمِ أَوْ) بِالصِّفَاتِ كَالْبَيَاضِ أَوْ السَّوَادِ، أَوْ (بِالْغِنَى أَوْ بِالْفَقْرِ أَوْ بِالعِلْمِ أَوْ بِالجَهْلِ إِلَى غَيْرِ ذَلِكَ) كَالْمَقَادِيرِ كَالطَّوْلِ أَوْ القِصَرِ، وَكَالأَزْمِنَةِ كَكَوْنِهِ فِي زَمَنِ إِبْرَاهِيْمَ أَوْ فِي زَمَنِ عِيْسَى عَلَيْهِمَا السَّلَامُ، وَالأَمْكِنَةِ كَكَوْنِهِ فِي مَكَّةَ أَوْ فِي الطَّائِفِ، وَالْجِهَاتِ كَكَوْنِهِ فِي جِهَةِ الْمَشْرِقِ أَوْ فِي جِهَةِ الْمَغْرِبِ.

‹Will (*irādah*) is necessary for Allah (Exalted is He).› The term *mashīʾah* is synonymous with it.[93] ‹It is a›n existent ‹pre-eternal attribute subsistent in His divine essence (Exalted is He) through which He specifies contingent things› with some of their possibilities[94] – either ‹with existence or nonexistence,› with attributes like whiteness or blackness, ‹with wealth or poverty, with knowledge or

---

91 Cf. Qur'an, 2:20, 41:39: "Truly, Allah is capable of all things."

92 *Fatḥ al-majīd*, 42. Cf. *Al-Jawharah*, 27; *Tuḥfat*, 170.

93 *Al-Jawharah*, 27; *Tuḥfat*, 171.

94 *Al-Jawharah*, 27; *Tuḥfat*, 171; *Fatḥ al-majīd*, 42–43.

ignorance, and so forth.› This also applies to proportions such as tallness or shortness, to times such as during the time of Ibrāhīm or ʿĪsā (peace be upon them both), to places such as Mecca or Ṭāʾif, and to directions such as the east or the west.[95]

(وَضِدُّهَا)، أَيْ: الإِرَادَةِ (الكَرَاهَةُ) بِمَعْنَى عَدَمِ الإِرَادَةِ.

‹Its› that is, will's **‹contrary is aversion (karāhah)›** in the sense of the absence of will.[96]

وَاعْلَمْ أَنَّ الإِرَادَةَ عِنْدَ أَهْلِ السُّنَّةِ غَيْرُ الأَمْرِ وَالرِّضَا وَالعِلْمِ.

١. فَقَدْ يُرِيدُ وَيَأْمُرُ وَيَرْضَى كَإِيمَانِ مَنْ عَلِمَ اللَّهُ إِيمَانَهُ مِثْلُ أَبِي بَكْرٍ رَضِيَ اللَّهُ عَنْهُ، وَهَـذَا يُقَالُ لَهُ «وَاجِـبٌ لِغَيْرِهِ» لأَنَّهُ حَيْـثُ تَعَلَّقَ عِلْمُ اللَّهِ وَإِرَادَتُهُ بِوُجُودِهِ فِي وَقْتٍ وَجَبَ وُجُودُهُ فِيهِ، وَيَسْتَحِيلُ عَدَمُهُ فِي ذَلِكَ الوَقْتِ، وَيُقَالُ لَهُ: «مُسْتَحِيلٌ لِغَيْرِهِ».

Know that will, according to Ahl al-Sunnah, is distinct from command (*amr*), approval (*riḍā*), and knowledge (*ʿilm*).

1. He may will, command, and approve of something, such as the belief of one whom Allah knew would believe, like Abū Bakr (may Allah be pleased with him). This is called "extrinsically necessary" (*wājib li-ghayrihi*), because once Allah's knowledge and will are connected to its existence at a specific time, its existence in that time becomes necessary, and its nonexistence in that time is impossible. This is referred to as "extrinsically impossible" (*mustaḥīl li-ghayrihi*).[97]

٢. وَقَدْ لَا يُرِيدُ وَلَا وَيَأْمُرُ وَلَا يَرْضَى كَالكُفْرِ مِمَّنْ ذُكِرَ، بَلْ هُوَ مُسْتَحِيلٌ كَمَا مَرَّ.

---

95   Cf. *Al-Jawharah*, 27; *Tuḥfat*, 171; *Fatḥ al-majīd*, 44.

96   *Al-Jawharah*, 43; *Tuḥfat*, 283; *Fatḥ al-majīd*, 49.

97   Our author defines extrinsically necessary and impossible in a different discussion in *Fatḥ al-majīd* but does not use them in his other books. *Fatḥ al-majīd*, 40.

2. He may neither will, nor command, nor approve of something, such as disbelief from the aforementioned person (whom He knew would believe). Rather, it is impossible, as previously mentioned.

٣. وَقَدْ يُرِيدُ وَلَا وَيَأْمُرُ وَلَا يَرْضَى كَالْكُفْرِ مِمَّنْ عَلِمَ اللَّهُ عَدَمَ إِيْمَانِهِ مِثْلُ فِرْعَـوْنَ وَهَامَانُ وَقَارُوْنَ، وَكَالْمَعَاصِـي الْوَاقِعَةِ فِي الْكَوْنِ، فَإِنَّ الْجَمِيْعَ وَاقِعٌ بِإِرَادَتِهِ تَعَالَى.

3. He may will something but neither command nor approve of it, such as disbelief from someone whom Allah knew would never believe' – like Fir'awn, Hāmān, and Qārūn – and such as acts of disobedience that occur in the cosmos. For all of these occur by His will (Exalted is He).[98]

٤. وَقَـدْ يَأْمُـرُ وَلَا يُرِيْـدُ كَإِيْمَانِ مَنْ عَلِـمَ اللَّهُ أَنَّهُ لَا يُؤْمِـنُ كَالْإِيْمَانِ مِمَّنْ ذُكِـرَ، وَإِنَّمَا أَمَرَهُمْ بِـهِ مَعَ كَوْنِهِ لَمْ يُرِدْهُ مِنْهُمْ لِحِكْمَـةٍ يَعْلَمُهَا اللَّهُ تَعَالَى لَا يَسْأَلُ عَمَّا يَفْعَلُ.

4. He may command but not will something, such as belief from someone whom Allah knew would never believe, like the belief of the aforementioned. However, He commanded them with it even though He did not will it from them, for a wisdom that Allah knows (Exalted is He), and He is not asked about what He does.

فَالْأَقْسَامُ أَرْبَعَةٌ، وَالرِّضَا لَازِمٌ لِلْأَمْرِ.

Thus, the categories are four, and approval is inseparable from the command.[99]

وَتَتَعَلَّـقُ الْإِرَادَةُ بِـكُلِّ مُمْكِـنٍ كَالْقُدْرَةِ، لَكِنْ تَعَلُّقُ الْقُـدْرَةِ تَعَلُّقُ إِيْجَادٍ وَإِعْدَامٍ، وَتَعَلُّقُ الْإِرَادَةِ تَعَلُّقُ تَخْصِيْصٍ، فَلَا تَتَعَلَّقَ بِالْوَاجِبِ وَلَا بِالْمُسْتَحِيْلِ، وَشَـمَلَ الْمُمْكِنُ الْخَيْرَ وَالشَّـرَّ فَلَا يَقَعُ فِي الْكَوْنِ شَيْءٌ مِنْ خَيْرٍ أَوْ شَرٍّ إِلَّا

---

98 That is, they all occur by His will, though He does not command or approve of them.

99 From first "He may will": *Al-Jawharah*, 27; *Tuḥfat*, 174. Cf. *Fatḥ al-majīd*, 47–48.

بِإِرَادَتِهِ تَعَالَى؛ إِذْ لَا يَصِحُّ أَنْ يَقَعَ فِي الكَوْنِ شَيْءٌ قَهْرًا عَنْهُ تَعَالَى خِلَافًا لِلْمُعْتَزِلَةِ القَائِلِينَ بِأَنَّ إِرَادَتَهُ تَعَالَى لَا تَتَعَلَّقُ بِالشُّرُورِ وَالقَبَائِحِ، وَلَكِنِ يَجِبُ عَلَيْنَا الأَدَبُ مَعَ اللَّهِ تَعَالَى بِأَنْ لَا نُنْسِبَ الشُّرُورَ وَالقَبَائِحَ إِلَيْهِ تَعَالَى إِلَّا فِي مَقَامِ التَّعْلِيمِ، فَإِنَّ ذَلِكَ لَا يَجُوزُ كَنِسْبَةِ خَلْقِ الأُمُورِ الخَسِيسَةِ إِلَيْهِ تَعَالَى، فَلَا يَجُوزُ أَنْ يُقَالَ فِي غَيْرِ مَقَامِ التَّعْلِيمِ: «اللَّهُ خَالِقُ القِرَدَةِ وَالخَنَازِيرِ».

Will connects to every contingent thing, just as capability does. However, the linkage of capability is a linkage of bringing into existence and nonexistence, while the linkage of will is a linkage of specification,[100] so it does not relate to what is necessary or what is impossible.[101]

"Contingent things" (*mumkināt*) include both good and evil, and no good or evil occurs in the cosmos except by His will (Exalted is He), since nothing can occur in existence contrary to His will (Exalted is He). This is contrary to the Mu'tazilah, who assert that His will (Exalted is He) does not apply to evil or reprehensible acts.[102]

However, we must observe propriety (*adab*) with Allah (Exalted is He) by not ascribing evil and reprehensible acts to Him (Exalted is He), for that – and likewise ascribing despicable things to Him – is impermissible, except in the context of instruction. Thus, it is not permissible to say, "Allah created apes and swine," outside the context of instruction.[103]

(وَالدَّلِيـلُ عَلَى ذَلِكَ) أَيْ: ثُبُـوتُ الإِرَادَةِ لَهُ تَعَالَى وُجُوْدُ العَالَمِ، وَتَرْكِيْبُهُ (أَنَّـهُ) تَعَالَـى (لَـوْ) لَمْ يَتَّصَفْ بِالإِرَادَةِ لَكَانَ كَارِهًـا، وَلَوْ (كَانَ كَارِهَا) أَيْ: عَادِمُ الإِرَادَةِ، لَمْ يَتَّصَفْ بِالقُدْرَةِ، لَكِنْ عَدَمُ اتِّصَافِهِ بِهَا مُحَالٌ؛ إِذْ لَوْ لَمْ يَتَّصَفْ بِهَا (لَكَانَ عَاجِزًا، وَكَوْنُهُ عَاجِزًا مُحَالٌ)؛ إِذْ لَوْ عَجَزَ لَمَا أَوْجَدَ شَيْئًا

---

100   Cf. *Al-Jawharah*, 34; *Tuḥfat*, 230.
101   Our author provides even more details in *Fatḥ al-majīd*, 43–44.
102   *Al-Jawharah*, 27; *Tuḥfat*, 171; *Fatḥ al-majīd*, 47–48.
103   *Fatḥ al-majīd*, 47; Cf. *Al-Jawharah*, 27; *Tuḥfat*, 173.

الصَّمَّـاءِ فِي اللَّيْلَـةِ الظَّلْمَـاءِ بِعِلْمٍ قَدِيْمٍ أَزَلِـيٍّ لَمْ يَزَلْ مَوْصُوْفَا بِهِ فِي أَزَلِ الآزَالِ، لَا بِعِلْمٍ مُتَجَدِّدٍ مُوْصُوْفٍ بِالْحُلُوْلِ والِانْتِقَالِ، فَلَا تَتَنَاهَى مَعْلُوْمَاتُهُ.

‹**Knowledge (***ilm***) is necessary for Allah (Exalted is He). It is a**›n existent ‹**pre-eternal attribute subsistent in Allah's divine essence (Exalted is He) through which He knows things**› that are necessary, possible and impossible,[105] with complete encompassment of all things as they truly are, in full detail. He (Majestic and Exalted is He) knows without limit and in full detail – such as His perfections and the breaths of the people of Paradise.[106]

The linkage of knowledge is a single, pre-eternal, executive linkage.[107]

Thus, Allah knows all that is known and comprehends all that occurs, from beneath the depths of the earth to the highest heavens. Nothing, even the tiniest particle in the earth or heavens, escapes His knowledge. Rather, He knows the movement of a black ant on a solid rock in the darkness of the night,[108] with pre-eternal, everlasting knowledge. He has never ceased being attributed with this knowledge in all eternities, and He is not described with renewed knowledge characterised by indwelling or transference. What He knows is without end.

(وَضِدُّهَا)، أَيْ: صِفَةُ العِلْمِ (الجَهْلُ).

‹**Its**› meaning the attribute of knowledge's ‹**contrary is ignorance (***jahl***).**[109]›

فَائِـدَةٌ: تَعَلُّـقُ الإِرَادَةِ تَابِـعٌ لِتَعَلُّقِ العِلْمِ فِـي التَّعَقُّلِ فَقَطْ لَا فِي الخَـارِجِ لِأَنَّهُمَـا قَدِيْمَـانِ، بِمَعْنَـى أَنَّـكَ تَتَعَقَّـلُ أَوَّلًا تَعَلُّقَ العِلْـمِ ثُمَّ تَتَعَقَّلُ تَعَلُّقَ

---

105   *Fatḥ al-majīd*, 49. Cf. *Al-Jawharah*, 28; *Tuḥfat*, 178.

106   *Al-Jawharah*, 28; *Tuḥfat*, 180; *Fatḥ al-majīd*, 49.

107   *Al-Jawharah*, 28; *Tuḥfat*, 178; *Fatḥ al-majīd*, 50.

108   Cf. al-Jāwī, *Bahjat al-wasāʾil* (Cairo: Dār al-Ṭālib al-Azharī, 2019), 78.

109   *Al-Jawharah*, 43; *Tuḥfat*, 283. In *Fatḥ al-majīd* (p52) he has: "and whatever is of the same meaning, like doubt, delusion, and sleep."

الإِرَادَةِ، وَتَعَلُّقُ القُـدْرَةِ التَّنْجِيْـزِيُّ تَابِـعٌ لِلتَّعَلُّقَينِ وَبَيْنَهُ وَبَيْنَهُمَـا تَرْتِيْبٌ فِي التَّعَقُّلِ وَالخَارِجِ، لِأَنَّهُ حَادِثٌ وَهُمَا قَدِيْمَانِ.

Beneficial Point. The linkage of will depends upon the linkage of knowledge in intellection only, not in actuality, since both are pre-eternal. This means that one first conceives the linkage of knowledge, then conceives the linkage of will.

The executive linkage of capability depends upon both linkages. Between it and them is a sequence both in conception and in actuality, since the executive link of capability is originated while the two [linkages of knowledge and will] are pre-eternal.[110]

(وَالدَّلِيْلُ عَلَى ذَلِكَ) أَي: ثُبُوْتِ العِلْمِ لَهُ تَعَالَى، وُجُوْدُ العَالَمِ. وَتَرْكِيْبُهُ: (أَنَّهُ) تَعَالَى (لَوْ) لَمْ يَتَّصَـفْ بِالعِلْمِ لَاتَّصَفَ بِالجَهْلِ، وَلَوْ (كَانَ جَاهِلًا) لَـمْ يَتَّصَـفْ بِـالإِرَادَةِ، وَلَوْ (لَمْ يَكُنْ مُرِيْدًا) لَمْ يُوْجَدْ شَـيْءٌ مِنْ العَالَمِ (وَهُوَ مُحَـالٌ) لِمُشَـاهَدَةِ وُجُـوْدِهِ بِالحِسِّ وَالعِيَانِ، وَحَيْثُ وَجَبَ لَـهُ تَعَالَى العِلْمُ اِسْتَحَالَ عَلَيْهِ ضِدُّهُ.

‹The proof of this› meaning establishing knowledge for Him (Exalted is He) is the existence of the world. Its formulation ‹is that if He› (Exalted is He) were not attributed with knowledge, He would be attributed with ignorance. If He ‹were ignorant,› He would not be attributed with will. If ‹He were not willing› nothing of the world would exist‹. And this is impossible› due to observing the world's existence through sense and sight‹.› Since knowledge is necessary for Him (Exalted is He), its contrary is impossible for Him.[111]

---

110 *Al-Jawharah*, 35; *Tuḥfat*, 233; *Taḥqīq al-maqām*, 130–132; *Fatḥ al-majīd*, 44.
111 *Fatḥ al-majīd*, 52; Cf. *Al-Jawharah*, 43; *Tuḥfat*, 181.

LIFE

(وَيَجِبُ فِي حَقِّهِ تَعَالَى الحَيَاةُ، وَهِيَ صِفَةٌ وُجُودِيَّةٌ قَدِيْمَةٌ قَائِمَةٌ بِذَاتِهِ تَعَالَى، تُصَحِّحُ)، أَيْ: تِلْكَ الصِّفَةَ (لَهُ) تَعَالَى (أَنْ يَتَّصَفَ بِالعِلْمِ وَغَيْرِهِ مِنَ الصِّفَاتِ)، أَيْ: صِفَاتِ المَعَانِي، كَالقُدْرَةِ وَالإِرَادَةِ وَالسَّمْعِ وَالبَصَرِ وَالكَلَامِ، وَحَيَاةُ اللَّهِ تَعَالَى بِذَاتِهِ لَيْسَتْ بِرُوْحٍ.

‹Life (*ḥayāt*) is necessary for Allah (Exalted is He). It is a pre-eternal, existential attribute subsistent in Allah's divine essence (Exalted is He). It› meaning this attribute ‹makes it possible for Him› (Exalted is He) ‹to be attributed with knowledge and other attributes[112]› meaning entitative attributes (*ṣifāt al-maʿānī*), such as capability, will, hearing, sight, and speech‹.› Allah's life (Exalted is He) is through His very essence, not through a spirit.[113]

(وَضِدُّهَا: المَوْتُ)، فَهُوَ تَعَالَى لَا تَأْخُذُهُ سِنَةٌ وَلَا نَوْمٌ، وَلَا يُعَارِضُهُ فَنَاءٌ وَلَا مَوْتٌ.

‹Its contrary is death (*mawt*).› He (Exalted is He) is not overtaken by drowsiness or sleep,[114] nor is He subjected to perishing or death.[115]

(وَالدَّلِيْلُ عَلَى ذَلِكَ) أَيْ: ثُبُوْتُ الحَيَاةِ لَهُ تَعَالَى، وُجُوْدُ العَالَمِ. وَتَرْكِيْبُهُ (أَنَّهُ) تَعَالَى (لَوْ لَمْ يَتَّصِفْ بِالحَيَاةِ لَاتَّصَفَ بِالمَوْتِ، وَلَوْ (كَانَ مَيِّتًا لَمْ يَكُنْ قَادِرًا وَلَا مُرِيْدًا وَلَا عَالِمًا، وَهُوَ)، أَيْ: عَدَمُ اتِّصَافِهِ تَعَالَى بِالقُدْرَةِ وَالإِرَادَةِ وَالعِلْمِ (مُحَالٌ)؛ إِذْ لَوْ كَانَ تَعَالَى كَذَلِكَ لَمْ يُوْجَدْ شَيْءٌ مِنَ العَالَمِ، وَذَلِكَ بَاطِلٌ لِأَنَّهُ خِلَافُ الحِسِّ وَالعِيَانِ.

---

112 *Al-Jawharah*, 29; *Tuḥfat*, 186; *Taḥqīq al-maqām*, 53.

113 *Al-Jawharah*, 29; *Tuḥfat*, 187; *Fatḥ al-majīd*, 53.

114 Our author mentions this in the context of being capable in *Bahjat al-wasāʾil*, 78.

115 *Al-Jawharah*, 43; *Tuḥfat*, 283; *Fatḥ al-majīd*, 54.

‹**The proof of this**› meaning establishing life for Him (Exalted is He) is the existence of the world. Its formulation ‹**is that if He**› (Exalted is He) were not attributed with life, He would be attributed with death (*mawt*). If He ‹**were dead, He would not be capable, willing, or knowing. And that**› meaning the absence of Him (Exalted is He) being attributed with capability, will, and knowledge ‹**is impossible**[116]›, because if Allah (Exalted is He) were that way, nothing in the world would exist‹.› This is invalid, contrary to sense and direct observation.[117]

وَالْحَيَاةُ لَا تَتَعَلَّقُ بِشَيِّءٍ، وَهِيَ شَـرْطٌ عَقْلِيٌّ فِي صِفَاتِ الْمَعَانِي يَلْزَمُ مِنْ وُجُوْدِهَا وُجُوْدُ صِفَاتِ الْمَعَانِي مَا عَدَاهَا، وَمِنْ عَدَمِهَا الْعَدَمُ، وَحَيْثُ وَجَبَتْ لَهُ تَعَالَى الْحَيَاةُ اسْتَحَالَ عَلَيْهِ ضِدُّهَا.

Life does not link to anything.[118] It is a rational condition (*shart ʿaqlī*) for entitative attributes. The existence of all other entitative attributes depends on its existence, and their absence depends on its absence. Since life is necessary for Him (Exalted is He), its contrary is impossible for Him.

HEARING AND SIGHT

(وَيَجِبُ فِي حَقِّهِ تَعَالَى السَّـمْعُ وَالْبَصَرُ، وَهُمَا صِفَتَانِ قَدِيْمَتَانِ قَائِمَتَانِ بِذَاتِهِ تَعَالَى يَنْكَشِـفُ بِهَا الْمَوْجُوْدُ) مِـنْ ذَوَاتٍ وَأَصْوَاتٍ وَأَلْـوَانٍ وَغَيْرِهَا، وَتَعَلُّقُهَا تَعَلُّقُ انْكِشَافٍ كَتَعَلُّقِ الْعِلْمِ.

‹**Hearing and sight (*samʿ* and *baṣar*) are necessary for Allah (Exalted is He). They are pre-eternal attributes subsistent in Allah's divine essence (Exalted is He), through which what exists is disclosed**›

---

116 Allah (Exalted is He) says, "Allah – there is no god but He, the Living, the Self-Subsisting." [Qur'an, 2:255]

117 *Fatḥ al-majīd*, 54; Cf. *Al-Jawharah*, 29; *Tuḥfat*, 187.

118 *Al-Jawharah*, 37; *Tuḥfat*, 244; *Fatḥ al-majīd*, 54.

including entities, sounds, colours, and other things.[119] Their linkage is a linkage of disclosure, like the linkage of knowledge.[120]

وَيَجِبُ عَلَيْنَا أَنْ نَعْتَقِدَ أَنَّ الإِنْكِشَافَ الحَاصِلَ بِالسَّمْعِ غَيْرُ الإِنْكِشَافِ الحَاصِلِ بِالبَصَرِ، وَأَنَّ الإِنْكِشَافَ الحَاصِلَ بِكُلٍّ مِنْهُمَا غَيْرُ الإِنْكِشَافِ الحَاصِلِ بِالعِلْمِ، وَأَنْ لِكُلٍّ مِنَ الإِنْكِشَافَاتِ الثَّلَاثَةِ حَقِيقَةٌ يُفَوَّضُ عِلْمُهَا إِلَى اللَّهِ تَعَالَى. وَلَيْسَ الأَمْرُ عَلَى مَا نَعْهَدُهُ مِنْ أَنَّ البَصَرَ يُفِيدُ بِالمُشَاهَدَةِ وُضُوحًا فَوْقَ العِلْمِ، بَلْ جَمِيْعُ صِفَاتِهِ تَعَالَى تَامَّةٌ كَامِلَةٌ يَسْتَحِيلُ عَلَيْهَا الخَفَاءُ وَالزِّيَادَةُ وَالنَّقْصُ إِلَى غَيْرِ ذَلِكَ، فَهُوَ تَعَالَى لَا يَعْزُبُ عَنْ سَمْعِهِ مَوْجُودٌ وَإِنْ خَفِيَ، وَلَا يَغِيْبُ عَنْ بَصَرِهِ شَيْءٌ وَإِنْ دَقَّ، وَلَا يَدْفَعُ سَمْعَهُ بُعْدٌ، وَلَا يَحْجَبُ رُؤْيَتَهُ ظَلَامٌ، يَسْمَعُ تَعَالَى مِنْ غَيْرِ أَصْمِخَةٍ وَآذَانٍ، وَيَرَى مِنْ غَيْرِ حَدَقَةٍ وَأَجْفَانٍ، كَمَا يَعْلَمُ بِغَيْرِ قَلْبٍ، وَيَبْطِشُ مِنْ غَيْرِ جَارِحَةٍ، وَيَخْلُقُ بِغَيْرِ آلَةٍ؛ إِذْ لَا تُشْبِهُ صِفَاتُهُ صِفَاتِ الخَلْقِ كَمَا لَا تُشْبِهُ ذَاتُهُ ذَوَاتِ الخَلْقِ.

It is obligatory for us to believe that the disclosure achieved through hearing is not the same as the disclosure achieved through sight, that the disclosure achieved through each of the two is not the same as the disclosure achieved through knowledge, and that each of the three forms of disclosure has a reality the knowledge of which is consigned to Allah (Exalted is He).

The matter is not as we are accustomed to – where sight, through direct observation, contributes clarity beyond knowledge. Rather, all of His attributes (Exalted is He) are complete and perfect, and it is impossible for anything to be hidden from them, for them to increase or decrease, or for them to be subject to any deficiency.[121]

---

119 *Al-Jawharah*, 29; *Tuḥfat*, 194, 196; *Fatḥ al-majīd*, 54, 56.
120 *Al-Jawharah*, 37; *Tuḥfat*, 242; *Fatḥ al-majīd*, 56.
121 *Al-Jawharah*, 29; *Tuḥfat*, 195; Cf. *Fatḥ al-majīd*, 56–57.

He (Exalted is He) does not miss anything with His hearing, even if it is concealed, nor does anything escape His sight, even if it is subtle. Distance does not block His hearing, and darkness does not veil His vision. Allah (Exalted is He) hears without an auditory canal or ears and sees without pupils or eyelids, just as He knows without a heart, grasps without a limb, and creates without a tool. For His attributes do not resemble the attributes of created things, just as His essence does not resemble the essences of created things.[122]

وَاعْلَمْ أَنَّ لِلسَّمْعِ وَالبَصَرِ ثَلَاثَةُ تَعَلُّقَاتٍ:

١. تَنْجِيزِيًّا قَدِيْمًا: وَهُوَ التَّعَلُّقُ بِذَاتِ اللَّهِ تَعَالَى وَصِفَاتِهِ.

٢. وَصَلَاحِيًّا قَدِيمًا: وَهُوَ التَّعَلُّقُ بِنَا قَبْلَ وُجُوْدِنَا.

٣. وَتَنْجِيزِيًّا حَادِثًا: وَهُوَ التَّعَلُّقُ بِنَا بَعْدَ وُجُوْدِنَا.

فَالتَّعَلُّقُ مُتَّحِدٌ، وَالصِّفَةُ مُتَعَدِّدَةٌ، حَقَائِقُهَا مُتَغَايِرَةٌ.

Know that hearing and sight have three linkages:

1. Pre-eternally executive – a linkage to Allah's entity (Exalted is He) and His attributes.
2. Pre-eternally aptitudinal – a linkage to us before our existence.
3. Originated executive – a linkage to us after our existence.[123]

The linkage is unified, while the attributes are multiple, their realities being distinct.[124]

(وَضِدُّهُمَا) أَيْ: السَّمْعِ وَالبَصَرِ (الصَّمَمُ وَالعَمَى).

‹Their› meaning hearing and sight's ‹**contraries are deafness and blindness (ṣamam and ʿamā).**›[125]

---

122 *Fatḥ al-majīd*, 57.
123 *Al-Jawharah*, 36; *Tuḥfat*, 241; *Fatḥ al-majīd*, 55–56.
124 *Fatḥ al-majīd*, 57. Cf. *Al-Jawharah*, 36; *Tuḥfat*, 239.
125 *Al-Jawharah*, 43; *Tuḥfat*, 283; *Fatḥ al-majīd*, 56, 58.

(وَالدَّلِيلُ عَلَى ذَلِكَ) أَيْ: ثُبُوتُ السَّمْعِ وَالبَصَرِ لَهُ تَعَالَى سَمْعِيٌّ، وَهُوَ (قَوْلُـهُ تَعَالَى: ﴿وَهُوَ السَّمِيعُ البَصِيرُ﴾ [الشورى: ١١]) وَقَوْله تَعَالَى: ﴿وَاللَّهُ بَصِيرٌ بِمَا يَعْمَلُونَ﴾ [الحجرات، ١٨] وَقَوْلُهُ ﷺ: «ارْبَعُوا عَلَى أَنْفُسِكُمْ فِي الدُّعَـاءِ، فَإِنَّكُمْ لَا تَدْعُـونَ أَصَمَّ ولا غائبًا، إِنَّكُمْ تَدْعُونَ سَمِيعًا قَرِيًّا مُجِيبًا»، وَمَعْنَى «ارْبَعُوا عَلَى أَنْفُسِكُمْ» أَيْ: أَشْفِقُوا عَلَيْهَا، بِمَعْنَى: لَا تَرْفَعُوا أَصْوَاتَكُمْ بِالدُّعَاءِ.

The proof of this meaning hearing and sight for Him (Exalted is He) being established is revelation. It **is His statement (Exalted is He), "He is the Hearer, the Seer,"**[126] and "And Allah is seeing of what you do."[127]

And [its textual proofs include] his statement (may Allah bless him and give him peace), "Show mercy to yourselves, for you do not supplicate to One who is deaf nor absent. Indeed, you supplicate to One who is hearing, near, and responsive."[128]

The meaning of "show mercy to yourselves" is to be gentle with yourselves, meaning not to raise your voices in supplication.[129]

وَقَدْ أَجْمَعَ أَهْلُ المِلَلِ وَالأَدْيَانِ عَلَى أَنَّهُ سَمِيعٌ بَصِيرٌ.

And [among its proofs is that] the followers of the [various] sects and religions are unanimous in that He is hearing and seeing.[130]

وَأَيْضًا لَوْ لَمْ يَتَّصِفْ سُبْحَانَهُ وَتَعَالَى بِالسَّمْعِ وَالبَصَرِ لَزِمَ أَنْ يَتَّصَفَ بِالصَّمَمِ وَالعَمَى، لَكِنِ اتِّصَافُهُ بِهَا بَاطِلٌ لِأَنَّهُمَا صِفَتَا نَقْصٍ، وَالنَّقْصُ عَلَيْهِ تَعَالَى مُحَالٌ، فَبَطَلَ مَا أَدَّى إِلَيْهِ، فَثَبَتَ لَهُ السَّمْعُ وَالبَصَرُ.

---

126 Qur'an, 42:11.

127 Qur'an, 49:18.

128 Imām al-Suyūṭī's *Jāmi' al-aḥādīth* (Cairo: n.p., 2002/1423) lists the hadith under numbers 25689 and 25690. The first is sourced to al-Bukhārī, Muslim and Abū Dāwūd. The second is sourced to Aḥmed and al-Ṭabarānī.

129 *Fatḥ al-majīd*, 57. Cf. *Al-Jawharah*, 29; *Tuḥfat*, 201.

130 *Al-Jawharah*, 29; *Tuḥfat*, 202; *Fatḥ al-majīd*, 56.

Also, if He were not attributed (Majestic and Exalted is He) with hearing and sight, it would entail Him being attributed with deafness and blindness. However, attributing Him with these is invalid, as they are attributes of deficiency, and deficiency is impossible for Him (Exalted is He). Thus, what leads to it is invalidated. So hearing and sight are established for Him.[131]

SPEECH

(وَيَجِبُ فِي حَقِّهِ تَعَالَى الْكَلَامُ، وَهُوَ صِفَةٌ قَدِيمَةٌ قَائِمَةٌ بِذَاتِهِ تَعَالَى، لَيْسَتْ بِحَرْفٍ وَلَا صَوْتٍ) وَهِيَ مُنَزَّهَةٌ عَنِ التَّقَدُّم وَالتَّأَخُّرِ، وَعَنِ الْإِعْرَابِ وَالبِنَاءِ، وَعَنِ السُّكُوتِ النَّفْسِيِّ بِأَنْ لَا يَسُرُّ فِي نَفْسِهِ تَعَالَى الكَلَامُ مَعَ القُدْرَةِ عَلَيْهِ، وَمُنَزَّهَةٌ عَنِ الآفَةِ البَاطِنِيَّةِ بِأَنْ لَا يَقْدِرُ عَلَى ذَلِكَ كَمَا فِي حَالِ الخَرَسِ وَالطُّفُوْلِيَّةِ، وَعَنْ جَمِيعِ صِفَاتِ كَلَامِ الحَوَادِثِ.

‹**Speech (kalām) is necessary for Allah (Exalted is He). It is a pre-eternal attribute subsistent in Allah's divine essence (Exalted is He) and is not composed of letters or sounds.**› It is free from temporal sequence, grammatical inflexion, and non-inflexion. It is also free from internal silence – meaning He does not withhold speech from Himself despite having the capability for it.

Furthermore, His speech is free from all internal defects – such as an inability to speak due to mute silence or infancy[132] – and from all the attributes of the speech of originated things.[133]

وَهُوَ صِفَةٌ وَاحِدَةٌ لَا تَعَدُّدَ فِيهَا، لَكِنْ لَهُ أَقْسَامٌ اعْتِبَارِيَّةٌ: فَمِنْ حَيْثُ تَعَلُّقِهِ بِطَلَبِ فِعْلِ الصَّلَاةِ مَثَلًا: أَمْرٌ، وَمِنْ حَيْثُ تَعَلُّقِهِ بِطَلَبِ تَرْكِ الزِّنَا مَثَلًا: نَهْيٌّ، وَمِنْ حَيْثُ تَعَلُّقِهِ بِأَنَّ فِرْعَوْنَ فَعَلَ كَذَا أَوْ فَعَلَ كَذَا مَثَلًا:

---

131 *Fatḥ al-majīd*, 55, 57.
132 *Al-Jawharah*, 29; *Tuḥfat*, 189.
133 Cf. *Fatḥ al-majīd*, 57–60.

خَبَرٌ، وَمِنْ حَيْثُ تَعَلُّقِهِ بِأَنَّ الطائِعَ لَهُ الجَنَّةُ: وَعْدٌ، وَمِنْ حَيْثُ تَعَلُّقِه بِأَنَّ العَاصِي يَدْخُلُ النَّارَ: وَعِيدٌ، إِلَى غَيْرِ ذَلِكَ.

It is a single attribute; there is no plurality to it. However, it has notional divisions:

- Insofar as it links to demanding the performance of prayer, for example, it is a command.
- Insofar as it links to demanding the abstention from fornication, for example, it is a prohibition.
- Insofar as it links to stating that Fir'awn did such-and-such, for example, it is a declarative statement.
- Insofar as it links to the obedient being granted Paradise, it is a promise.
- Insofar as it links to the disobedient entering the Fire, it is a threat. And so forth.[134]

وَيَتَعَلَّـقُ بِجَمِيعِ الوَاجِبَـاتِ وَالجَائِزَاتِ وَالمُسْـتَحِيلَاتِ، كَالعِلْمِ، لَكِنْ تَعَلَّقَ العِلْمِ تَعَلُّقُ انْكِشَافٍ وَتَعَلُّقُ الكَلَامِ تَعَلُّقُ دَلَالَة.

It links to all that is necessary, possible, and impossible, just like knowledge.[135] However, the linkage of knowledge is a linkage of disclosure, while the linkage of speech is a linkage of signification.[136]

وَتَعَلُّقُهُ بِالنِّسْبَةِ لِغَيْرِ الأَمْرِ وَالنَّهْي تَنْجِيزِيٌّ قَدِيمٌ، وَأَمَّا بِالنِّسْبَةِ لَهُمَا، فَإِنْ لَمْ يَشْتَرِطْ فِيهِمَا وُجُودُ المَأْمُورِ وَالمَنْهِي فَكَذَلِكَ، وَإِنْ اشْتُرِطَ فِيهِمَا ذَلِكَ كَانَ التَّعَلُّـقُ فِيهِمَـا صُلُوحِيَّـةً قَدِيمَـةً قَبْلَ وُجُودِ المَأْمُـورِ وَالمَنْهِي وَتَنْجِيزِيَّةً حَادِثَةً بَعْدَ وُجُودِهِمَا.

Its linkage with respect to things other than commands and prohibitions is pre-eternally executive.

---

134 *Al-Jawharah*, 29; *Tuḥfat*, 190; *Fatḥ al-majīd*, 59.
135 *Al-Jawharah*, 45; *Tuḥfat*, 234, 242; *Tuḥfat al-Murīd*, 58.
136 *Fatḥ al-majīd*, 58, 68.

With commands and prohibitions, it depends. If the existence of the person commanded or prohibited is not made a condition, then the relation is likewise eternally executive. But if their existence is made a condition, then the linkage is pre-eternally aptitudinal before that person exists, and originated executive after their existence.[137]

فَهُوَ تَعَالَى مُتَكَلِّمٌ آمِرٌ نَاهٍ وَوَاعِدٌ مُتَوَعِّدٌ بِكَلَامٍ قَدِيمٍ قَائِمٍ بِذَاتِهِ، لَا يُشْبِهُهُ كَلَامُ الْخَلْقِ، فَلَيْسَ بِصَوْتٍ يَحْدُثُ مِنْ إِنْسِلَالِ هَوَاءٍ أَوْ اِصْطِكَاكِ أَجْسَامٍ، وَلَا بِحَرْفٍ يَنْقَطِعُ بِانْطِبَاقِ شَفَةٍ أَوْ تَحَرُّكِ لِسَانٍ، وَمُوسَى - عَلَيْهِ السَّلَامُ - سَمِعَ كَلَامَ اللَّهِ بِغَيْرِ حَرْفٍ وَلَا صَوْتٍ، كَمَا يَرَى الْأَبْرَارُ ذَاتَ اللَّهِ تَعَالَى فِي الْآخِرَةِ مِنْ غَيْرِ جَوْهَرٍ وَلَا عَرَضٍ.

Thus, He (Exalted is He) speaks, commands, prohibits, promises, and threatens with everlasting, pre-eternal speech that subsists in His essence. The speech of created things does not resemble it.

It is not composed of sound that results from the drawing forth of air or the collision of objects, nor is it a phoneme that is interrupted by the closing of lips or the movement of the tongue.

Mūsā (peace be upon him) heard Allah's speech without phoneme or sound, just as the virtuous will see Allah's essence (Exalted is He) in the Hereafter without substance or accident.[138]

(وَضِدُّهَا) أَيْ: صِفَةِ الْكَلَامِ (الْبَكَمُ، وَهُوَ الْخَرَسُ) وَالْمُرَادُ بِالْبَكَمِ عَدَمُ الْكَلَامِ النَّفْسِيِّ، سَوَاءٌ كَانَ بِآفَةٍ أَمْ لَا، فَدَخَلَ فِيهِ السُّكُوتُ، وَالْمُرَادُ بِالْخَرَسِ آفَةٌ تَمْنَعُ مِنَ الْكَلَامِ النَّفْسِيِّ، وَمِثَالُهُ فِي الشَّاهِدِ أَنْ يَمْنَعَ اللَّهُ عَنِ الْإِنْسَانِ التَّفَكُّرَ فَلَا يَجْرِي عَلَى قَلْبِهِ كَلَامٌ نَفْسِيٌّ.

---

137 *Al-Jawharah*, 29; *Tuḥfat*, 190; *Fatḥ al-majīd*, 59; Muḥammad al-Dumyāṭi, *Nihāyat al-amal* (Cairo: Al-Maṭbaʿah al-Maymuniyyah, 1313), 11.

138 Cf. *Fatḥ al-majīd*, 66.

‹Its› meaning the attribute of speech's ‹**contrary is muteness (bakam),**[139] **which is inarticulacy (kharas).**›

What is meant by "muteness" (*bakam*) is the absence of self-speech, whether or not it results from a deficiency – thus, even silence falls under it.

What is meant by "inarticulacy" (*kharas*) is a defect that prevents self-speech. An example of this in the witnessed realm (*shāhid*) is when Allah blocks a person from pondering, so that no self-speech occurs in his heart.

وَاعْلَـمْ أَنَّ كَلَامَ اللَّـهِ تَعَالَى يُطْلِقُ عَلَى: الكَلَام القَدِيـم القَائِم بِذَاتِهِ تَعَالَـى، وَعَلَـى الـكَلَام اللَّفْظِيِّ المَقْـرُوْءِ بِمَعْنَى: أَنَّهُ تَعَالَى خَلَقَهُ، وَلَيْسَ لِأَحَدٍ فِي أَصْلِ تَرْكِيْبِهِ كَسْبٌ.

Know that "Allah's speech" (Exalted is He) refers to:

1. Pre-eternal speech, which subsists in His essence (Exalted is He).
2. Uttered speech, which is recited in the sense that He (Exalted is He) creates it and that no one has a role in its original composition.[140]

فَمَنْ أَنْكَرَ أَنَّ مَا بَيْنَ دُفَّتَي المُصْحَفَ كَلَامُ اللَّهِ فَقَدْ كَفَرَ، إِلَّا أَن يُرِيْدَ أَنـَّهُ لَيْـسَ هُوَ الصِّفَـةُ القَائِمَةُ بِذَاتِهِ تَعَالَى، وَمَعَ كَـوْنِ الأَلْفَاظِ الَّتِي نَقْرَؤُهَا حَادِثَةً لَا يَجُوْزُ أَنْ يُقَالَ: القُرْآنُ حَادِثٌ، إِلَّا فِي مَقَام التَّعْلِيْم؛ لِأَنَّ القُرْآنَ يُطْلَقُ عَلَى الصِّفَةِ القَائِمَةِ بِذَاتِهِ تَعَالَى أَيْضًا، لَكِنْ مَجَازًا، فَرُبَّمَا يُتَوَهَّمُ مَنْ أَطْلَقَ أَنَّ القُرْآنَ حَادِثٌ أَنَّ الصِّفَةَ القَائِمَةَ بِذَاتِهِ تَعَالَى حَادِثَةٌ.

Whoever denies that what lies between the two covers of the *mushaf* is Allah's speech has committed disbelief – unless he intends that it itself is not the attribute subsistent in His essence (Exalted is He).

---

139 *Al-Jawharah*, 43; *Tuḥfat*, 283; *Fatḥ al-majīd*, 63.
140 *Al-Jawharah*, 29; *Tuḥfat*, 191; *Fatḥ al-majīd*, 61.

Despite the utterances that we recite being originated, it is not permissible to say that the Qur'an is originated, except in the context of instruction, because "the Qur'an" also refers to the attribute subsistent in His essence (Exalted is He) – though figuratively.

Thus, someone who states that the Qur'an is originated may mistakenly imagine that the attribute subsisting in Allah's essence is originated.[141]

وَالتَّحْقِيقُ: أَنَّ مَدْلُولَ الْأَلْفَاظِ الَّتِي نَقْرَؤُهَا بَعْضُ مَدْلُولِ الصِّفَةِ الْقَدِيمَةِ؛ لِأَنَّ الصِّفَةَ تَدُلُّ عَلَى جَمِيعِ الْوَاجِبَاتِ وَالْجَائِزَاتِ وَالْمُسْتَحِيلَاتِ، وَالْأَلْفَاظُ الَّتِي نَقْرَؤُهَا تَدُلُّ عَلَى بَعْضِ ذَلِكَ.

The truth is that what is indicated by the utterances we recite is part of what is indicated by the pre-eternal attribute. This is because the attribute indicates all that is necessary, possible and impossible, whereas the utterances we recite indicate some of that.[142]

(وَالدَّلِيلُ عَلَى ذَلِكَ) أَيْ: ثُبُوتِ الْكَلَامِ لَهُ تَعَالَى سَمْعِيٌّ، وَهُوَ (قَوْلُهُ تَعَالَى: ﴿وَكَلَّمَ اللَّهُ مُوسَىٰ تَكْلِيمًا﴾ [النساء، ١٦٤]) أَيْ: أَزَالَ اللَّهُ عَنْهُ الْحِجَابَ وَأَسْمَعَهُ الْكَلَامَ الْقَدِيمَ، ثُمَّ عَادَ عَلَيْهِ الْحِجَابُ. وَلَيْسَ الْمُرَادُ أَنَّهُ تَعَالَى ابْتَدَأَ كَلَامًا ثُمَّ سَكَتَ؛ لِأَنَّهُ لَمْ يَزَلْ مُتَكَلِّمًا دَائِمًا وَأَبَدًا،

وَرُوِيَ أَنَّ مُوسَى عَلَيْهِ السَّلَامُ كَانَ يَسُدُّ أُذُنَيْهِ عِنْدَ قُدُومِهِ مِنَ الْمُنَاجَاةِ، لِئَلَّا يَسْمَعَ كَلَامَ الْخَلْقِ، لِكَوْنِهِ لَا يَسْتَطِيعُ سَمَاعَهُ، لِأَنَّهُ صَارَ عِنْدَهُ كَأَشَدِّ مَا يَكُونُ مِنْ أَصْوَاتِ الْبَهَائِمِ الْمُنْكَرَةِ بِسَبَبِ مَا ذَاقَ مِنَ اللَّذَّاتِ الَّتِي لَا يُحَاطُ بِهَا عِنْدَ سَمَاعِ كَلَامِ مَنْ لَيْسَ كَمِثْلِهِ شَيْءٌ. وَقَدْ أَشْرَقَ وَجْهُهُ مِنَ النُّورِ فَمَا رَآهُ أَحَدٌ إِلَّا عَمِيَ، فَتَبَرْقَعَ وَبَقِيَ الْبُرْقَعُ عَلَى وَجْهِهِ إِلَى أَنْ مَاتَ.

---

141 *Al-Jawharah*, 29; *Tuḥfat*, 191; *Fatḥ al-majīd*, 60–61.
142 *Al-Jawharah*, 29; *Tuḥfat*, 193; *Fatḥ al-majīd*, 61.

‹The proof of this› meaning establishing speech for Him (Exalted is He) is revelation ‹**is His statement (Exalted is He), "And Allah spoke directly to Mūsā."**[143]› That is, Allah removed the veil and made him hear the pre-eternal speech, then returned the veil. It is not meant that He (Exalted is He) began speaking and then became silent, for He never ceased speaking – pre-eternally and forever.[144]

It has been related that Mūsā (peace be upon him) covered his ears when returning from his intimate conversation with Allah, so that he would not hear the speech of creation, as he could no longer bear listening to them. To him, their voices had become like the harshest, most jarring cries of beasts, due to what he had experienced of an indescribable delight when hearing the speech of the One for whom there is nothing like unto Him.

His face became radiant with divine light, such that whoever saw him went blind. Thus, he covered his face, and the veil remained upon him until he passed away.[145]

وَقَدْ أَجْمَعَ أَهْلُ الأَدْيَانِ وَالمِلَلِ عَلَى أَنَّهُ تَعَالَى مُتَكَلِّمٌ.

The followers of the [various] sects and religions are unanimous in that He (Exalted is He) is speaking.[146]

وَأَيْضًا كُلُّ حَيٍّ قَابِلٌ لِلِاتِّصَافِ بِالكَلَامِ، وَالقَابِلُ لِلشَّيْءِ لَا يَخْلُو عَنْهُ أَوْ عَنْ ضِدِّهِ، فَلَوْ لَمْ يَتَّصَفْ سُبْحَانَهُ وَتَعَالَى بِالكَلَام لَاتَّصَفَ بِضِدِّهِ، لَكِنِ اتِّصَافُهُ بِهِ مُحَالٌ لِأَنَّهُ نَقْصٌ، وَالنَّقْصُ عَلَيْهِ تَعَالَى مُحَالٌ.

---

143 Al-Nisā', 4:164.

144 *Al-Jawharah*, 29; *Tuḥfat*, 199.
      Fatḥ al-majīd, 63.

145 Imām al-Bājūrī states that most of the well-known accounts concerning Mūsā's conversation are lies, unbefitting of Mūsā (peace be upon him). *Al-Jawharah*, 29; *Tuḥfat*, 201.
      The account is mentioned in *Nūr al-ẓalām*, 43.

146 *Al-Jawharah*, 29; *Tuḥfat*, 202.

Also, every living being is capable of being attributed with speech, and whatever is capable of something cannot be devoid of it or of its contrary. If He (Majestic and Exalted is He) were not attributed with speech, He would necessarily be attributed with its contrary. However, attributing Him with its contrary is impossible, because it is a deficiency, and deficiency is impossible for Him (Exalted is He).[147]

RECAP: ENTITATIVE ATTRIBUTES

وَهَـٰذِهِ الصِّفَـاتُ السَّـبْعَةُ - وَهِيَ : القُـدْرَةُ وَالإِرَادَةُ وَالعِلْمُ وَالحَيَاةُ وَالسَّـمْعُ وَالبَصَـرُ وَالـكَلَامُ - تُسَـمَّى : «صِفَاتُ المَعَانِي»، وَهِيَ وُجُودِيَّةٌ بِحَيْثُ لَوْ كُشِـفَ الحِجَـابُ لَرُؤِيَتْ أَوْ سُـمِعَتْ، وَهَذِهِ السَّـبْعَةُ تُلَازِمُ السَّـبْعَةَ الَّتِي تُسَمَّى : «مَعْنَوِيَّةٌ»، وَهِيَ أُمُورٌ اِعْتِبَارِيَّةٌ.

These seven attributes – capability, will, knowledge, life, hearing, sight, and speech – are called "entitative attributes" (*ṣifāt al-maʿānī*). They are existential, such that if the veil were removed, they would be seen or heard.

These seven are inseparable from the seven attributes, which are called "qualitative attributes" (*ṣifāt maʿnawiyyah*) and are notional entities (*umūr iʿtibāriyyah*).[148]

BEING CAPABLE

(وَيَجِبُ فِي حَقِّهِ تَعَالَى كَوْنُهُ قَادِرًا) فَالكَوْنِيَّةُ المَذْكُورَةُ صِفَةٌ ثَابِتَةٌ فِي نَفْسِهَا قَائِمَةٌ بِالـذَّاتِ لَازِمَةٌ لِلقُـدْرَةِ. فَمَعْنَى كَوْنِهِ قَـادِرًا هُوَ: قِيَامُ القُـدْرَةِ بِذَاتِهِ

---

147 Cf. *Fatḥ al-majīd*, 54; Muḥammad bin Yūsuf bin ʿUmar al-Sanūsī, *Al-ʿAqīdat al-kubrā* in *Sharh al-ʿAqīdat al-kubrā* (Damascus: Dār al-Taqwā, 1441 AH/2019 CE), 93.

148 *Fatḥ al-majīd*, 67–68.

تَعَالَى، وَلَيْسَ هُنَاكَ صِفَةٌ أُخْرَى زَائِدَةٌ عَلَى قِيَامِ القُدْرَةِ بِالذَّاتِ ثَابِتَةٌ فِي خَارِجِ الذِّهْنِ.

‹**Being capable (*kawnuhu qādiran*) is necessary for Allah (Exalted is He).**› The aforementioned "being" is established in itself, subsistent in His essence, inseparable from capability.

Thus, the meaning of being capable is that capability subsists in His essence (Exalted is He).[149] There is no additional attribute beyond the subsistence of capability in His essence that is established extra-mentally.[150]

(وَضِدُّهُ كَوْنُهُ عَاجِزًا).

‹**Its contrary is being incapable (*kawnuhu ʿājizan*).**›[151]

(وَالدَّلِيْلُ عَلَى ذَلِكَ)، أَيْ: ثُبُوْتُ كَوْنِهِ قَادِرًا (دَلِيْلُ القُدْرَةِ) وَإِنْ شِئْتَ قُلْتَ: وَالدَّلِيْلُ عَلَى وُجُوْبِهِ لَهُ تَعَالَى أَنَّ الكَوْنَ قَادِرًا لَازِمٌ لِقِيَامِ القُدْرَةِ بِذَاتِهِ تَعَالَى، وَإِذَا ثَبَتَ لَهُ تَعَالَى كَوْنُهُ قَادِرًا اسْتَحَالَ عَلَيْهِ كَوْنُهُ عَاجِزًا.

‹**The proof of this**› meaning establishing His being capable ‹**is the proof of capability (*qudrah*).**› Alternatively, one might say: The proof of its necessity for Him (Exalted is He) is that being capable is inseparable from the subsistence of capability in His essence (Exalted is He). If being capable is established for Him (Exalted is He), then being incapable is impossible for Him.[152]

---

149 *Fatḥ al-majīd*, 63.
150 *Fatḥ al-majīd*, 63.
151 *Fatḥ al-majīd*, 64.
152 *Fatḥ al-majīd*, 64.

BEING WILLING

(وَيَجِبُ فِي حَقِّهِ تَعَالَى كَوْنُهُ مُرِيدًا) وَهُوَ صِفَةٌ لَهُ تَعَالَى أَزَلِيَّةٌ مُغَايِرَةٌ لِلْإِرَادَةِ، لَكِنَّهَا لَازِمَةٌ لِلْإِرَادَةِ، وَهُوَ أَمْرٌ اِعْتِبَارِيٌّ لَيْسَ لَهُ تَحَقَّقَ فِي خَارِجِ الْأَذْهَانِ، بَلْ لَهُ تَحَقَّقٌ فِي نَفْسِهِ وَفِي الذِّهْنِ فَقَطْ.

‹**Being willing (*kawnuhu murīdan*) is necessary for Allah (Exalted is He).**› It is an everlasting attribute that is distinct from will, though it is inseparable from it. It is a notional entity that has no extra-mental reality but is realised only in itself and in the mind.[153]

(وَضِدُّهُكَوْنُهُ كَارِهًا) أَي: عَادِمُ الْإِرَادَةِ.

‹**Its contrary is being averse (*kawnuhu kārihan*)**› that is, not having will.[154]

(وَالدَّلِيْلُ عَلَى ذَلِكَ) أَي: ثُبُوْتُ كَوْنُهُ تَعَالَى مُرِيْدًا (دَلِيْلُ الْإِرَادَةِ) وَإِنْ شِئْتَ قُلْتَ: وَالدَّلِيْلُ عَلَى وُجُوْبِهِ لَهُ تَعَالَى أَنَّ الْكَوْنَ مُرِيْدًا لَازِمٌ لِقِيَامِ الْإِرَادَةِ بِذَاتِهِ تَعَالَى، وَحَيْثُ وَجَبَتْ لَهُ تَعَالَى هَذِهِ الصِّفَةُ اِسْتَحَالَ عَلَيْهِ ضِدُّهَا.

‹**The proof of this**› meaning establishing His being willing (Exalted is He) ‹**is the proof of will.**› Alternatively, one might say:

The proof of its necessity for Him (Exalted is He) is that being willing is inseparable from the subsistence of will in His essence (Exalted is He). Since this attribute is necessary for Him, its contrary is impossible for Him.[155]

---

153 *Fatḥ al-majīd*, 64.
154 *Fatḥ al-majīd*, 65.
155 *Fatḥ al-majīd*, 65.

(وَيَجِبُ فِي حَقِّهِ تَعَالَى كَوْنُهُ عَالِمًا) وَهُوَ صِفَةٌ لِلَّهِ تَعَالَى أَزَلِيَّةٌ مُغَايِرَةٌ لِلعِلْمِ، لَكِنَّهَا لَازِمَةٌ لَـهُ، وَهُوَ أَمْـرٌ اِعْتِبَارِيٌّ لَيْسَ لَـهُ تَحَقَّقٌ فِي الخَـارِجِ، بَلْ فِي نَفْسِهِ، وَفِي الذِّهْنِ فَقَطْ.

‹Being knowing (*kawnuhu ʿāliman*) is necessary for Allah (Exalted is He).› It is an everlasting attribute that is distinct from knowledge, though it is inseparable from it. It is a notional entity that has no external realisation, but exists only in itself and in the mind.[156]

(وَضِدُّهُكَوْنُهُ جَاهِلًا).

‹Its contrary is being ignorant (*kawnuhu jāhilan*).›[157]

(وَالدَّلِيْلُ عَلَى ذَلِكَ دَلِيْلُ العِلْمِ) وَإِنْ شِئْتَ قُلْتَ: وَالدَّلِيْلُ عَلَى وُجُوْبِهِ لَهُ تَعَالَى أَنَّ الكَوْنَ عَالِمًا لَازِم لِقِيَامِ العِلْمِ بِهِ تَعَالَى، وَحَيْثُ وَجَبَتْ لَهُ تَعَالَى هَذِهِ الصِّفَةُ اِسْتَحَالَ عَلَيْهِ ضِدُّهَا.

‹The proof of this is the proof of knowledge.› Alternatively, one might say:

The proof of its necessity for Him (Exalted is He) is that being knowing is inseparable from the subsistence of knowledge in His essence (Exalted is He). Since this attribute is necessary for Him, its contrary is impossible for Him.[158]

BEING LIVING

(وَيَجِبُ فِي حَقِّهِ تَعَالَى كَوْنُهُ حَيًّا) وَهُوَ صِفَةٌ لِلَّهِ تَعَالَى أَزَلِيَّةٌ مُغَايِرَةٌ لِلحَيَاةِ، لَكِنَّهَا لَازِمَةٌ لَهَا، وَهُوَ أَمْرٌ اِعْتِبَارِيٌّ لَيْسَ لَهُ تَحَقَّقٌ إِلَّا فِي نَفْسِهِ فَقَطْ.

---

156 *Fatḥ al-majīd*, 65.
157 *Fatḥ al-majīd*, 65.
158 *Fatḥ al-majīd*, 65.

‹Being living (*kawnuhu ḥayyan*) is necessary for Allah (Exalted is He).› It is an everlasting attribute that is distinct from life, though it is inseparable from it. It is a notional entity that is realised only in itself.[159]

$$ (\text{وَضِدُّهُ كَوْنُهُ مَيِّتًا}) . $$

‹Its contrary is being dead (*kawnuhu mayyitan*).›[160]

(وَالدَّلِيْلُ عَلَى ذَلِكَ دَلِيْلُالحَيَاةِ) وَإِنْ شِئْتَ قُلْتَ: وَالدَّلِيْلُ عَلَى وُجُوْبِهِ لَهُ تَعَالَى أَنَّ الكَـوْنَ حَيًّا لَازِمٌ لِقِيَامِ الحَيَاةِ بِهِ تَعَالَى، وَحَيْثُ وَجَبَتْ لَهُ تَعَالَى هَذِهِ الصِّفَةُ اسْتَحَالَ عَلَيْهِ ضِدُّهَا.

‹The proof of this is the proof of life.› Alternatively, one might say: The proof of its necessity for Him (Exalted is He) is that being living is inseparable from the subsistence of life in His essence (Exalted is He). Since this attribute is necessary for Him, its contrary is impossible for Him.[161]

BEING HEARING AND SEEING

(وَيَجِـبُ فِي حَقِّهِ تَعَالَى كَوْنُهُ سَمِيْعًا بَصِيْرًا) وَهُمَـا صِفَتَانِ لَهُ تَعَالَى أَزَلِيَّتَانِ مُغَايِرَتَـانِ لِلسَّـمْعِ وَالبَصَرِ، لَكِنَّهُمَـا لَازِمَتَانِ لَهُمَا، وَهُمَا أَمْـرَانِ اعْتِبَارِيَّانِ، وَلِكُلٍّ مِنْهُمَا تَحَقُّقٌ فِي نَفْسِهِ فَقَطْ.

‹Being hearing and being seeing (*kawnuhu samīʿan* and *baṣīran*) are necessary for Allah (Exalted is He).› These are everlasting attributes, distinct from hearing (*samʿ*) and sight (*baṣar*), though they are inseparable from them. They are notional matters, and each is realised only in itself.[162]

---

159 *Fatḥ al-majīd*, 65.
160 *Fatḥ al-majīd*, 65.
161 *Fatḥ al-majīd*, 65.
162 *Fatḥ al-majīd*, 66.

(وَضِدُّهُمَا كَوْنُهُ أَصَمُّ وَكَوْنُهُ أَعْمَى).

‹Their contraries are being deaf and blind (*kawnuhu aṣamma and a'mā*).›[163]

(وَالدَّلِيْلُ عَلَى ذَلِكَ دَلِيْلُ السَّمْعِ وَدَلِيْلُ البَصَرِ) وَإِنْ شِئْتَ قُلْتَ: وَالدَّلِيْلُ عَلَى وُجُوْبِهِمَا لَهُ تَعَالَى أَنَّ الكَوْنَ سَمِيْعًا لَازِمٌ لِقِيَامِ السَّمْعِ بِذَاتِهِ تَعَالَى، وَالكَوْنَ بَصِيْرًا لَازِمٌ لِقِيَامِ البَصَرِ بِهِ تَعَالَى، وَحَيْثُ وَجَبَتْ لَهُ تَعَالَى هَاتَانِ الصِّفَتَانِ اِسْتَحَالَ عَلَيْهِ ضِدُّهُمَا.

‹The proof of this is the proof of hearing and the proof of sight.› Alternatively, one might say:

The proof of their necessity for Him (Exalted is He) is that being hearing (*kawnuhu sami'an*) is inseparable from the subsistence of hearing (*sam'*) in His essence (Exalted is He), and being seeing (*kawnuhu baṣiran*) is inseparable from the subsistence of sight (*baṣar*) in Him (Exalted is He). Since these two attributes are necessary for Him, their contraries are impossible for Him.[164]

BEING SPEAKING

(وَيَجِبُ فِي حَقِّهِ تَعَالَى كَوْنُهُ مُتَكَلِّمًا) وَهُوَ صِفَةٌ لَهُ تَعَالَى أَزَلِيَّة مُغَايِرَة لِلكَلَامِ، لَكِنَّهَا لَازِمَةٌ لَهُ، فَيَلْزَمُ مِنْ قِيَامِ الكَلَامِ بِذَاتِهِ تَعَالَى كَوْنُهُ تَعَالَى مُتَكَلِّمًا، وَلَيْسَ لَهُ تَحَقُّقٌ إِلَّا فِي نَفْسِهِ فَقَطْ.

‹Being speaking (*kawnuhu mutakalliman*) is necessary for Allah (Exalted is He).› It is an everlasting attribute for Him (Exalted is He), distinct from speech, though inseparable from it. The subsistence of speech in His essence (Exalted is He) necessitates His being speaking (Exalted is He). It has no realisation except in itself.[165]

---

163 *Fatḥ al-majīd*, 66.
164 *Fatḥ al-majīd*, 66.
165 *Fatḥ al-majīd*, 66.

(وَضِدُّهُ كَوْنُهُ أَبْكَمُ).

‹Its contrary is being mute (*kawnuhu abkam*).›[166]

(وَالدَّلِيلُ عَلَى ذَلِكَ دَلِيلُ الكَلَامِ) وَإِنْ شِئْتَ قُلْتَ: وَالدَّلِيلُ عَلَى وُجُوبِهِ لَـهُ تَعَالَى أَنَّ الكَـوْنَ مُتَكَلِّمًا لَازِمٌ لِقِيَامِ الكَلَامِ بِذَاتِـهِ تَعَالَى، وَإِذَا ثَبَتَ لَهُ تَعَالَى كَوْنُهُ مُتَكَلِّمًا اسْتَحَالَ عَلَيْهِ تَعَالَى كَوْنُهُ أَخْرَسَ وَمَا فِي مَعْنَاهُ الَّذِي هُوَ ضِدُّ كَوْنِهِ تَعَالَى مُتَكَلِّمًا.

‹The proof of this is the proof of speech.› Alternatively, one may say: The proof of its necessity for Him (Exalted is He) is that being speaking (*kawnuhu mutakalliman*) is inseparable from the subsistence of speech in His essence (Exalted is He). If being speaking is established for Him (Exalted is He), then being mute and whatever has the same meaning – the contrary of being speaking – is impossible for Him.[167]

RECAP OF HIS ATTRIBUTES

فَهَذِهِ الصِّفَاتُ الوَاجِبَةُ لَهُ تَعَالَى العِشْرُونَ وَالمُسْتَحِيلَاتُ العِشْرُونَ الَّتِي يَجِبُ عَلَى كُلِّ مُكَلَّفٍ مَعْرِفَتُهَا تَفْصِيلًا بِالدَّلِيلِ وَلَوْ إِجْمَالِيًا، ثُمَّ يَجِبُ أَنْ يَعْتَقِـدَ إِجْمَـالًا أَنَّهُ تَعَالَى مُتَّصَفٌ بِجَمِيْعِ الكَمَالَاتِ الَّتِي لَا يُحْصِيهَا إِلَّا اللَّهُ تَعَالَى، وَأَنَّهُ مُنَزَّهٌ عَنْ جَمِيْعِ النَّقَائِصِ الَّتِي لَا يُحْصِيهَا إِلَّا هُوَ.

These are the twenty attributes that are necessary for Allah (Exalted is He) and the twenty that are impossible, which every legally responsible person is obligated to know in detail with proof – even if that proof is general.

It is then obligatory to believe as a whole that He (Exalted is He) is attributed with every perfection – which no one can enumerate

---

166 *Fatḥ al-majīd*, 67.
167 *Fatḥ al-majīd*, 66.

except Allah (Exalted is He) – and that He is free from every deficiency, which no one can enumerate except Him.[168]

تَنْبِيهَانِ:

الأَوَّلُ: عُلِمَ مِمَّا مَرَّ أَنَّ الصِّفَاتِ العِشْرِينَ أَرْبَعَةُ أَقْسَامٍ:

١. نَفْسِيَّةٌ وَهِيَ الوُجُودُ.

٢. وَسَلْبِيَّةٌ وَهِيَ خَمْسَةٌ: القِدَمُ وَالبَقَاءُ وَالقِيَامُ بِالنَّفْسِ وَالمُخَالَفَةُ لِلحَوَادِثِ وَالوَحْدَانِيَّةُ.

٣. وَصِفَاتُ معانٍ وَهِيَ سَبْعَةٌ: القُدْرَةُ وَالإِرَادَةُ وَالعِلْمُ وَالحَيَاةُ وَالسَّمْعُ وَالبَصَرُ وَالكَلَامُ.

٤. وَصِفَاتٌ مَعْنَوِيَّةٌ وَهِيَ كَوْنُهُ قَادِرًا وَمُرِيدًا وَعَالِمًا وَحَيًّا وَسَمِيعًا وَبَصِيرًا وَمُتَكَلِّمًا.

First Notice It is known from what has preceded that the twenty attributes fall into four categories:

1. Essential (*nafsiyyah*): existence.
2. Negative (apophatic) attributes (*salbiyyah*): pre-eternity, everlastingness, self-subsistence, dissimilarity to originated things, and unicity.
3. Entitative attributes (*ṣifāt maʿānī*): capability, will, knowledge, life, hearing, sight, and speech.
4. Qualitative attributes (*ṣifāt maʿnawiyyah*): being capable, willing, knowing, living, hearing, seeing, and speaking.[169]

---

168 *Fatḥ al-majīd*, 68.
169 *Fatḥ al-majīd*, 67–68.

الثَّانِي: لَا يَتَعَلَّقُ إِلَّا مَا كَانَ مِنْ صِفَاتِ الْمَعَانِي، وَهِيَ مِنْ حَيْثُ التَّعَلُّقُ وَعَدَمُهُ، وَمِنْ حَيْثُ عُمُومُهُ لِلْوَاجِبَاتِ وَالْجَائِزَاتِ وَالْمُسْتَحِيلَاتِ وَخُصُوصُهُ بِالْمُمْكِنَاتِ وَبِالْمَوْجُودَاتِ أَقْسَامٌ أَرْبَعَةٌ:

الْأَوَّلُ: مَا يَتَعَلَّقُ بِالْمُمْكِنَاتِ، وَهِيَ الْقُدْرَةُ وَالإِرَادَةُ، لَكِنْ تَعَلُّقُ الْأَوَّلِ تَعَلُّقُ إِيجَادٍ وَإِعْدَامٍ، وَتَعَلُّقُ الثَّانِيَةِ تَعَلُّقُ تَخْصِيصٍ.

وَالثَّانِي: مَا يَتَعَلَّقُ بِالْوَاجِبَاتِ وَالْجَائِزَاتِ وَالْمُسْتَحِيلَاتِ، وَهُوَ الْعِلْمُ وَالْكَلَامُ، لَكِنْ تَعَلُّقُ الْأَوَّلِ تَعَلُّقُ انْكِشَافٍ، وَتَعَلُّقُ الثَّانِي تَعَلُّقُ دَلَالَةٍ.

وَالثَّالِثُ: مَا يَتَعَلَّقُ بِالْمَوْجُودَاتِ، وَهُوَ السَّمْعُ وَالْبَصَرُ.

وَالرَّابِعُ: مَا لَا يَتَعَلَّقُ بِشَيْءٍ، وَهُوَ الْحَيَاةُ.

وَلَا يَجِبُ عَلَى الْمُكَلَّفِ مَعْرِفَةُ هَذِهِ التَّعَلُّقَاتِ؛ لِأَنَّ ذَلِكَ مِنْ غَوَامِضِ عِلْمِ الْكَلَامِ.

Second Notice Only the entitative attributes have a linkage (*ta'al-luq*).[170] This applies both to whether they relate or not and to the scope of their linkage.

With respect to encompassing what is necessary, possible, and impossible, and being restricted to possible and existent things, they are divided into four categories.

First Category: What links to contingent things (*mumkināt*), namely capability and will. However, the linkage of capability is a linkage of bringing into existence and bringing into nonexistence, while the linkage of will is a linkage of specification.

Second Category: What links to what is necessary, possible, and impossible, namely knowledge and speech.

However, the linkage of knowledge is a linkage of disclosure, while the linkage of speech is a linkage of signification.

---

170 Cf. *Al-Jawharah*, 33; *Tuḥfat*, 223.

Third Category: What links to existent beings, namely hearing and sight.

Fourth Category: What does not connect to anything, namely life.

A legally responsible person is not required to know these linkages, since they are among the abstruse matters of the science of theology.[171]

WHAT IS POSSIBLE FOR ALLAH

(وَالجَائِزُ فِي حَقِّهِ تَعَالَى فِعْلُ كُلِّ مُمْكِنٍ أَوْ تَرْكِهِ) وَالمُمْكِنُ هُوَ الَّذِي يَجُوزُ عَلَيْهِ الوُجُودُ وَالعَدَمُ وَلَوْ شَرًّا كَالكُفْرِ وَالمَعَاصِي وَالخَلْقِ وَالرِّزْقِ وَنَحْوِهَا، فَلَا مُمْكِنٌ إِلَّا وَهُوَ حَادِثٌ بِفِعْلِهِ وَفَائِضٌ مِنْ عَدْلِهِ.

‹**What is possible for Allah (Exalted is He) is performing or forgoing every contingent thing.**› A "contingent thing" (*mumkin*) is that for which both existence and nonexistence are rationally possible, even if it is evil – such as disbelief, disobedience, creation, sustenance, and similar matters.

There is no contingent thing save that it is originated by His action and emanates from His justice.[172]

(وَالدَّلِيْلُ عَلَى ذَلِكَ أَنَّهُ لَوْ وَجَبَ عَلَيْهِ سُبْحَانَهُ وَتَعَالَى فِعْلُ شَيْءٍ أَوْ تَرْكُهُ لَصَارَ الجَائِزُ وَاجِبًا أَوْ مُسْتَحِيْلًا) أَي: وَالدَّلِيْلُ عَلَى أَنَّ فِعْلَ المُمْكِنَاتِ أَوْ تَرْكَهَا جَائِزٌ فِي حَقِّهِ تَعَالَى أَنْ تَقُوْلَ: قَدْ اِتَّفَقَ عَلَى جَوَازِ المُمْكِنَاتِ، فَلَوْ وَجَبَ عَلَيْهِ تَعَالَى فِعْلُ شَيْءٍ مِنْهَا لَصَارَ الجَائِزُ وَاجِبًا، وَلَوْ اِمْتَنَعَ عَلَيْهِ فِعْلُ شَيْءٍ لَصَارَ الجَائِزُ مُسْتَحِيْلًا (وَهُوَ) أَي: صَيْرُوْرَةُ الجَائِزِ وَاجِبًا أَوْ مُسْتَحِيْلًا (مُحَالٌ) فَبَطَلَ مَا أَدَّى إِلَيْهِ هُوَ وُجُوْبُهَا أَوْ اِمْتِنَاعُهَا وَثَبَتَ جَوَازُهَا وَهُوَ المَطْلُوْبُ.

---

171 Since the last footnote: *Al-Jawharah*, 33; *Tuḥfat*, 224. The entire second notice is in *Fatḥ al-majīd*, 68.

172 *Fatḥ al-majīd*, 68.

‹The proof of this is that if it was necessary for Him (Sublime and Exalted is He) to perform or forgo something, then what is possible would become either necessary or impossible.›

That is, the proof that performing and forgoing contingent things is rationally possible for Allah (Exalted is He) is to say: There is agreement that contingent things are possible. If it were necessary for Him (Exalted is He) to perform one of them, then what is rationally possible would become necessary. If He were barred from performing something, then what is rationally possible would become impossible.

‹However, it› that is, the contingent becoming necessary or impossible ‹is impossible.›[173] Thus, what leads to it – namely, its necessity or impossibility – is also invalid. Therefore, the rational possibility of performing or forgoing contingent things is established, which is the desired conclusion.[174]

RECAP OF MATTERS RELATED TO ALLAH

فَهَـٰذِهِ إِحْـدَى وَأَرْبَعُوْنَ عَقِيْدَةً تَتَعَلَّـقُ بِالإِلَهِ عَزَّ وَجَلَّ: عِشْـرُوْنَ واجِبات، وَعِشْرُوْنَ مستحيلَات، وواحِدَة جَائِزَة. وقَدْ تَمَّ القِسم الأَوَّل مِنْ هَذَا الفَنّ وَهُوَ الإلهيات.

These are forty-one points of doctrine pertaining to the Divine (Mighty and Majestic is He): twenty necessary, twenty impossible, and one possible.

With this, the first section of this discipline is complete – namely, the section concerning Divine Attributes (*ilāhiyyāt*).

---

173 Qur'an, 28:68: "And your Lord creates what He wills and chooses."
174 *Fatḥ al-majīd*, 73.

KNOWING THE PROPHETS

(و) أَمَّا القِسْـمُ الثَّاني وَهُوَ النَّبَوِيَّاتُ، فَيَشْـتَمِلُ عَلَى مَا يَجِبُ لِلأَنْبِيَاءِ وَمَا يَسْتَحِيْلُ فِي حَقِّهِمْ وَمَا يَجُوْزُ عَلَيْهِمْ.

‹**And**› as for the second section – which concerns matters related to the prophets [peace be upon them] – it includes what is necessary for the prophets, impossible for them, and what is possible for them.

WHAT IS NECESSARY AND IMPOSSIBLE FOR THEM

TRUTHFULNESS

فَالَّذِي (يَجِبُ فِي حَقِّ الرُّسُـلِ عَلَيْهِمْ الصَّلَاةُ وَالسَّلَامُ الصِّدْقُ) وَهُوَ مُطَابَقَةُ خَبَرِهِـمْ لِلْوَاقِع وَلَوْ بِحَسَـبِ اِعْتِقَادِهِمْ، كَمَـا فِي قَوْلِهِ ﷺ: «كُلُّ ذَلِكَ لَمْ يَكُنْ»، لَمَّا قَالَ ذُو الْيَدَيْنِ حِينَ سَلَّمَ ﷺ مِنْ رَكْعَتَيْنِ مِنْ الظُّهْرِ: «أَقَصِرَتِ الصَّلَاةُ أَمْ نَسِتَ يَا رَسُوْلَ اللَّهِ»؟

‹**Truthfulness (*ṣidq*) is necessary for the Messengers (blessings and peace be upon them).**› It is defined as their report corresponding to reality, even if only in accordance with their beliefs.[175]

---

175 In *Fatḥ al-majīd* the author mentions that Shaykh Aḥmad al-Suhaymī said that the truthfulness that is necessary for the Prophets (peace be upon them) is their message corresponding to reality and their beliefs, and that it is impossible for their message to correspond to reality while diverging from their beliefs. But as for truthfulness itself, it is the message corresponding to reality, whether or not it corresponds to one's beliefs.

    Al-Jawharah, 59; *Tuḥfat*, 408; *Fatḥ al-majīd*, 74.

An example of this is found in the statement of the Prophet (may Allah bless him and give him peace): "None of that happened," in response to Dhu l-Yadayn saying to him (may Allah bless him and give him peace) after he said "*As-Salāmu 'alaykum*" following two *rak'ahs*[176] of the Ẓuhr Prayer: "Was prayer shortened, or did you forget, O Messenger of Allah?"[177]

(وَضِدُّهُالْكِذْبُ) أَيْ: عَدَمُ مُطَابَقَةِ خَبَرِهِمْ لِلْوَاقِعِ وَافَقَ الْاِعْتِقَادَ أَمْ لَا .

‹**Its contrary is lying (*kadhib*)**› meaning their message not corresponding to reality, whether or not it aligns with their beliefs‹.›[178]

(وَالدَّلِيـلُ عَلَـى ذَلِكَ) أَيْ: وُجُوْبُ الصِّدْقِ لَهُــمْ عَلَيْهِمْ الصَّلَاةُ وَالسَّلَامُ (أَنَّهُمْ لَوْ) لَمْ يَصْدُقُوْا لَلَزِمَ كَذِبُهُمْ؛ لِأَنَّهُ لَا وَاسِـطَةَ بَيْنَ الصِّدْقِ وَالْكَذِبِ، وَلَـوْ (كَذَبُـوْا لَكَانَ خَبَرُ اللَّهِ سُبْحَانَهُ وَتَعَالَى) بِأَنَّهُمْ صَادِقـُونَ (كَاذِبًا) وَالْمُرَادُ خَبَرُهُ تَعَالَى الْحُكْمِيُّ، وَهُوَ الْمُعْجِزَةُ، وَهُوَ فِعْلُ اللَّهِ تَعَالَى؛ لِأَنَّ اللَّهَ تَعَالَى صَدَّقَهُــمْ بِالْمُعْجِزَاتِ، فَإِنَّهُ تَعَالَى لَمْ يُجْرِ عَادَتَهُ مِــنْ أَوَّلِ الدُّنْيَا إِلَى الْآنَ بِتَمْكِيـنِ الْـكَاذِبِ مِنْ الْمُعْجِزَاتِ، بَلْ أَجْرَى عَادَتَـهُ بِوُقُوعِهَا مِنْ الصَّادِقِ دُوْنَ الْـكَاذِبِ، وَإِذَا خَيَّـلَ بِسِـحْرٍ أَوْ نَحْوِهِ أَظْهَـرَ فَضِيحَتَهُ عَنْ قُرْبِ ذَلِكَ، وَمَعْلُـومٌ أَنَّ تَصْدِيقَ الْـكَاذِبِ كَـذِبٌ (وَهُـوَ) أَيْ: كَوْنُ خَبَرِهِ تَعَالَى كَاذِبًا (مُحَالٌ)؛ لِأَنَّ خَبَرَهُ تَعَالَى عَلَى وُفْقِ عِلْمِهِ، وَالْخَبَرُ الَّذِي عَلَى وُفْقِ الْعِلْمِ لَا يَكُوْنُ إِلَّا حَقًّا، وَإِذَا اِسْتَحَالَ كَذِبُهُ تَعَالَى ثَبَتَ صِدْقُهُ، وَإِذَا ثَبَتَ صِدْقُهُ صَحَّ تَصْدِيقُهُ لِلرُّسُلِ، وَإِذَا صَحَّ ذَلِكَ ثَبَتَ صِدْقُهُمْ، وَهُوَ الْمَطْلوبُ .

‹**The proof of this**› meaning truthfulness being necessary for them (peace be upon them) ‹**is that if they**› were not truthful, it would

---

176 *Al-Jawharah*, 59; *Tuḥfat*, 408.

177 Imam al-Suyūṭī's *Jāmi' al-aḥādīth* lists variations of this hadith under number 42443, sourced to 'Abd al-Razzāq's *Muṣannaf*, Muslim, and al-Nasā'ī.

178 *Al-Jawharah*, 60; *Tuḥfat*, 415; *Fatḥ al-majīd*, 76.

necessitate their dishonesty, since there is no middle ground between truthfulness and lying. If they ‹**were to lie, then Allah's declaration (Sublime and Exalted is He)**› that they are truthful ‹**would itself be a lie.**›

What is intended [by Allah's declaration] here is His implicit message (*ḥukmī*) – namely, the miracle – which is an act of Allah (Exalted is He)[179]. For Allah (Exalted is He) confirmed their truthfulness through miracles.[180] Since it has never been His norm (Exalted is He) – from the beginning of the world until now – to furnish a liar with miracles, but rather His norm has been that miracles occur only for the truthful, not the liars.

If a liar were to deceive people through magic or something similar, his deception would soon be exposed. And it is known that validating the claim of a liar is itself a lie.[181]

‹**And that**› meaning His declaration (Exalted is He) being false ‹**is impossible**› since His declaration (Exalted is He) corresponds to His knowledge, and a declaration that corresponds to knowledge can only be true‹.›[182] If falsehood is impossible for Him (Exalted is He), then His truthfulness is established. And if His truthfulness is established, then His confirmation of the messengers' truthfulness is valid. If this confirmation is valid, then their truthfulness is necessarily established – and that is the desired conclusion.[183]

---

179 This concerns the linguistic message implied by a non-linguistic event, viz. the linguistic message implied in a miracle, that message being: "My servant is truthful in what he has conveyed from Me."

180 *Fatḥ al-majīd*, 74–75. Cf. *Al-Jawharah*, 59; *Tuḥfat*, 409.

181 *Al-Jawharah*, 59; *Tuḥfat*, 409; *Fatḥ al-majīd*, 75.

182 *Al-Jawharah*, 59; *Tuḥfat*, 409; *Fatḥ al-majīd*, 75–76.

183 *Al-Jawharah*, 59; *Tuḥfat*, 409; *Fatḥ al-majīd*, 76.

TRUSTWORTHINESS

(وَيَجِـبُ فِي حَقِّهِـمْ عَلَيْهِمْ الصَّلَاةُ وَالـسَّلَامُ الْأَمَانَةُ) وَهِيَ حِفْـظُ ظَوَاهِرِهِمْ وَبَوَاطِنِهِـمْ مِـنْ التَّلَبُّسِ بِمَنْهِـيٍّ عَنْهُ، وَلَوْ نَهِـيَ كَرَاهَـةٍ أَوْ خِلَافَ الْأَوْلَى، فَهُـمْ مَعْصُومُونَ عَنْ جَمِيْعِ الْمَعَاصِي الْمُتَعَلِّقَةِ بِظَاهِرِ الْبَدَنِ كَالزِّنَى وَشُرْبِ الْخَمْرِ وَالْكَـذِبِ وَغَيْـرِ ذَلِكَ مِنْ مَنْهِيَّاتِ الظَّاهِـرِ، وَمَعْصُومُونَ عَنْ جَمِيْعِ الْمَعَاصِي الْمُتَعَلِّقَةِ بِالْبَاطِنِ مِـنْ الْحَسَـدِ وَالْكِبْـرِ وَالرِّيَاءِ وَغَيْـرِ ذَلِكَ مِنْ مَنْهِيَّـاتِ الْبَاطِنِ، وَالْمُرَادُ الْمَنْهِيُّ عَنْهُ وَلَوْ صُوْرَةً فَيَشْمَلُ مَا قَبْلَ النُّبُوَّةِ وَمَا فِي حَالَـةِ الصِّغَرِ، وَلَا يَقَعُ مِنْهُمْ مَكْـرُوْهٌ وَلَا خِلَافُ الْأَوْلَى، بَلْ وَلَا مُبَاحٌ عَلَى وَجْهِ كَوْنِ ذَلِكَ مَكْرُوهًا أَوْ خِلَافَ الْأَوْلَى أَوْ مُبَاحًا، وَإِذَا وَقَعَ صُوْرَةُ ذَلِكَ مِنْهُمْ فَهُوَ لِلتَّشْرِيعِ فَيَصِيرُ وَاجِبًا أَوْ مَنْدُوبًا فِي حَقِّهِمْ، فَأَفْعَالُهُمْ عَلَيْهِمْ الـصَّلَاةُ وَالـسَّلَامُ دَائِرَةٌ بَيْنَ الْوَاجِبِ وَالْمَنْدُوبِ، بَلْ فِي الْأَوْلِيَاءِ الَّذِينَ هُمْ أَتْبَاعُهُمْ مَنْ يَصِلُ إِلَى مَقَامٍ تَصِيرُ فِيْهِ حَرَكَاتُهُ وَسَكَنَاتُهُ طَاعَاتٍ بِالنِّيَّاتِ.

‹Trustworthiness (*amānah*) is necessary for the Messengers (blessings and peace be upon them).› It is defined as their external bodies and inner selves[184] being safeguarded from engaging in what is forbidden, even if it is forbidden out of being detested (*makrūh*) or contrary to what is best (*khilāf al-awlā*).

They are safeguarded from all acts of disobedience related to the exterior of the body, like fornication, drinking wine, lying, and other external prohibitions. Likewise, they are safeguarded from all internal acts of disobedience, such as envy, arrogance, ostentation, and other internal prohibitions.

What is intended is everything that is forbidden, even in form. This includes protection prior to prophethood and during childhood. Thus, no act that is detested or contrary to what is best occurs from

---

184 Lit. their externals and internals.

them – indeed, not even a merely permissible act – in a way that it remains detested, sub-optimal, or merely permissible.

If such an act does appear from them in form, it is for the sake of legislation, and thus becomes obligatory or recommended for them. For their actions (may Allah bless them and give them peace) fall within the range of the obligatory and the recommended.

Indeed, among their followers, the *awliyā'*, there are those who reach a station where their motions and stillness become acts of worship by virtue of their intentions.[185]

(وَضِدُّهَا الْخِيَانَةُ).

‹Its contrary is treachery (*khiyānah*).›[186]

(وَالدَّلِيْلُ عَلَى ذَلِكَ) أَيْ: وُجُوْبِ الْأَمَانَةِ لَهُمْ (أَنَّهُمْ لَوْ خَانُوا) أَيْ: خَالَفُوا أَمَرَ اللَّهِ تَعَالَى (بِفِعْلٍ مُحَرَّمٍ، أَوْ مَكْرُوهٍ) أَوْ خِلَافِ الْأَوْلَى لِغَيْرِ التَّشْرِيعِ (لَكُنَّا مَأْمُورِيْنَ بِمِثْلِ ذَلِكَ) أَيْ: مَا يَفْعَلُوْنَهُ، وَالْمُرَادُ بِالْفِعْلِ مَا يَعُمُّ فِعْلَ اللِّسَانِيِّ وَهُوَ الْقَوْلُ، وَفِعْلَ الْقَلْبِ؛ لِأَنَّ اللَّهَ تَعَالَى أَمَرَنَا بِاتِّبَاعِهِمْ فِي أَفْعَالِهِمْ وَأَقْوَالِهِمْ وَأَحْوَالِهِمْ مِنْ غَيْرِ تَفْصِيلٍ مَا عَدَا مَا ثَبَتَ اخْتِصَاصُهُمْ بِهِ وَمَا عَدَا الْأُمُوْرَ الْجِبَلِيَّةَ: كَالْقِيَامِ وَالْقُعُودِ وَالْمَشْي، فَإِنَا لَمْ نُؤْمَرْ بِالِاتِّبَاع فِي ذَلِكَ. (وَلَا يَصِحُّ أَنْ نُؤْمَرَ بِمُحَرَّمٍ أَوْ مَكْرُوهٍ) أَوْ خِلَافِ الْأَوْلَى؛ لِأَنَّ اللَّهَ تَعَالَى لَا يَأْمُرُ بِالْفَحْشَاءِ، فَتَعَيَّنَ أَنَّهُمْ لَا يَفْعَلُونَ إِلَّا الطَّاعَةَ إِمَّا وَاجِبَةً أَوْ مَنْدُوبَةً، فَلَا تَكُوْنُ أَفْعَالُهُمْ مُحَرَّمَةً أَوْ مَكْرُوهَةً وَلَا خِلَافَ الْأَوْلَى. فَأَفْعَالُهُمْ دَائِرَةٌ بَيْنَ الْوَاجِبِ وَالْمَنْدُوبِ وَلَا يَدْخُلُهَا الْمُبَاحُ؛ لِأَنَّهُمْ إِذَا فَعَلُوْهُ يَكُوْنُ لِبَيَانِ الْجَوَازِ وَالتَّشْرِيعِ، وَهُوَ إِمَّا وَاجِبٌ أَوْ مَنْدُوبٌ.

‹The proof of this› meaning trustworthiness being necessary for them ‹is that if they were to commit treachery› meaning if they

---

185 *Al-Jawharah*, 61; *Tuḥfat*, 406; *Fatḥ al-majīd*, 78–79.
186 *Fatḥ al-majīd*, 79.

contradicted the command of Allah (Exalted is He) ‹**by performing something unlawful or detested**› or an act contrary to what is best for non-legislative purposes‹, **then we would have been commanded to do the same**›, meaning we would have been commanded to follow their actions‹.›[187]

What is intended by "act" is what extends to acts of the tongue (that is, speech) or acts of the heart. This is because Allah (Exalted is He) has commanded us to follow them in their actions, speech, and states, without distinction[188], except for what has been established as unique to them and natural actions (such as standing, sitting, and walking), since we were not commanded to follow them in those matters.

‹**Furthermore, it is not valid that we would be commanded to perform something unlawful or detested**› or contrary to what is best‹.› This is because Allah (Exalted is He) does not command immorality.

Thus, it necessarily follows that they do nothing except acts of obedience, which are either obligatory or recommended. Therefore, their actions are never unlawful, detested, or contrary to what is superior.

Their actions remain within the range of the obligatory and the recommended, and the merely permissible does not enter that range. If they were to perform a merely permissible act, it would be to clarify its permissibility and establish its legislative status – which itself is either obligatory or recommended.[189]

وَهَذِهِ الْحُجَّةُ سَمْعِيَّةٌ أَوْ شَرْعِيَّةٌ، وَإِنْ كَانَتْ عَلَى صُورَةِ الدَّلِيْلِ الْعَقِيلِيِّ؛ لِأَنَّ دَلِيْـلَ الْمُلَازِمَـةِ شَـرْعِيٌّ وَهُـوَ قَوْلُهُ تَعَالَى : ﴿قُلْ إِنْ كُنْتُـمْ تُحِبُّونَ اللَّهَ فَاتَّبِعُونِـي﴾ [آلَ عِمْـرَانَ، ٣١] وَأَنَّ بُـطْلَانَ التَّالِي بِدَلِيلٍ شَـرْعِيٍّ وَهُوَ قَوْلُهُ تَعَالَى : ﴿إِنَّ اللَّـهَ لَا يَأْمُرُ الْفَحْشَـاءَ﴾ [الْأَعْـرَافِ، ٢٨] بِخِلَافِ الْحُجَّةِ

---

187 *Fath al-majīd*, 78. Cf. *Al-Jawharah*, 59; *Tuḥfat*, 407.
188 This reason: *Al-Jawharah*, 59; *Tuḥfat*, 407.
189 *Fath al-majīd*, 78.

عَلَى وُجُوبِ صِدْقِهِمْ فَإِنَّهَا عَقْلِيَّةٌ، وَلِذَا قَالَ السَّنُوسِيُّ: وَيَسْتَحِيلُ عَلَيْهِمُ الْكِذْبُ عَقْلًا وَالْمَعَاصِي شَرْعًا.

This argument is textual (*sam'iyyah*) or legislative (*shar'iyyah*), even though it takes the form of a rational proof. This is because the proof of its necessitation (*dalīl al-mulāzamah*) is legislative, as indicated by Allah's statement (Exalted is He): "Say, 'If you love Allah, then follow me....'"[190]

Likewise, the proof of the invalidity of the implicative consequent (*buṭlān al-tālī*) is based on a legislative proof, as Allah (Exalted is He) states: "Indeed, Allah does not command immorality."[191]

This contrasts with the argument for the necessity of their truthfulness, which is rational (*'aqliyyah*). For this reason, al-Sanūsī stated: "It is rationally impossible for them to lie and legislatively impossible for them to commit disobedience."[192]

CONVEYANCE

(وَيَجِبُ فِي حَقِّهِمْ عَلَيْهِمُ الصَّلَاةُ وَالسَّلَامُ تَبْلِيغُ مَا أُمِرُوْا بِتَبْلِيغِهِ لِلْخَلْقِ) بِخِلَافِ مَا أُمِرُوْا بِكِتْمَانِهِ وَمَا خُيِّرُوْا فِيْهِ فَلَيْسَ تَبْلِيغُ كُلٍّ مِنْهُمَا وَاجِبَةً، بَلْ يَجِبُ كِتْمَانُ مَا أُمِرُوْا بِكِتْمَانِهِ، وَلَا يَجِبُ عَلَيْهِمْ شَيْءٌ فِيْمَا خُيِّرُوْا فِيْهِ.

‹**Conveyance of what they were commanded to convey to the creation (*tablīgh li-l-khalq*) is necessary for the Messengers (blessings and peace be upon them).**› This is in contrast to what they were ordered to conceal or given the option to convey or conceal, for neither of these is necessarily required to be conveyed.

---

190 Qur'an, 3:31.

191 Qur'an, 7:28.

192 al-Sanūsī, *Al-'Aqīdat al-kubrā* in Muḥammad bin Yūsuf bin 'Umar al-Sanūsī, *Sharh al-'Aqīdat al-kubrā* (Damascus: Dār al-Taqwā, 1441 AH/2019 CE),112. Cf. *Al-Jawharah*, 59; *Tuḥfat*, 407.

Rather, it is necessary to conceal what they were commanded to conceal, and nothing that was optional for them is obligatory upon them.[193]

(وَضِدُّهُكِتْمَانُ ذَلِكَ) أَيْ: جَمِيْعُ مَا أُمِرُوْا بِتَبْلِيْغِهِ لِلْخَلْقِ.

‹Its contrary is concealing this (*kitmān dhālik*)› meaning concealing all that they were commanded to convey to creatures‹.›[194]

(الدَّلِيْـلُ عَلَـى ذَلِكَ) أَيْ: جَمِيْـعُ مَا أُمِـرُوْا بِتَبْلِيْغِهِ (أَنَّهُمْ لَوْ) لَـمْ يَبْلُغُوْا لَكَتَمُـوْا؛ إِذْ لَا وَاسِـطَةَ بَيْـنَ الْكِتْمَـانِ وَالتَّبْلِيـغِ، لَكِنَّهُمْ لَـمْ يَكْتُمُوْا؛ إِذْ لَوْ (كَتَمُـوْا شَـيْئًا) أَيْ: بَعْضًا (مِمَّا أُمِرُوْا بِتَبْلِيْغِهِ) لِلْخَلْـقِ (لَكُنَّا مَأْمُورِّينَ بِكِتْمَانِ الْعِلْـمِ) لِأَنَّ اللَّـهَ تَعَالَى أَمَرَنَا بِالِاقْتِـدَاءِ بِهِمْ حَيْثُ قَالَ فِي حَقِّ نَبِيِّنَا: ﴿إِنَّ اللَّـهَ لَا يَأْمُـرُ الْفَحْشَاءَ﴾ [الأعراف، ٢٨] (وَلَا يَصِـحُّ أَنْ نُؤْمَـرَ بِهِ) أَيْ: بِكِتْمَانِ الْعِلْمِ (لِأَنَّ كَاتِمَ العِلْمِ مَلْعُونٌ) قَالَ اللَّهُ تَعَالَى: ﴿إِنَّ الَّذِينَ يَكْتُمُونَ مَـا أَنزَلْنَـا مِنَ الْبَيِّنَـاتِ وَالْهُدَىٰ مِن بَعْدِ مَا بَيَّنَّاهُ لِلنَّـاسِ فِي الْكِتَابِ أُولَٰئِكَ يَلْعَنُهُمُ اللَّهُ وَيَلْعَنُهُمُ اللَّاعِنُونَ﴾ [البقرة، ١٥٩].

‹The proof of this› meaning that they conveyed all that they were commanded to convey ‹is that if they› had not conveyed it, they would have concealed it, since there is no middle ground between concealing and conveying. However, they did not conceal anything, because if they had ‹concealed anything› meaning any part ‹of what they were ordered to convey› to creation‹, then we would have been commanded to conceal knowledge.›

This is because Allah (Exalted is He) commanded us to emulate them[195], as He (Exalted is He) says concerning our Prophet (may Allah bless him and give him peace): "Indeed, Allah does not com-

---

193 *Fatḥ al-majīd*, 80. Cf. *Al-Jawharah*, 60; *Tuḥfat*, 414.

194 *Al-Jawharah*, 60; *Tuḥfat*, 415. *Fatḥ al-majīd*, 80.

195 *Fatḥ al-majīd*, 80. Cf. *Al-Jawharah*, 60; *Tuḥfat*, 414.

mand immorality."[196] ‹**Furthermore, it is not valid that we would be commanded with this**› meaning to conceal knowledge ‹**since the one who conceals knowledge is cursed.**› Allah (Exalted is He) said, "Indeed! Those who conceal the proofs and the guidance which We revealed, after We made it clear to mankind in the Book – those are whom Allah curses and the cursers curse."[197]

ACUITY

(وَيَجِبُ فِي حَقِّهِمْ عَلَيْهِمْ الصَّلَاةُ وَالسَّلَامُ الْفَطَانَةُ) وَهِيَ التَّيَقُّظُ لِإِلْزَامِ الْخُصُومِ وَإِبْطَالِ دَعَاوِيهِمْ الْبَاطِلَةِ.

‹**Acuity (*faṭānah*) is necessary for the Messengers (blessings and peace be upon them).**›[198] It is defined as alertness for the purpose of compelling opponents with argument and to invalidate their false claims.[199]

(وَضِدُّهَا الْبَلَادَةُ)، أَيْ: الْغَفْلَةُ.

‹**Its contrary is dullness (*balādah*)**› meaning inattentiveness or slow-wittedness.[200]

(وَالدَّلِيلُ عَلَى ذَلِكَ) أَيْ: وُجُوبِ الْفَطَانَةِ لَهُمْ عَلَيْهِمْ الصَّلَاةُ وَالسَّلَامُ (أَنَّهُ) أَيْ: الشَّأْنَ (لَوْ انْتَفَتْ عَنْهُمْ الْفَطَانَةُ لَمَا قَدَرُوا أَنْ يُقِيمُوا حُجَّةً عَلَى الْخَصْمِ وَهُوَ) أَيْ: عَدَمُ الْقُدْرَةِ عَلَى إِقَامَةِ الْحُجَّةِ (مُحَالٌ؛ لِأَنَّ الْقُرْآنَ دَلَّ فِي مَوَاضِعَ كَثِيرَةٍ عَلَى إِقَامَتِهِمْ الْحُجَّةَ عَلَى الْخَصْمِ) كَقَوْلِهِ تَعَالَى: ﴿وَتِلْكَ﴾ أَيْ: حُجَّةُ إِبْرَاهِيمَ عَلَى قَوْمِهِ ﴿حُجَّتُنَا آتَيْنَاهَا إِبْرَاهِيمَ﴾ [الأنعام، ٨٣]،

---

196 Qur'an, 7:28.
197 Qur'an, 2:159. *Fatḥ al-majīd*, 80. Cf. *Al-Jawharah*, 60; *Tuḥfat*, 414.
198 *Al-Jawharah*, 59; *Tuḥfat*, 410; *Fatḥ al-majīd*, 81.
199 *Al-Jawharah*, 59; *Tuḥfat*, 410; *Fatḥ al-majīd*, 81.
200 *Al-Jawharah*, 60; *Tuḥfat*, 415; *Fatḥ al-majīd*, 81.

وَكَقَوْلِهِ تَعَالَى حِكَايَةً عَنْ قَوْمِ نُوحٍ: ﴿يَا نُوحُ قَدْ جَادَلْتَنَا فَأَكْثَرْتَ جِدَالَنَا﴾ [هود، ٣٢]، وَكَقَوْلِهِ تَعَالَى: ﴿وَجَادِلْهُمْ بِالَّتِي هِيَ أَحْسَنُ﴾ [النحل، ١٢٥]، أَيْ: بِالطَّرِيقِ الَّتِي تَشْتَمِلُ عَلَى نَوْعِ إِرْفَاقٍ بِهِمْ، وَمَنْ لَمْ يَكُنْ فَطِنًا لَا يُمْكِنُهُ إِقَامَةُ الْحُجَّةِ وَلَا الْمُجَادَلَةُ. وَهَذِهِ الْآيَاتُ وَإِنْ كَانَتْ وَارِدَةً فِي بَعْضِهِمْ إِلَّا أَنَّ مَا ثَبَتَ لِبَعْضِهِمْ مِنَ الْكَمَالِ الَّذِي لَا يَتِمُّ الْمَقْصُودُ إِلَّا بِهِ يَثْبُتُ لِجَمِيعِهِمْ، فَثَبَتَتِ الْفَطَانَةُ لِلْجَمِيعِ، وَإِنْ لَمْ يَكُونُوا رُسُلًا بَلْ أَنْبِيَاءُ فَقَطْ، نَعَمْ الْوَاجِبُ لِلْأَنْبِيَاءِ مُطْلَقُ الْفِطْنَةِ، وَأَمَّا الرُّسُلُ فَالْوَاجِبُ لَهُمْ كَمَالُ الْفِطْنَةِ.

‹**The proof of this**› meaning the necessity of acuity (*faṭānah*) for the Messengers (blessings and peace be upon them) ‹**is that if acuity were absent from them, they would be unable to establish arguments against their opponents. But that**› meaning the absence of the ability to establish arguments ‹**is impossible, because the Qur'an repeatedly affirms that they established arguments against their opponents.**›

For example, Allah (Exalted is He) says: "This" – meaning Ibrāhīm's argument against his people – "is Our argument. We gave it to Ibrāhīm."[201]

He (Exalted is He) relates from the people of Nūḥ: "O Nūḥ! You have disputed with us and made frequent disputes with us."[202]

And He (Exalted is He) says: "And dispute with them in a way that is best"[203] – that is, in a manner that includes employing gentleness and wisdom with them.[204]

Whoever lacks acuity is incapable of establishing arguments or engaging in meaningful disputation.[205]

---

201 Qur'an, 6:83.
202 Qur'an, 11:32.
203 Qur'an, 16:125.
204 Cf. *Al-Jawharah*, 59; *Tuḥfat*, 410; *Fatḥ al-majīd*, 81.
205 *Al-Jawharah*, 59; *Tuḥfat*, 411; *Fatḥ al-majīd*, 81.

Even if these verses were revealed concerning only some of the prophets, it is a principle that any perfection necessary to fulfil the prophetic function – if established for some – is affirmed for all.

Thus, acuity is established for all prophets, even those who are not messengers, but rather, just prophets.[206] Indeed, for prophets, what is necessary is basic acuity. For messengers, what is necessary is complete acuity.[207]

وَإِذَا ثَبَتَ لَهُمْ هَذِهِ الصِّفَاتُ الْأَرْبَعَةُ اسْتَحَالَ عَلَيْهِمْ أَضْدَادُهَا، وَمَعْنَى اسْتِحَالَتِهَا: عَدَمُ قَبُولِهَا الثُّبُوتَ بِالدَّلِيْلِ الشَّرْعِيِّ.

If these four attributes are established for them, their contraries are impossible for them.[208] The meaning of their impossibility is that they do not admit of being established, [and[209]] by legislative evidence.[210]

WHAT IS POSSIBLE

(وَالْجَائِزُ فِي حَقِّهِمْ عَلَيْهِمْ الصَّلَاةُ وَالسَّلَامُ الْأَعْرَاضُ الْبَشَرِيَّةُ الَّتِي لَا تُؤَدِّي إِلَى نَقْصٍ فِي مَرَاتِبِهِمْ الْعَلِيَّةِ كَالْمَرَضِ) غَيْرِ الْمُنَفِّرِ (وَنَحْوِهِ) كَالْجُوعُ وَالْعَطَشُ وَالنَّوْمُ وَالْأَكْلُ وَالشُّرْبُ وَالْمَشْيُ وَالرُّكُوبُ وَالْبَيْعُ وَالشِّرَاءُ وَالْجِمَاعُ لِلنِّسَاءِ عَلَى وَجْهِ الْحِلِّ بِالنِّكَاحِ أَوْ بِالْمِلْكِ، بِخِلَافِ الْجُنُونِ قَلِيلِهِ وَكَثِيرِهِ وَالْجُذَامِ وَالْبَرَصِ وَالْعَمَى وَغَيْرِ ذَلِكَ مِنْ الْأُمُورِ الْمُنَفِّرَةِ، وَبِخِلَافِ الْأُمُورِ الْمُخِلَّةِ بِالْمُرُوءَةِ كَالْأَكْلِ عَلَى الطُّرُقِ وَالْحِرَفِ الدَّنِيئَةِ وَنَحْوِ ذَلِكَ مِمَّا لَا يَلِيْقُ بِهِمْ، فَلَا يَجُوزُ ذَلِكَ.

‹What is possible (*jāʾiz*) for the Messengers (blessings and peace be upon them) are human conditions that do not detract from their lofty stations, such as illness› provided it is not repulsive (*munaffir*) ‹and

---

206 *Al-Jawharah*, 59; *Tuḥfat*, 411; *Fatḥ al-majīd*, 81.
207 *Al-Jawharah*, 59; *Tuḥfat*, 411; *Fatḥ al-majīd*, 81.
208 *Al-Jawharah*, 60; *Tuḥfat*, 415; *Fatḥ al-majīd*, 76, 79–81.
209 Added from *Tuḥfat al-murīd*. *Al-Jawharah*, 60; *Tuḥfat*, 416.
210 *Al-Jawharah*, 60; *Tuḥfat*, 416; Cf. *Fatḥ al-majīd*, 81; *Al-Thimār al-yāniʿ*, 15.

the like.› Among these conditions are hunger, thirst, sleep, eating,[211] drinking, walking, riding, selling, buying, engaging in intercourse with women in a lawful manner – either through marriage or ownership (*milk al-yamīn*).[212] This is in contrast to repulsive conditions, such as insanity (*junūn*), whether mild or severe; leprosy (*judhām*) and vitiligo (*baraṣ*); blindness (*'amā'*); and other similarly repulsive states.[213] It also excludes conditions incompatible with decorum (*muru'ah*), such as eating openly on roads, engaging in lowly trades, and similar actions unbecoming of their elevated status – all of these are impossible for them.[214]

وَلَمْ يَصِحَّ أَنَّ شُعَيْبًا كَانَ ضَرِيرًا، وَمَا كَانَ بِأَيُّوبَ مِنَ الْبَلَاءِ فَكَانَ بَيْنَ الْجِلْدِ وَالْعَظْمِ فَلَمْ يَكُنْ مُنَفِّرًا، وَمَا كَانَ بِيَعْقُوبَ فَهُوَ حِجَابٌ عَلَى الْعَيْنِ مِنْ تَوَاصُلِ الدُّمُوعِ.

It is not authentically established that Shu'ayb (peace be upon him) was blind. The affliction Ayyūb experienced was limited to the area between his skin and bone and thus was not repulsive. As for Ya'qūb, his condition was merely a film (*ḥijāb*) over the eyes due to incessant weeping.[215]

أَمَّا خُرُوجُ الْمَنِيِّ مِنِ امْتِلَاءِ الْأَوْعِيَةِ فَجَائِزٌ عَلَيْهِمْ، بِخِلَافِ الْإِحْتِلَامِ فَلَا يَجُوزُ عَلَيْهِمْ؛ لِأَنَّهُ مِنْ تَلَاعُبِ الشَّيْطَانِ، لِأَنَّهُ لَا سَبِيلَ لَهُ عَلَيْهِمْ.

As for seminal emission occurring due to the fullness of the seminal vessels, that is possible for them. However, seminal emission resulting from nocturnal emissions (*iḥtilām*) is impossible for them, as this stems from the manipulations of Shayṭān, and he has no authority (*sabīl*) over them.[216]

---

211 *Al-Jawharah*, 61; *Tuḥfat*, 418; *Fatḥ al-majīd*, 86.
212 *Al-Jawharah*, 61; *Tuḥfat*, 420; *Fatḥ al-majīd*, 86.
213 *Al-Jawharah*, 61; *Tuḥfat*, 423; *Fatḥ al-majīd*, 87.
214 *Fatḥ al-majīd*, 86–87.
215 Cf. *Al-Jawharah*, 61; *Tuḥfat*, 423; *Nūr al-ẓalām*, 163.
216 *Fatḥ al-majīd*, 87; Cf. *Al-Jawharah*, 61; *Tuḥfat*, 422.

أَمَّا السَّهْوُ فَمُمْتَنِعٌ عَلَيْهِمْ فِي الْأَخْبَارِ الْبَلَاغِيَّةِ، أَيْ: الَّتِي طُلِبَ مِنْهُمْ تَبْلِيغُهَا عَنِ اللَّهِ تَعَالَى، كَقَوْلِهِمْ: «الْجَنَّةُ أُعِدَّتْ لِلْمُتَّقِينَ» وَ «عَذَابُ الْقَبْرِ وَاجِبٌ» وَهَكَذَا، وَفِي غَيْرِ الْبَلَاغِيَّةِ: كَـ «قَامَ زَيْدٌ وَقَعَدَ بَكْرٌ» وَهَكَذَا، وَجَائِزٌ عَلَيْهِمْ فِي الْأَفْعَالِ الْبَلَاغِيَّةِ لِلتَّشْرِيعِ كَالسَّهْوُ فِي الصَّلَاةِ. وَسَهْوُهُمْ إِنَّمَا هُوَ لِاشْتِغَالِهِمْ بِرَبِّهِمْ.

As for absentmindedness (*sahw*), it is impossible for the Messengers with respect to messages to be conveyed – that is, messages whose transmission Allah (Exalted is He) has commanded of them, such as their statements: "Paradise is prepared for the righteous," and "The punishment of the grave is real," and similar pronouncements – as well as with respect to non-conveyed statements, such as "Zayd stood," or "Bakr sat," and the like. However, absentmindedness is possible for them concerning actions intended to be conveyed (*af'āl balāghiyyah*), such as absentmindedness during prayer. Their absentmindedness in such instances occurs only due to their being occupied with their Lord.[217]

وَأَمَّا النِّسْيَانُ فَمُمْتَنِعٌ عَلَيْهِمْ فِي الْبَلَاغِيَّاتِّ قَبْلَ تَبْلِيغِهَا، قَوْلِيَّةً كَانَتْ أَوْ فِعْلِيَّةً، فَالْقَوْلِيَّةُ كَقَوْلِهِمْ: «الْجَنَّةُ أُعِدَّتْ لِلْمُتَّقِينَ»، وَالْفِعْلِيَةُ: كَصَلَاةِ الضُّحَى؛ إِذْ أَمَرَهُمُ اللَّهُ بِفِعْلِهَا لِيَقْتَدِيَ بِهِمْ فِيهَا، فَلَا يَجُوزُ نِسْيَانُ كُلٍّ مِنْهُمَا قَبْلَ تَبْلِيغِ الْأُولَى بِالْقَوْلِ وَالثَّانِيَةِ بِالْفِعْلِ، أَمَّا بَعْدُ التَّبْلِيغِ فَيَجُوزُ عَلَيْهِمْ نِسْيَانُ مَا ذُكِرَ مِنَ اللَّهِ تَعَالَى لَا مِنَ الشَّيْطَانِ؛ لِأَنَّهُ لَا سَبِيلَ لَهُ عَلَيْهِمْ، وَقَدْ قَالَ ﷺ: «إِنِّي لَا أَنْسَى، وَلَكِنْ أُنَسَّى».

Forgetfulness (*nisyān*) is impossible for the Messengers concerning messages intended to be conveyed (*balāghiyyāt*) prior to their conveyance, whether verbal or performative. Examples of verbal messages include statements such as, "Paradise is prepared for the righteous," while performative messages include prescribed actions,

---

217 *Al-Jawharah*, 61; *Tuḥfat*, 424; *Fatḥ al-majīd*, 87.

such as the Ḍuḥā prayer, which Allah commanded them to perform so that people could emulate them. Thus, it is impossible for them to forget either category – verbal messages before conveying them verbally or prescribed actions before demonstrating them practically. However, after conveyance, forgetfulness regarding these matters is possible for them, though such forgetfulness originates from Allah and not from Shayṭān, as Shayṭān has no authority over them.[218] Indeed, the Prophet (may Allah bless him and give him peace) said, "I do not forget, but I am made to forget."[219]

وَبِالْجُمْلَةِ فَيَجُوزُ عَلَى ظَوَاهِرِهِمْ مَا يَجُوزُ عَلَى الْبَشَرِ مِمَّا لَا يُؤَدِّي إِلَى نَقْصٍ. وَأَمَّا بَوَاطِنُهُمْ فَهِيَ مُنَزَّهَةٌ عَنْ ذَلِكَ لِتَعَلُّقِهَا بِاللَّهِ تَعَالَى.

In summary, whatever is possible for customary humans, provided it does not imply deficiency (*naqṣ*), is also possible for the Messengers in terms of their outward states (*ẓawāhir*).[220]

As for their inward states (*bawāṭin*), these are entirely free (*munazzahah*) from such possibilities, due to their connection with Allah (Exalted is He).[221]

(وَالدَّلِيلُ عَلَى ذَلِكَ) أَيْ: جَوَازِ وُقُوعِ الْأَعْرَاضِ، أَيْ: الصِّفَاتِ الْحَادِثَةِ الْبَشَرِيَّةِ (مَشَاهِدُهَا بِهِمْ عَلَيْهِمُ الصَّلَاةُ وَالسَّلَامُ) لِمَنْ عَاصَرَهُمْ وَبُلُوغُ ذَلِكَ بِالتَّوَاتُرِ لِغَيْرِهِ، فَوُقُوعُهَا بِهِمْ أَقْوَى دَلِيلٍ عَلَى الْجَوَازِ؛ لِأَنَّ الْوُقُوعَ فَرْعٌ عَنِ الْجَوَازِ، وَأَيْضًا هُمْ يَتَرَقَّوْنَ دَائِمًا فِي الْمَرَاتِبِ الْعَلِيَّةِ، وَوُقُوعُ الْأَمْرَاضِ بِهِمْ مَثَلًا سَبَبٌ فِي زِيَادَةِ مَرَاتِبِهِمُ الْعَلِيَّةِ، وَلِأَجْلِ أَنْ يَتَسَلَّى بِهِمْ غَيْرُهُمْ وَيَعْرِفَ الْعَاقِلُ أَنَّ الدُّنْيَا لَيْسَتْ دَارَ جَزَاءٍ لِأَحْبَابِهِ تَعَالَى؛ إِذْ لَوْ كَانَتْ دَارَ جَزَاءٍ لَهُمْ لَمْ يُصِبْهُمْ شَيْءٌ مِنْ كُدُورَاتِهَا، فَهُوَ زِيَادَةٌ فِي عُلُوِّ مَرَاتِبِهِمْ عَلَيْهِمُ الصَّلَاةُ وَالسَّلَامُ.

---

218   *Al-Jawharah*, 61; *Tuḥfat*, 425.
219   This is one of the four hadiths in *Al-Muwaṭṭa'* mentioned without a chain.
220   Lit. externals.
221   *Al-Jawharah*, 61; *Tuḥfat*, 425.

‹The proof (*dalīl*) for this› meaning the possibility of human conditions, meaning originated human attributes ‹**is their observable occurrence in the case of the Messengers (peace and blessings be upon them)**› by those who lived contemporaneously with them and the transmission of those occurrences to subsequent generations through recurrent mass transmission (*tawātur*)‹.› Indeed, the very occurrence of these conditions is itself the strongest proof for their possibility, since occurrence logically follows possibility. Furthermore, the Messengers continuously ascend in their elevated ranks (*marātib ʿaliyyah*), and the occurrence of illnesses or similar conditions serves as a means to further elevate these ranks. Moreover, such occurrences serve as consolation for others, enabling those endowed with reason to understand that this world is not an abode of reward for His beloveds (Exalted is He). If it were a place of reward for them, they would not have experienced any of its hardships. Thus, these conditions only result in further elevation of their lofty stations (may peace and blessings be upon them).[222]

RECAP OF MATTERS RELATED TO THE PROPHETS

فَهَـذِهِ تِسْـعُ عَقَائِدَ تَتَعَلَّقُ بِالرُّسُـلِ عَلَيْهِمُ الصَّلَاةُ وَالسَّلَامُ، وَتَقَدَّمُ إِحْدَى وَأَرْبَعُوْنَ تَتَعَلَّقُ بِالإِلَهِ سُبْحَانَهُ وَتَعَالَى، فَالْجُمْلَةُ خَمْسُوْنَ عَقِيْدَةً يَجِبُ عَلَى كُلِّ مُكَلَّفٍ مَعْرِفَتُهَا بِأَدِلَّتِهَا عَلَى مَا مَرَّ.

These are nine points of doctrine (*ʿaqāʾid*) concerning the Messengers (peace and blessings be upon them). Previously, forty-one points relating to Allah (Glory be to Him and Exalted is He) were presented. Thus, there are a total of fifty doctrinal points that every legally responsible person must know along with their proofs, as mentioned earlier.[223]

---

222 *Fatḥ al-majīd*, 87–88.
223 *Fatḥ al-majīd*, 89.

CONCLUSION

خَاتِمَةٌ. نَسْأَلُ اللَّهَ تَعَالَى حُسْنَهَا.

Conclusion. We ask Allah (Exalted is He) to grant us the best thereof.

HIS LINEAGE

(يَجِبُ عَلَى الشَّخْصِ) أَيْ: الذَّكَرِ وَالْأُنْثَى (أَنْ يَعْرِفَ نَسَبَهُ ﷺ مِنْ جِهَةِ أَبِيهِ، وَمِنْ جِهَةِ أُمِّهِ) إِلَى عَدْنَانَ فَقَطْ، أَمَّا مَا بَعْدَهُ فَلَا يَجِبُ مَعْرِفَتُهُ بِلَا خِلَافٍ، بَلْ كَرِهَهُ مَالِكٌ.

‹Individuals› meaning male and female ‹**are required to know the lineage of the Prophet (may Allah bless him and give him peace) from his father's side and his mother's side**›, but only up to ʿAdnān‹.› Beyond this point, knowledge of his lineage is not required by consensus[224]; [Imām] Mālik considered it disliked.

(فَأَمَّا نَسَبُهُ ﷺ مِنْ جِهَةِ أَبِيهِ فَهُوَ سَيِّدُنَا مُحَمَّدُ بْنُ عَبْدِ اللَّهِ) فَمِنْ كَلَامِهِ رَضِيَ اللَّهُ عَنْهُ مِنَ الطَّوِيْلِ:

لَقَـدْ حَكَـمَ الْبَـادُونَ فِي كُلِّ بَلْدَةٍ بِأَنَّ لَنَا فَـضْلًا عَلَى سَـادَةِ الْأَرْضِ

وَأَنَّ أَبِي ذُو الْمَجْدِ وَالسُّؤْدُدِ الَّذِي يَسَارُ بِهِ مَا بَيْنَ نَشْـرٍ إِلَى خَفْضِ

---

224 Al-Faḍālī in *Kifāyat al-ʿawām* mentions the ruling and attributes it to al-Ajhūrī. See: al-Bājūrī, *Taḥqīq al-maqām*, 187–188. *Nūr al-ẓalām* and *Al-Thimār al-yāniʿ* both mention the ruling and details, but without attribution. See: *Nūr al-ẓalām*, 111; *Al-Thimār al-yāniʿ*, 27.

(بْنُ عَبْدِ الْمُطَّلِبِ) اِسْمُهُ عَامِرٌ أَوْ شَيْبَةُ الْحَمْدِ (بْنِ هَاشِمٍ) اِسْمُهُ عَمْرُو أَوْ عُمَرُ (بْنِ عَبْدِ مَنَافٍ) اِسْـمُهُ الْمُغِيرَةُ (بْنِ قُصَيٍّ)، بِضَمٍّ فَفَتْحٍ، اِسْـمُهُ زَيْدٌ أَوْ يَزِيدُ، (بْنِ كِلَابٍ) اِسْمُهُ حَكِيمٌ بِفَتْحٍ فَكَسْرٍ، أَوِ الْمُغِيرَةِ أَوِ الْمُهَذَّبُ (بْنِ مُرَّةَ) بِضَمِّ الْمِيمِ وَفَتْحِ الرَّاءِ الْمُشَـدَّدَةِ (بْنِ كَعْبٍ) بِفَتْحٍ وَسُكُونٍ (بْنِ لُؤَيٍّ) بِالْهَمْـزِ وَتَرْكِهِ لَكِنِ الْأَكْثَرَ الْأَوَّلَ (بْنِ غَالِبٍ) بِالْغَيْنِ الْمُعْجَمَةِ وَكَسْـرِ اللَّامِ (بْنِ فِهْرٍ) بِكَسْـرٍ فَسُـكُونٍ (بْنِ مَالِكٍ) وَكُنْيَتُهُ أَبُو حَارِثٍ (بْنُ النَّضْرِ) اِسْـمُهُ قَيْسٌ (بْنِ كِنَانَةَ) كَانَ شَيْخًا حَسَنًا عَظِيمَ الْقَدْرِ تَقْصِدُ الْعَرَبُ إِلَيْهِ لِعِلْمِهِ وَفَضْلِهِ (بْنِ خُزَيْمَةَ) بِالتَّصْغِيرِ (بْنِ مُدْرِكَةَ) بِضَمٍّ فَسُكُونٍ فَكَسْرٍ وَاِسْمُهُ عُمَرُ عَلَى الصَّحِيحِ، وَكَانَ فِيهِ نُورُ النَّبِيِّ ﷺ ظَاهِرًا (بْنِ إِلْيَاسَ) وَاِسْمُهُ حُسَيْنٌ، وَكُنْيَتُهُ أَبُو عَمْرٍو، وَكَانَ يَسْمَعُ فِي صُلْبِهِ تَلْبِيَةَ النَّبِيِّ الْمَعْرُوفَةَ فِي الْحَجِّ (بْنِ مُضَرَ) بِضَمٍّ فَفَتْحٍ، اِسْمُهُ عَمْرٌو، وَكُنْيَتُهُ أَبُو إِلْيَاسَ (بْنِ نِزَارٍ) وَاِسْمُهُ خَلْدَانُ (بْنِ مَعْدٍ) وَلَمَّا سَـلَّطَ اللَّهُ بُخْتَنَصَّرَ عَلَى الْعَرَبِ أَمَرَ اللَّهُ أُرْمِيَاءَ أَنْ يَحْمِلَهُ عَلَى الْبُرَاقِ كَيْلَا تُصِيبُهُ النَّقْمَةُ، فَفَعَلَ ذَلِكَ أُرْمِيَاءُ وَاحْتَمَلَهُ مَعَهُ إِلَى أَرْضِ الشَّامِ فَنَشَأَ فِي بَنِي إِسْرَائِيلَ، ثُمَّ عَادَ بَعْدَ أَنْ سَكَنَتِ الْفِتْنَةُ بِمَوْتِ بُخْتَنَصَّرَ (بْنِ عَدْنَانَ) وَكَانَ فِي زَمَنِ مُوسَى عَلَيْهِ السَّلَامُ عَلَى الصَّحِيحِ.

‹The lineage of the Prophet (may Allah bless him and give him peace) from his father's side, is as follows:›

‹Our Master Muḥammad son of› ‹'Abd Allāh› who said (may Allah be pleased with him) [*al-ṭawīl metre*]:

The Bedouins from every land have judged that we surpass
    the lords of the earth

And that my father possesses glory and honour, by which he
    ascends from the lowlands to the heights.[225]

---

225 The earliest mention I could find is Alī Ibn Ibrāhīm al-Ḥalabī (d. 1044 AH), *Al-Sīrat al-Ḥalabiyyah* (Beirut: Dār al-Kutub al-'Ilmiyyah, 1427), 1:59.

‹son of ʿAbd al-Muṭṭalib› his name was ʿĀmir or Shaybat al-Ḥamd‹,›

‹son of Hāshim› his name was ʿAmr or ʿUmar‹,›

‹son of ʿAbd Manāf› his name was al-Mughīrah‹,›

‹son of Quṣayy› – with a *dammah* then a *fatḥah* – his name was Zayd or Yazīd‹,›

‹son of Kilāb› his name Ḥakīm – with a *fatḥah* then a *kasrah* – or al-Mughīrah or al-Muhadhdhab‹,›

‹son of Murrah› with a *mīm* and a doubled *rāʾ*‹,›

‹son of Kaʿb› with a *fatḥah* and *sukūn*‹,›

‹son of Luʾayy› with or without a *hamzah*, though the former is more frequent‹,›

‹son of Ghālib› with a *ghayn* having a single dot and the *lām* having a kasrah‹,›

‹son of Fihr› with a *kasrah* then a *sukūn*‹,›

‹son of Mālik› his *kunyah* is Abū Ḥārith‹,

‹son of al-Naḍr› his name was Qays‹,›

‹son of Kinānah› who was an esteemed elder sought by Arabs for his knowledge and virtue‹,›

‹son of Khuzaymah› with the diminutive form‹,›

‹son of Mudrikah› – with a *sukūn* then a *kasrah* – his name was ʿUmar according to the soundest opinion, and the light of the Prophet – may Allah bless him and give him peace – was visibly manifest in him‹,›

‹son of Ilyās› whose name was Ḥusayn and whose *kunyah* is Abū ʿAmr, and from whose loins the *talbiyah*[226] uttered by the Prophet (may Allah bless him and give him peace) during Hajj was audible‹,›

‹son of Muḍar› with a *dammah* then a *fatḥah*; his name was ʿAmr, and his *kunyah* is Abū Ilyās‹,›

‹son of Nizār› his name was Khaldān‹,›

‹son of Maʿd› when Allah gave Bukhtanaṣṣar victory over the Arabs,

---

226 The wording of the *talbiyah* is: "*Labbayka Llāhumma labbayk, labbayka lā sharīka laka labbayk, inna al-ḥamda wa-l-niʿmata laka wa-l-mulk, lā sharīka lak*" ("Here I am, O Allah, here I am. Here I am, You have no partner, here I am. Indeed, praise and blessing are Yours, and dominion. You have no partner").

He commanded Armiyā' to carry Ma'd upon Burāq, protecting him from harm. Armiyā' took him to the Levant, where he grew up among the Children of Isrā'īl, returning after the tribulations ceased upon Bukhtanaṣṣar's death‹.›

‹**son of 'Adnān**› who lived during the time of Mūsā, peace be upon him, according to the sound opinion‹.›

وَأَجْمَعَ الْعُلَمَاءُ عَلَى أَنَّ رَسُوْلَ اللَّهِ ﷺ إِنَّمَا انْتَسَبَ إِلَى عَدْنَانَ (وَلَيْسَ فِيْمَا بَعْدَهُ)، أَيْ: عَدْنَانَ (إِلَى آدَمَ عَلَيْهِ الصَّلَاةُ وَالسَّلَامُ طَرِيْقٌ صَحِيْحٌ فِيْمَا يُنْقَلُ) لِمَا وَقَعَ فِيْهِ مِنَ الْأَقْوَالِ الْمُخْتَلِفَةِ الْمُتَبَاعِدَةِ.

The scholars agree unanimously that the Messenger of Allah (may Allah bless him and give him peace) traces his lineage [authentically only] to 'Adnān. ‹**Beyond him**› meaning 'Adnān ‹**extending back to Ādam (peace and blessings be upon him), no authentic lineage has been transmitted**›, due to vastly divergent opinions‹.[227]›

(وَأَمَّا نَسَبُهُ ﷺ مِنْ جِهَةِ أُمِّهِ فَهُوَ سَيِّدُنَا مُحَمَّدُ بْنُ آمِنَةَ بِنْتِ وَهْبِ بْنِ عَبْدِ مَنَافِ ابْنِ زُهْرَةَ) بِضَمِّ الزَّايِ وَسُكُوْنِ الْهَاءِ، وَهُوَ اسْمُ رَجُلٍ عَلَى الصَّوَابِ (بْنِ كِلَابٍ) وَعَبْدُ مَنَافٍ الَّذِي فِي نَسَبِهِ ﷺ مِنْ جِهَةِ أُمِّهِ غَيْرُ عَبْدِ مَنَافٍ جَدِّهِ ﷺ مِنْ جِهَةِ أَبِيهِ، وَكِلَابٌ هَذَا أَحَدُ أَجْدَادِهِ ﷺ (فَتَجْتَمِعُ) أَيْ: آمِنَةُ (مَعَهُ فِي جَدِّهِ كِلَابٌ)

‹The lineage of the Prophet (may Allah bless him and give him peace) from his mother's side is as follows:›
‹**Our Master Muḥammad (may Allah bless him and give him peace),**›
‹**son of Āminah,**›
‹**daughter of Wahb,**›
‹**son of 'Abd Manāf,**›

227　*Nūr al-ẓalām* and *Al-Thimār al-yāni'* both mention being traced to 'Adnān. *Al-Thimār al-yāni'* mentioned the lack of an authentic transmitted path. See: *Nūr al-ẓalām*, 111; *Al-Thimār al-yāni'*, 27.

‹son of Zuhrah› – with a *ḍammah* on the *zāy* and a *sukūn* on the *hā'* – which is correctly considered a man's name‹,›
‹son of Kilāb.›

The ʿAbd Manāf found in his maternal lineage is distinct from the paternal ʿAbd Manāf who is among his forefathers.

Kilāb is one of his grandfathers.

‹She› meaning Āminah **‹meets him [(may Allah bless him and give him peace)] at his grandfather Kilāb.›**[228]

وَنَسَبُهُ ﷺ مُطَهَّرٌ مِنْ سِفَاحِ الْجَاهِلِيَّةِ، وَلَمْ يَلِدْهُ إِلَّا نِكَاحٌ كنِكَاحِ الْإِسْلَامِ مِنْ لَدُنْ آدَمَ إِلَى أَنْ وَلَدَهُ ﷺ أَبُوهُ وَأُمُّهُ، وَاسْتَدَلَّ بَعْضُهُمْ بِقَوْلِهِ ﷺ: «لَمْ أَزَلْ أَنْقُلُ مِنْ أَصْلَابِ الطَّاهِرِينَ إِلَى أَرْحَامِ الطَّاهِرَاتِ»، أَنَّ جَمِيعَ آبَائِهِ ﷺ وَجَمِيعَ أُمَّهَاتِهِ إِلَى آدَمَ وَحَوَّاءَ لَيْسَ فِيهِمْ كَافِرٌ؛ لِأَنَّهُ لَا يُوصَفُ بِالطَّهَارَةِ إِلَّا الْمُؤْمِنُ.

His lineage (may Allah bless him and give him peace) is purified from the fornication of the pre-Islamic era. From Ādam's time until the birth of the Prophet by his parents, he descended only through lawful unions akin to those recognised in Islamic law.[229]

Some scholars inferred from the Prophet's own words (may Allah bless him and give him peace), "I did not cease transferring from the loins of purified men to the wombs of purified women,"[230] that all his forefathers and foremothers, from Ādam and Ḥawwā' downwards, were believers, since purity is a quality exclusively attributed to believers.

---

228 *Nūr al-ẓalām* and *Al-Thimār al-yāniʿ* both mention this. See: *Nūr al-ẓalām*, 111; *Al-Thimār al-yāniʿ*, 27.

229 In other words: All of his ancestors are the product of a marriage sanctioned by Islamic Law.

230 The earliest mention I found is in Imām al-Rāzī's *Mafātīḥ al-ghayb* (Beirut: Dār Iḥyā' al-Turāth al-ʿArabī, 1420), 24:537, 13:33–34, for Q26:221–223 and 6:74–75.

HIS BASIN

(وَمِمَّـا يَجِـبُ أَيْضًـا أَنْ يَعْلَمَ أَنَّ لَـهُ) ﷺ (حَوْضًا) أَعْطَاهُ اللَّـهُ تَعَالَى إِيَّاهُ فِي الْآخِرَةِ، لَكِـنْ لَا يَكْفُـرُ مَـنْ أَنْكَرَهُ وَإِنَّمَا يَفْسُقُ، وَأَوْحَى اللَّهُ تَعَالَى إِلَى عِيْسَى عَلَيْهِ السَّلَامُ أَنَّ لِمُحَمَّدٍ حَوْضًا أَبْعَدَ مِنْ مَكَّةَ إِلَى مَطْلَعِ الشَّمْسِ، فِيْهِ آنِيَةٌ مِثْلَ عَدَدِ نُجُوْمِ السَّمَاءِ، وَلَهُ لَوْنُ كُلِّ شَـرَابِ الْجَنَّـةِ وَطَعْمُ كُلِّ ثِمَارِهَـا أهـ. أَيْ: بَعْضُهُ لَوْنُـهُ أَحْمَرُ وَبَعْضُهُ لَوْنُهُ أَبْيَـضُ وَهَكَذَا، وَلَهُ طَعْمُ الْخَوْخِ وَالْمَوْزِ وَالْمِشْمِشِ وَغَيْرِهَا، فَمَنْ يَشْرَبُ مِنْهُ يَجِدُ طَعْمَ ثِمَارِ الْجَنَّةِ.

‹**It is also required to know that he**› (may Allah bless him and give him peace) ‹**has a Basin (*ḥawḍ*)**› that Allah (Exalted is He) grants him in the Hereafter. Denying it does not render one a disbeliever (*kāfir*), but rather morally corrupt (*fāsiq*)‹.›[231]

Allah (Exalted is He) revealed to ʿĪsā (peace be upon him) that Muḥammad has a Basin whose expanse is greater than the distance from Mecca to the rising-place of the sun. Within it are drinking vessels as numerous as the stars of the sky. It exhibits the colours of all the beverages of Paradise and has the flavour of all its fruits. [End of quote.][232] That is, some of it is red, some white, and other such colours, tasting of peaches, bananas, apricots, and similar fruits. Whoever drinks from it finds the flavours of Paradise's fruits.[233]

وَاخْتُلِـفَ فِـي مَحَلِّـهِ، فَعِنْـدَ الْجُمْهُـوْرِ أَنَّهُ قَبْـلَ الصِّـرَاطِ؛ لِأَنَّ النَّاسَ يَخْرُجُونَ مِـنْ قُبُوْرِهِمْ عِطَاشًـا فَيَرِدُونَ الْحَوْضَ لِلشُّـرْبِ، وَعِنْدَ بَعْضِهِمْ أَنَّهُ بَعْدَهُ؛ لِأَنَّهُ يَنْصُبُ فِيهِ الْمَاءُ مِنْ الْكَوْثَرِ وَهُوَ النَّهْرُ الَّذِي فِي دَاخِلِ الْجَنَّةِ،

---

231 From "that Allah": *Al-Jawharah*, 111; *Tuḥfat*, 699.

232 The author does not indicate the beginning of this quotation nor its source. The passage itself is from a report concerning something revealed to ʿĪsā (peace be upon him). See *Al-Jawharah*, 111; *Tuḥfat*, 704.

233 *Fatḥ al-majīd*, 100–101; Cf. *Al-Jawharah*, 111; *Tuḥfat*, 704.

فَيَكُوْنُ الْحَوْضُ بَعْدَ الصِّرَاطِ بِجَانِبِ الْجَنَّةِ وَلَوْ كَانَ قَبْلَهُ لَحَالَتِ النَّارُ بَيْنَهُ

وَبَيْـنَ الْمَـاءِ الَّذِي يَنْصُبُ فِيْهِ مِنْ الْكَوْثَرِ، وَهُمْ يُحْبَسُـونَ هُنَاكَ فِي مَوْقِفِ

الْقِصَاصِ لِأَجْلِ الْمَظَالِمِ الَّتِي بَيْنَهُمْ حَتَّى يَتَحَلَّلُوْا مِنْهَا. وَصَحَّحَ الْقُرْطُبِيُّ

أَنَّ لَهُ ﷺ حَوْضَيْنِ: حَوْضًا قَبْلَ الصِّرَاطِ وَحَوْضًا بَعْدَهُ، وَاخْتَارَهُ السَّنُوسِيُّ

فِي «شَرْحِ الكُبْرَى»، ثُمَّ الَّذِي يَجِبُ اعْتِقَادُهُ أَنَّ لَهُ ﷺ حَوْضًا.

Scholars differ about its location. The majority hold that it is situated before the Bridge (*ṣirāṭ*), since people exit their graves thirsty,
[so they] are then brought to the Basin to drink.

Others assert that it is situated after the Bridge, as water pours
into it from Kawthar – the river within Paradise – placing the Basin
at the side of Paradise after crossing the Bridge. If it were positioned
before, the Fire would obstruct the flow of Kawthar's water into it.
Additionally, at that point people are detained at the Station (*mawqif*)
for reciprocal retribution regarding interpersonal grievances, and
they remain there until all such grievances are resolved.

Al-Qurṭubī authenticated the view that the Prophet (may Allah
bless him and give him peace) has two Basins – one Basin before
the Bridge and one Basin after it.[234] Al-Sanūsī preferred this position
in *Sharḥ al-kubrā*.[235]

Ultimately, the obligatory point of belief is simply to affirm that
the Prophet (may Allah bless him and give him peace) has a Basin
(*ḥawḍ*).[236]

---

234 *Al-Jawharah*, 111; *Tuḥfat*, 705; *Fatḥ al-majīd*, 100.

235 Muḥammad bin Yūsuf bin ʿUmar al-Sanūsī, *Sharḥ al-ʿAqīdat al-kubrā* (Damascus: Dār al-Taqwā, 1441 AH/2019 CE), 642.

236 *Al-Jawharah*, 111; *Tuḥfat*, 705.

HIS INTERCESSION

(و) يَجِبُ أَنْ يَعْلَمَ (أَنَّهُ يَشْفَعُ فِي فَصْلِ الْقَضَاءِ) أَيْ: فِي الْقَضَاءِ الْفَاصِلِ بَيْنَ النَّاسِ.

‹**And**› it is obligatory to know ‹**that he (may Allah bless him and give him peace) will intercede in rendering judgement**› meaning in the decisive judgement among people.[237]

رُوِيَ أَنَّهُ إِذَا جَمَعَ اللَّهُ النَّاسَ فِي صَعِيدٍ وَاحِدٍ يَوْمَ الْقِيَامَةِ أَقْبَلَتِ النَّارُ يَرْكَبُ بَعْضُهَا بَعْضًا، وَخَزَنَتُهَا يَكُفُّونَهَا عَنِ النَّاسِ وَهِيَ تَقُولُ: وَعِزَّةِ رَبِّي لَيُخَلِّيَنَّ بَيْنِي وَبَيْنَ أَزْوَاجِي، فَيَقُولُونَ لَهَا: وَمَنْ أَزْوَاجِكِ؟ فَتَقُولُ: كُلُّ مُتَكَبِّرٍ جَبَّارٍ. فَلَا يَزَالُ النَّاسُ يَمُوجُ بَعْضُهُمْ فِي بَعْضٍ أَلْفَ عَامٍ، وَاللَّهُ تَعَالَى لَا يُكَلِّمُهُمْ كَلِمَةً وَاحِدَةً، فَيَشْتَدُّ الْهَوْلُ عَلَى أَهْلِ الْمَوْقِفِ حَتَّى يَتَمَنَّوُا الِانْصِرَافَ مِنْ هَذَا الْمَوْقِفِ، وَلَوْ إِلَى جَهَنَّمَ. فَيَقُولُ بَعْضُهُمْ لِبَعْضٍ: اذْهَبُوا إِلَى أَبِيكُمْ آدَمَ، فَيَأْتُونَ آدَمَ، فَيَقُولُونَ: يَا أَبَا الْبَشَرِ، الْأَمْرُ عَلَيْنَا شَدِيدٌ، وَأَنْتَ الَّذِي خَلَقَكَ اللَّهُ بِيَدِهِ وَأَسْجَدَ لَكَ مَلَائِكَتَهُ وَنَفَخَ فِيكَ مِنْ رُوحِهِ، اشْفَعْ لَنَا فِي فَصْلِ الْقَضَاءِ، اشْفَعْ لَنَا إِلَى رَبِّكَ لِيَقْضِيَ بَيْنَنَا. فَيَقُولُ: لَسْتُ هُنَاكَ إِنِّي قَدْ أُخْرِجْتُ مِنَ الْجَنَّةِ بِخَطِيئَةٍ، وَأَنَّهُ لَيْسَ يُهِمُّنِي الْيَوْمَ إِلَّا نَفْسِي، وَلَكِنْ عَلَيْكُمْ بِنُوحٍ، فَإِنَّهُ أَوَّلُ الْمُرْسَلِينَ. فَيَأْتُونَ نُوحًا وَيَقُولُونَ لَهُ: اشْفَعْ لَنَا إِلَى رَبِّكَ لِيَقْضِيَ بَيْنَنَا. فَيَقُولُ: لَسْتُ هُنَاكَ إِنِّي دَعَوْتُ دَعْوَةً أَغْرَقْتُ أَهْلَ الْأَرْضِ، وَأَنَّهُ لَيْسَ يُهِمُّنِي الْيَوْمَ إِلَّا نَفْسِي، وَلَكِنِ ائْتُوا إِبْرَاهِيمَ الَّذِي اتَّخَذَهُ اللَّهُ خَلِيلًا. فَيَأْتُونَ إِبْرَاهِيمَ فَيَقُولُونَ: اشْفَعْ لَنَا إِلَى رَبِّكَ لِيَقْضِيَ بَيْنَنَا، فَيَقُولُ: لَسْتُ هُنَاكَ، إِنِّي قَدْ كَذَبْتُ فِي الْإِسْلَامِ

---

237   *Fatḥ al-majīd*, 97. Cf. *Al-Jawharah*, 113; *Tuḥfat*, 709.

ثَلَاثَ كِذْبَاتٍ، وَهِيَ قَوْلُهُ: ﴿إِنِّي سَقِيمٌ﴾ [الصَّافَّاتِ]، هَذَا وَقَوْلُهُ: ﴿بَلْ فَعَلَهُ كَبِيرُهُمْ﴾ [الْأَنْبِيَاءُ]، وَقَوْلُهُ لِامْرَأَتِهِ: «إِنَّهَا أُخْتِي»، وَلَيْسَ يُهِمُّنِي الْيَوْمَ إِلَّا نَفْسِي، وَلَكِنْ ائْتُوا مُوسَى الَّذِي كَلَّمَهُ اللَّهُ تَكْلِيمًا. فَيَأْتُونَ مُوسَى، فَيَقُولُ: لَسْتُ هُنَاكَ إِنِّي قَتَلْتُ نَفْسًا بِغَيْرِ حَقٍّ لَيْسَ يُهِمُّنِي الْيَوْمَ إِلَّا نَفْسِي، وَلَكِنْ ائْتُوا عِيسَى رُوحَ اللَّهِ وَكَلِمَتَهُ. فَيَأْتُونَهُ، فَيَقُولُ: إِنِّي اتَّخَذْتُ وَأُمِّي إِلَهَيْنِ مِنْ دُونِ اللَّهِ، وَإِنِّي لَا يُهِمُّنِي الْيَوْمَ إِلَّا نَفْسِي، وَلَكِنْ أَرَأَيْتُمْ إِنْ كَانَ لِأَحَدِكُمْ بِضَاعَةٌ فَجَعَلَهَا فِي كِيسٍ ثُمَّ خَتَمَ عَلَيْهَا أَكَانَ يَصِلُ إِلَى مَا فِي الْكِيسِ حَتَّى يَفُضَّ الْخَتْمَ! فَيَقُولُونَ: لَا، فَيَقُولُ: إِنَّ مُحَمَّدًا ﷺ خَاتَمُ الْأَنْبِيَاءِ، وَقَدْ وَافَى الْيَوْمَ، وَقَدْ غَفَرَ اللَّهُ لَهُ مَا تَقَدَّمَ مِنْ ذَنْبِهِ وَمَا تَأَخَّرَ، ائْتُوهُ. فَيَأْتُونَهُ، فَيَقُولُ: أَنَا لَهَا، أُمَّتِي أُمَّتِي، ثُمَّ يَخِرُّ سَاجِدًا تَحْتَ الْعَرْشِ كَسُجُودِ الصَّلَاةِ. فَيُقَالُ: يَا مُحَمَّدُ، ارْفَعْ رَأْسَكَ وَسَلْ تُعْطَ وَاشْفَعْ تُشَفَّعْ، فَيَرْفَعُ رَأْسَهُ، يَشْفَعُ فِي فَصْلِ الْقَضَاءِ.

It is transmitted that when Allah gathers people in a single field on the Day of Resurrection (*Yawm al-Qiyāmah*), the Fire will advance, piling parts of itself upon other parts. Its keepers (*khazanah*) will restrain it from harming the people, and the Fire will cry out, "By the might of my Lord, you will surely clear the way between me and my spouses!" They will ask it, "Who are your spouses?" and it will reply, "Every arrogant tyrant."[238]

People will continue surging among one another in this state for a thousand years, during which Allah (Exalted is He) will not speak a single word to them. The horror and distress will intensify for those assembled at this Station, to the extent that they wish to leave it – even if it means entering the Fire. Some will say to others, "Go to your father, Ādam."

---

238 Abū Yaʿlā al-Mawṣilī, *Musnad Abī Yaʿlā*, ed. Ḥusayn Salīm Asad (Damascus: Dār al-Maʾmūn li-l-Turāth, 1984), no. 1145.

They will approach Ādam and say, "O father of humanity, our situation is dire. Allah created you with His hand, commanded the angels to prostrate to you, and breathed His spirit into you. Intercede for us concerning the final judgement; intercede with your Lord so that He may judge among us." Ādam will reply, "That is not for me – I was expelled from Paradise due to my offence. Today I am concerned only for myself. Rather, go to Nūḥ, for he was the first messenger sent by Allah."

They will then approach Nūḥ and say to him, "Intercede with your Lord so He may judge among us." Nūḥ will reply, "That is not for me – I made a supplication by which the people of the earth were drowned. Today I am concerned only for myself. Instead, go to Ibrāhīm, whom Allah took as His intimate friend (*khalīl*)."

They will approach Ibrāhīm and say, "Intercede with your Lord so He may judge among us." Ibrāhīm will reply, "That is not for me – I spoke three lies in Islam" – namely his statement: (1) "I am ill,"[239] (2) "Rather, the largest of them did it,"[240] and (3) saying to his wife, "She is my sister." – And he will say, "Today I am concerned only for myself. Instead, go to Mūsā, the one whom Allah directly addressed."

They will approach Mūsā, who will respond, "That is not for me – I killed a soul without justification. Today I am concerned only for myself. Instead, go to ʿĪsā, the spirit (*rūḥ*) of Allah and His word (*kalimah*)."

They will approach ʿĪsā, who will say, "I was taken along with my mother as two deities besides Allah. Today I am concerned only for myself. But tell me, if one of you placed some merchandise in a bag and then sealed it, could anyone reach its contents without breaking the seal?" They will reply, "No." He will then say, "Indeed, Muḥammad (may Allah bless him and give him peace) is the Seal (*khātam*) of the Prophets, and today he is present, having been forgiven by Allah for both his past and future sins. Go to him."

---

239 Qur'an, 37:89.
240 Qur'an, 21:63.

They will approach Muḥammad (may Allah bless him and give him peace), and he will say, "This is for me. My community, my community!" Then he will fall down in prostration beneath the Throne, like the prostration performed in prayer. It will then be said to him, "O Muḥammad, raise your head. Ask and you will be granted; intercede, and your intercession will be accepted." He will then raise his head and intercede for the rendering of judgement (*faṣl al-qaḍā*).[241]

ثُمَّ إِنَّ أَهْلَ الْمَوْقِفِ يَنْصَرِفُونَ مِنْ هَذَا الْمَوْقِفِ إِلَى الْحِسَابِ، وَلَا يَنَالُ شَيْءٌ مِنْ هَذَا الْهَوْلِ الْأَنْبِيَاءُ وَالْأَوْلِيَاءُ وَلَا سَائِرُ الْعُلَمَاءِ، لِقَوْلِهِ تَعَالَى: ﴿لَا يَحْزُنُهُمُ الْفَزَعُ الْأَكْبَرُ﴾ [الْأَنْبِيَاءُ، ١٠٣] فَهُمْ آمِنُونَ مِنْ عَذَابِ اللَّهِ لَكِنَّهُمْ يَخَافُونَ خَوْفَ إِجْلَالٍ وَإِعْظَامٍ.

Then, the people of the Station will depart it for the Reckoning (*ḥisāb*). However, none of this horror will affect the prophets, *awliyā'* and scholars, based on the statement of Allah (Exalted is He): "The Supreme Horror will not grieve them."[242] They are thus safe from Allah's punishment but still experience fear out of reverence and veneration for Him.

وَقِيلَ: إِنَّ الَّذِي يَذْهَبُ إِلَى الْأَنْبِيَاءِ لِطَلَبِ الشَّفَاعَةِ رُؤَسَاءُ أَهْلِ الْمَوْقِفِ وَمَا بَيْنَ إِتْيَانِهِمْ مِنْ نَبِيٍّ إِلَى نَبِيٍّ أَلْفُ عَامٍ، وَقِيلَ: الَّذِي يَسْعَى لِلْأَنْبِيَاءِ فِي طَلَبِ الشَّفَاعَةِ الْعُلَمَاءُ الْعَامِلُونَ.

It has been said that those who approach the Prophets to seek intercession (*shafā'ah*) are the leaders among the people at the Station, with a span of one thousand years passing between their approaching one Prophet and the next. It has also been said that those who hasten toward the Prophets seeking intercession are the practising scholars (*'ulamā' 'āmilūn*).

---

241 *Al-Jawharah*, 113; *Tuḥfat*, 713; *Fatḥ al-majīd*, 97–98. Imām al-Suyūṭī's *Jāmi' al-aḥādīth* lists variations of this hadith under number 39122, sourced to al-Ṭayālisī and Aḥmad.

242 Qur'an, 21:103.

وَهَـٰذِهِ الشَّـفَاعَةُ تُعَـمُّ جَمِيـعَ الْخَلْـقِ مِنْ إِنْسٍ وَجِـنٍّ وَمُؤْمِـنٍ وَكَافِرٍ مِنْ هَذِهِ الْأُمَّةِ وَمِنْ غَيْرِهَا، وَلِذَلِكَ تُسَـمَّى الشَّفَاعَةُ الْعُظْمَى وَهِيَ أَوَّلُ الْمَقَامِ الْمَحْمُـوْدِ، أَيْ: الَّـذِي يَحْمَـدُهُ فِيْهِ الْأَوَّلُوْنَ وَالْآخِرُوْنَ، وَآخِرُهُ اسْـتِقْرَارُ أَهْلِ الْجَنَّةِ فِي الْجَنَّةِ وَأَهْلِ النَّارِ فِي النَّارِ، وَتَجَمَعُ الْأَنْبِيَاءُ حَيْنَئِذٍ تَحْتَ لِوَائِهِ ﷺ.

This intercession encompasses all created things – human and jinn, believer and unbeliever – from this community and others. Thus, it is named the Greatest Intercession (*shafāʿah ʿuẓmā*). It constitutes the beginning of the Praiseworthy Station (*al-maqām al-maḥmūd*), meaning the station for which he is praised by all creation, the first and the last. It concludes with the people of Paradise residing permanently in Paradise and the people of the Fire permanently in the Fire.[243] At that time, all the Prophets will gather beneath his banner (may Allah bless him and give him peace).[244]

(وَهَذِهِ الشَّفَاعَةُ مُخْتَصَّةٌ بِهِ ﷺ) وَلَهُ شَفَاعَاتٌ أُخَرُ، بَلْ وَلِغَيْرِهِ مِنَ الْأَنْبِيَاءِ وَالْعُلَمَـاءِ وَالصَّالِحِيـنَ، إِلَّا أَنَّـهُ الَّـذِي يُفْتَـحُ لَهُمْ بَابُ الشَّـفَاعَةِ لِأَنَّهُمْ لَا يَتَجَاسَرُونَ عَلَى الشَّفَاعَةِ قَبْلَهُ لِعِظَمِ الْجَلَالِ يَوْمَئِذٍ.

‹This intercession is unique to him (may Allah bless him and give him peace).› He also has other intercessions, and likewise, other Prophets, scholars, and righteous individuals will intercede. However, this Greatest Intercession is the one that opens the door to intercession for all others,[245] since none of them dare to intercede before him, due to the tremendous majesty and awe of that day.

---

243 From "Thus…": *Al-Jawharah*, 113; *Tuḥfat*, 713.

244 *Fatḥ al-majīd*, 98.

245 *Fatḥ al-majīd*, 98. Cf. *Al-Jawharah*, 113–7; *Tuḥfat*, 713, 715.

MESSENGERS MENTIONED IN THE QUR'ĀN

(وَمِمَّا يَجِبُ أَيْضًا أَنْ يَعْرِفَ الرُّسُلُ الْمَذْكُورِينَ فِي الْقُرْآنِ تَفْصِيلًا) وَيَكْفِي فِي الْإِيمَانِ بِكُلٍّ مِنْهُمْ أَنْ يَكُونَ بِحَيْثُ لَوْ سُئِلَ عَنْ رِسَالَتِهِ لَاعْتَرَفَ بِهَا، فَلَا يَجِبُ أَنْ يَسْرُدَهُمْ عَنْ حِفْظٍ، وَمَنْ أَنْكَرَ وَاحِدًا مِنْهُمْ بَعْدَ أَنْ عَلِمَهُ كَفَرَ بِخِلَافِ مَا لَوْ سُئِلَ عَنْهُ اِبْتِدَاءً فَقَالَ: «لَا أَعْرِفُهُ»، فَلَا يُكفرُ

‹It is also obligatory to know, in detail, the Messengers explicitly mentioned in the Qur'ān.› It is sufficient for belief in each Messenger that, if asked about his prophethood, one would acknowledge it. However, it is not obligatory to enumerate them from memory. Whoever denies one of these Messengers after coming to know of him commits disbelief. In contrast, if one is asked about a Messenger before having learned of him and says, "I do not know him," this does not constitute disbelief.[246]

(وَأَمَّا غَيْرُهُمْ مِنَ الرُّسُلِ وَالْأَنْبِيَاءِ فَيَجِبُ عَلَيْهِ) أَيْ: كُلُّ مُكَلَّفٍ (أَنْ يَعْرِفَهُمْ) أَيْ: غَيْرَ الْمَذْكُورِينَ فِي الْقُرْآنِ (إِجْمَالًا) فَيَجِبُ التَّصْدِيقُ بِأَنَّ لِلَّهِ رُسُلًا وَأَنْبِيَاءَ عَلَى الْإِجْمَالِ لَا يَعْلَمُ عَدَدَهُمْ إِلَّا اللَّهُ فَهُمْ غَيْرُ مَحْصُورِينَ لَنَا.

‹As for messengers (*rusul*) and prophets (*anbiyāʾ*) other than those explicitly mentioned in the Qur'ān, it is obligatory for them› meaning every legally responsible person ‹to know them› meaning those not mentioned in the Qur'ān ‹in a general sense.› One must affirm, in general, that Allah has messengers and prophets whose number is known only to Him, as they are not enumerated for us.[247]

(وَقَدْ نَظَمَ بَعْضُهُمُ الْأَنْبِيَاءَ الَّتِي تَجِبُ مَعْرِفَتُهُمْ تَفْصِيلًا فَقَالَ:

---

246 *Al-Jawharah*, 18; *Tuḥfat*, 115; *Fatḥ al-majīd*, 82.
247 *Fatḥ al-majīd*, 83.

حَتْـمٌ عَلَى كُلِّ ذِي التَّكْلِيفِ مَعْرِفَةٌ * بِأَنْبِيَـاءٍ عَلَـى التَّفْصِيـلِ قَـدْ عُلِمُوا

فِي تِلْكَ حُجَّتُنَـا مِنْهُـمْ ثَمَانِـى * مِـنْ بَعْدَ عَشَرٍ وَيَبْقَى سَبْعَةٌ وَهُمْ

إِدْرِيـسُ هُوْدٌ شَعْـبُ صَالِـحٌ وَكَذَا * ذُو الْكِفْـلِ آدَمُ بِالْمُخْتَارِ قَدْ خَتَمُوا

Some scholars have composed verses listing the prophets whose detailed recognition is obligatory, saying:

‹Incumbent (*ḥatm*) upon every legally responsible individual is knowing (*ma'rifah*) In detail those prophets who are known.
In "That is Our argument"[248] are eight of them after ten. Seven remain; they are:
Idrīs, Hūd, Shu'ayb, Ṣāliḥ, and also Dhu al-Kifl, Ādam, with the Chosen One (*mukhtār*) they were sealed›[249]

وَفَقَوْلُ النَّاظِمِ «حَتْمُ» خَبَرٌ مُقَدَّمٌ، وَ «مَعْرِفَةُ» مُبْتَدَأٌ مُؤَخَّرًا.

In the versifier's statement, "*ḥatm*" is a predicate advanced forward, while "*ma'rifah*" is a subject detailed afterward.

وَقَوْلُهُ: «قَـدْ عُلِمُوا فِي تِلْكَ حُجَّتِنَا»، أَيْ: قَدْ عُلِمَ الْأَنْبِيَاءُ الْخَمْسَـةُ وَالْعِشْرُونَ فِي الْقُرْآنِ، لَكِنْ فِي سُورَةِ الْأَنْعَامِ ثَمَانِيَةَ عَشَرَ مِنْهُمْ، وَذَلِكَ قَوْلُهُ تَعَالَى: ﴿وَتِلْكَ حُجَّتُنَا آتَيْنَاهَا إِبْرَاهِيمَ عَلَى قَوْمِهِ﴾ ... ﴿وَكُلًّا فَضَّلْنَا عَلَى الْعَالَمِينَ﴾ [الأنعام، ٨٣ - ٨٦] فَاللَّهُ تَعَالَى ذَكَرَ هُنَا ثَمَانِيَةَ عَشَرَ نَبِيًّا مِنْ غَيْرِ تَرْتِبٍ لَا بِحَسَبِ الزَّمَانِ وَلَا بِحَسَبِ الْفَضْلِ، وَلَكِنْ هُنَا لَطِيفَةٌ أَوْجَبَتْ التَّرْتِيبَ هُنَا: وَهِيَ أَنَّ اللَّهَ ذَكَرَ أَوَّلًا نُوحًا وَإِبْرَاهِيمَ وَإِسْحَاقَ وَيَعْقُوبَ، لِأَنَّهُمْ أُصُولُ الْأَنْبِيَاءِ ثُمَّ مِنَ الْمَرَاتِبِ الْمُعْتَبَرَةِ بَعْدَ النُّبُوَّةِ الْمُلْكُ وَالْقُدْرَةُ وَالسُّلْطَانُ وَقَدْ أَعْطَى اللَّهُ دَاوُدَ وَسُلَيْمَانَ مِنْ ذَلِكَ حَظًّا وَافِرًا، ثُمَّ مِنَ الْمَرَاتِبِ الصَّبْرُ

---

248 Qur'an, 6:83–86.

249 *Fatḥ al-majīd*, 82–83. The earliest mention I could find is Ibn Daqīq al-'Īd (d. 702 AH), *Sharḥ al-arba'īn al-Nawawiyyah* (n.p.: Mu'assasat al-Rayān, 1424/2003), 10.

عِنْدَ نُزُولِ الْبَلَاءِ وَالْمِحَنِ وَالشَّدَائِدِ وَقَدْ خَصَّ اللَّهُ بِهَذِهِ أَيُّوبَ، ثُمَّ عَطَفَ عَلَى هَاتَيْنِ الْمَرْتَبَتَيْنِ مَنْ جَمَعَ بَيْنَهُمَا وَهُوَ يُوسُفُ، فَإِنَّهُ صَبَرَ عَلَى الْبَلَاءِ وَالشِّدَّةِ حَتَّى أَعْطَاهُ اللَّهُ مُلْكَ مِصْرَ مَعَ النُّبُوَّةِ، ثُمَّ مِنَ الْمَرَاتِبِ الْمُعْتَبَرَةِ فِي فَضْلِ الْأَنْبِيَاءِ كَثْرَةُ الْمُعْجِزَاتِ وَكَثْرَةُ الْبَرَاهِينِ، وَقَدْ خَصَّ اللَّهُ مُوسَى وَهَارُونَ مِنْ تِلْكَ بِالْحَظِّ الْوَافِرِ وَمِنَ الْمَرَاتِبِ الْمُعْتَبَرَةِ الزُّهْدُ فِي الدُّنْيَا، وَقَدْ خَصَّ بِذَلِكَ زَكَرِيَّا وَيَحْيَى وَعِيسَى وَإِلْيَاسَ، ثُمَّ ذَكَرَ اللَّهُ بَعْدَ هَؤُلَاءِ مَنْ لَمْ يَبْقِ لَهُ أَتْبَاعٌ وَلَا شَرِيعَةٌ، وَهُمْ إِسْمَاعِيلُ وَالْيَسَعُ وَيُونُسُ وَلُوطٌ، فَإِذَا اُعْتُبِرَتْ هَذِهِ اللَّطِيفَةُ كَانَ هَذَا التَّرْتِيبُ حَسَنًا، وَاللَّهُ أَعْلَمُ.

His statement, "are known in 'That is Our argument,'" means that the twenty-five prophets mentioned explicitly in the Qur'ān are known. Eighteen of these are mentioned specifically in Sūrat al-An'ām, in the verse where Allah (Exalted is He) says: "That is Our argument; We gave it unto Abraham against his people... and all [of them] We favoured over the worlds."[250]

Allah (Exalted is He) mentioned eighteen prophets here without following a chronological order or an order based on their virtue. However, there is a subtlety (*laṭīfah*) that imposes an implicit order: Allah first mentioned Nūḥ, Ibrāhīm, Isḥāq, and Ya'qūb, as these prophets represent the foundational roots of prophecy. Next, after prophethood itself, the significant rank is sovereignty, power, and authority, of which Allah granted Dāwūd and Sulaymān an abundant share. Another rank is steadfastness (*ṣabr*) during trials, hardships, and calamities, and Allah specifically distinguished Ayyūb with this quality. Then, Allah mentioned one who combined these two ranks – Yūsuf, who patiently endured trials and hardships until Allah granted him sovereignty over Egypt alongside prophethood. Another rank considered significant is an abundance of miracles and apodictic proofs (*barāhīn*), and Allah singled out Mūsā and Hārūn for a substantial portion of these. Additionally, renouncement of the

---

250 Qur'an, 6:83–86.

material world (*zuhd*) is considered an important rank, and Allah specifically distinguished Zakariyyā, Yaḥyā, 'Īsā, and Ilyās with this quality. Finally, Allah mentioned those who no longer have followers or a surviving religious law, who are Ismā'īl, al-Yasa', Yūnus, and Lūṭ. If this subtle point is understood, the ordering presented here becomes particularly meaningful. (And Allah knows best.)[251]

وَقَوْلُ النَّاظِمِ: «وَيَبْقَى سَبْعَةٌ»، أَيْ: وَيَبْقَى مِنْ الْخَمْسَةِ وَالْعِشْرِينَ بَعْدَ ثَمَانِيَةَ عَشَرَ سَبْعَةٌ مَذْكُورَةٌ فِي مَوَاضِعَ كَثِيرَةٍ فِي الْقُرْآنِ الْعَظِيمِ، وَلِذَلِكَ ذَكَرَهُمْ.

The versifier's phrase "seven remain" refers to the seven prophets remaining from the total of twenty-five after the eighteen mentioned previously. These seven are explicitly mentioned in numerous places throughout the Noble Qur'ān, which is why the versifier specifically identified them by name.[252]

وَقَوْلُهُ: «بِالْمُخْتَارِ قَدْ خَتَمُوا»، الْجَارُّ وَالْمَجْرُورُ مُتَعَلِّقٌ بِالْفِعْلِ مَعَ حَذْفِ الْعَاطِفِ، أَيْ: وَقَدْ خَتَمَ الْأَنْبِيَاءُ وَالرُّسُلُ بِالنَّبِيِّ الْمُخْتَارِ عَلَى جَمِيعِ الْخَلْقِ، وَهُوَ سَيِّدُنَا مُحَمَّدٌ ﷺ.

Regarding his statement, "with the Chosen One they were sealed": the prepositional phrase ("with the Chosen One") is grammatically linked to a verb from which the coordinating conjunction ("and") has been elided. Thus, the intended meaning is: "And the prophets and messengers were sealed with the Prophet chosen above all creation – our master Muḥammad (may Allah bless him and give him peace)."

فَأَفْضَلُ الْمَخْلُوقَاتِ نَبِيُّنَا، ثُمَّ سَيِّدُنَا إِبْرَاهِيمُ، فَسَيِّدُنَا مُوسَى، فَسَيِّدُنَا عِيسَى، فَسَيِّدُنَا نُوحٌ، وَهَؤُلَاءِ الْخَمْسَةُ هُمْ أُولُو الْعَزْمِ، ثُمَّ بَقِيَّةُ الرُّسُلِ، ثُمَّ بَقِيَّةُ الْأَنْبِيَاءِ غَيْرُ الرُّسُلِ مَعَ تَفَاوُتِ مَرَاتِبِهِمْ عِنْدَ اللَّهِ تَعَالَى.

---

251 *Fatḥ al-majīd*, 82.
252 *Fatḥ al-majīd*, 83.

The best of creation is our Prophet (may Allah bless him and give him peace),[253] then our master Ibrāhīm, then our master Mūsā, then our master ʿĪsā, and then our master Nūḥ. These five are the ones of Resolute Determination (*ūlu l-ʿazm*).[254] Next in rank are the remaining messengers, followed by the prophets who were not messengers – all possessing varying degrees of superiority with Allah [Exalted is He].[255]

فَالْوَاجِـبُ اعْتِقَـادُ أَفْضَلِيَةِ الْأَفْضَـلِ عَلَى وُفْقِ مَا وَرَدَ بِهِ الْحُكْمُ تَفْصِيلًا فِي التَّفْصِيلِيِّ وَإِجْمَالًا فِي الْإِجْمَالِيِّ، وَيَمْتَنِعُ الْهُجُومُ فِيمَا لَمْ يَرِدْ فِيهِ إِذْنٌ مِنِ الشَّرْعِ.

It is obligatory (*wājib*) to believe in the superiority of each individual according to the manner in which the religious ruling (*ḥukm*) was conveyed: detailed belief for those explicitly detailed and general belief for those mentioned in general. It is impossible to speculate or conclude superiority in matters for which explicit permission (*idhn*) from the Revealed Law has not been transmitted.[256]

THE GREATER VIRTUE OF SOME GENERATIONS

(وَمِمَّا يَجِبُ اعْتِقَادُهُ أَيْضًا أَنَّ قَرْنَهُ ﷺ (أَفْضَلُ الْقُرُونِ، ثُمَّ الْقَرْنُ الَّذِي بَعْدَهُ، ثُمَّ الْقَـرْنُ الَّذِي بَعْدَهُ) أَيْ: يَجِبُ أَنْ يَعْتَقِدَ أَنَّ أَصْحَابَهُ ﷺ أَفْضَلُ الْقُرُونِ الْمُتَأَخِّرَةِ وَالْمُتَقَدِّمَةِ مَا عَدَا الْأَنْبِيَاءَ وَالرُّسُلَ لِقَوْلِهِ: «إِنَّ اللَّهَ اخْتَارَ أَصْحَابِي عَلَى الْعَالَمِينَ سِوَى النَّبِيِّينَ وَالْمُرْسَلِينَ».)

‹**It is also obligatory to believe that the Prophet's generation is the best generation, followed by the one succeeding it, and then the one succeeding that.**› Meaning it is required to believe that his com-

---

253 *Al-Jawharah*, 65; *Tuḥfat*, 447; *Fatḥ al-majīd*, 85.
254 *Al-Jawharah*, 66; *Tuḥfat*, 450; *Fatḥ al-majīd*, 85.
255 *Al-Jawharah*, 66; *Tuḥfat*, 450; *Fatḥ al-majīd*, 85.
256 *Al-Jawharah*, 66; *Tuḥfat*, 451.

panions (may Allah bless him and give him peace) are superior to all previous and subsequent generations, excluding only the Prophets and Messengers (may Allah bless them and give them peace). This belief is based upon his statement (may Allah bless him and give him peace), "Indeed, Allah chose my companions over all of creation save the Prophets and the Messengers."[257]

وَلَا يَخْفَى تَرْجِيحُ رُتْبَةِ مَنْ لَازَمَهُ ﷺ وَقَاتَلَ مَعَهُ وَقُتِلَ تَحْتَ رَايَتِهِ عَلَى مَنْ لَمْ يَكُنْ كَذَلِكَ، وَإِنْ كَانَ شَرَفُ الصُّحْبَةِ حَاصِلًا لِلْجَمِيعِ.

It is evident that the rank (*rutbah*) of those who kept the Prophet's company (may Allah bless him and give him peace), fought at his side, and were slain under his banner holds a higher rank than those who did not – even though the honour (*sharaf*) of companionship applies to all of them.[258]

وَ «الْقَرْنُ»: أَهْلُ زَمَانٍ وَاحِدٍ مُتَقَارِبٌ اشْتَرَكُوا فِي أَمْرٍ مِنْ الْأُمُورِ الْمَقْصُودَةِ، كَالصَّحَابَةِ، فَإِنَّهُمْ اشْتَرَكُوا فِي الصُّحْبَةِ وَهَكَذَا مِنْ بَعْدِهِمْ.

A "generation" (*qarn*) refers to a group of people living at approximately the same time who share a common characteristic or goal, such as the Companions who shared companionship with the Prophet (may Allah bless him and give him peace). The same definition applies to the generations after them.[259]

ثُمَّ إِنَّ رُتْبَةَ التَّابِعِينَ تَلِي رُتْبَةِ الصَّحَابَةِ. وَ «التَّابِعِيُّ»: مَنْ اجْتَمَعَ بِالصَّحَابِيِّ اجْتِمَاعًا مُتَعَارَفًا، وَلَا يَشْتَرَطُ فِيهِ طُولُ الِاجْتِمَاعِ، كَمَا فِي

---

257   Imām al-Suyūṭī's *Jāmiʿ al-aḥādīth* lists variations of this hadith under numbers 6617 and 36945. The first is sourced to Abū Naʿīm's *Faḍāʾil al-ṣaḥābah*, al-Khaṭīb, and Ibn ʿAsākir. The second is sourced to Ibn ʿAsākir. Both variations have (جميع العالمين). The variation without (جميع) is attributed to al-Bazzār in *Kashf al-astār*, numbers 2763 and 16383.
        Cf. *Al-Jawharah*, 75; *Tuḥfat*, 485; *Fatḥ al-majīd*, 6; *Nūr al-ẓalām*, 55.
258   *Al-Jawharah*, 75; *Tuḥfat*, 485.
259   *Al-Jawharah*, 75; *Tuḥfat*, 486.

الصَّحَابِيٍّ مَعَ النَّبِيِّ ﷺ، وَلَا يَشْـتَـرِطُ التَّمَيُّزُ فِي التَّابِعِيِّ، كَمَا لَا يَشْـتَـرِطُ فِي الصَّحَابِيِّ.

Then, the rank of the Successors (*tābi'ūn*) follows that of the Companions (*ṣaḥābah*).[260] A Successor is anyone who met with a Companion in a recognised manner.[261] It is not a condition that this meeting be prolonged.[262] Additionally, discernment (*tamyīz*) is not stipulated as a condition for being a Successor, just as it is not stipulated for [being] a Companion.[263]

وَأَفْضَـلُ التَّابِعِيْـنَ أُوَيْسُ الْقَرْنِي، كَمَا أَنَّ أَفْضَلَ التَّابِعِياتِ حَفْصَةُ بِنْتُ سِيرِيْنَ، عَلَى خِلَافٍ فِي الْمَسْأَلَةِ.

The best of the Successors is Uways al-Qarnī, just as the best among the female Successors is Ḥafṣah bint Sīrīn – though there is scholarly disagreement concerning this issue.[264]

ثُمَّ إِنَّ رُتْبَةَ أَتْبَاعِ التَّابِعِيْنَ تَلِي رُتْبَةَ التَّابِعِيْنَ مِنْ غَيْرِ تَرَاخٍ كَبِيرٍ.

Then, the rank of the Successors of the Successors (*atbā' al-tābi'īn*) follows the rank of the Successors without a significant gap between them.[265]

وَالْأَصْـلُ فِي ذَلِكَ قَوْلُهُ ﷺ: «خَيْرُ أُمَّتِي الْقَرْنُ الَّذِيْنَ يَلُوْنِي ثُمَّ الَّذِيْنَ يَلُوْنَهُـمْ ثُمَّ الَّذِيْـنَ يَلُوْنَهُـمْ»، وَظَاهِرُهُ أَنَّ مَا بَعْدَ الْقُرُوْنِ الثَّلَاثَةِ سَوَاءٌ فِي

---

260 *Al-Jawharah*, 75; *Tuḥfat*, 488.

261 The author explains "recognised fashion" in *Fatḥ al-majīd* as it taking place on the earth, physically, while believing in him (may Allah bless him and give him peace), and it taking place after being assigned messengerhood. See *Fatḥ al-majīd*, 6.

262 *Al-Jawharah*, 75; *Tuḥfat*, 489.

263 *Al-Jawharah*, 75; *Tuḥfat*, 489.

264 *Al-Jawharah*, 75; *Tuḥfat*, 489.

265 *Al-Jawharah*, 75; *Tuḥfat*, 490.

الْفَضِيلَةِ كَمَا وَرَدَ فِي الْحَدِيثِ: «مَثَلُ هَذِهِ الْأُمَّةِ مَثَـلُ الْمَطَرِ، لَا يَدْرِي أَوَّلَهُ خَيْرٌ أَوْ آخِرَهُ».

The basis for this is the Prophet's statement (may Allah bless him and give him peace): "The best of my nation is the generation of those who come after me, then those who come after them, and then those who come after them."[266] Its apparent meaning is that the generations after these three are equal in virtue,[267] as indicated in another hadith: "The likeness of this nation is that of rain; it is not known whether its beginning is better or its end."[268]

THE GOODNESS OF MUḤAMMAD'S COMMUNITY

وَيَعْتَقِدُ أَهْلُ السُّنَّةِ أَنَّ أُمَّةَ مُحَمَّدٍ ﷺ خَيْرُ الْأُمَمِ أَجْمَعِينَ.

The People of the Sunnah (*Ahl al-Sunnah*) hold that the community of Muḥammad (may Allah bless him and give him peace) is the best of all communities.[269]

وَأَفْضَلُهُمْ أَهْلُ الْقُرُونِ الَّذِينَ شَاهَدُوهُ وَآمَنُوا بِهِ، وَصَدَّقُوهُ وَبَايَعُوهُ وَتَابَعُوهُ وَقَاتَلُوا بَيْنَ يَدَيْهِ وَفَدَّوْهُ بِأَنْفُسِهِمْ وَأَمْوَالِهِمْ وَعَزَّرُوهُ وَنَصَرُوهُ.

The best of them are those generations who witnessed him, believed in him, affirmed his truthfulness, pledged allegiance to him, followed him, fought alongside him, ransomed him with their lives and wealth, honoured him, and supported him.

---

266 Al-Bukhārī, 2652; Muslim, 2533.
     Imām al-Suyūṭī's *Jāmiʿ al-aḥādīth* lists variations under numbers 12036–38, 12094, 12097–99, and 12154.

267 *Al-Jawharah*, 75; *Tuḥfat*, 490.

268 Imām al-Suyūṭī's *Jāmiʿ al-aḥādīth* lists variations under number 20945, sourced to Aḥmad, al-Tirmidhī, Abū Yaʻlā, al-Ramhurmuzī, al-Ḥakīm, al-Ṭabarānī. *Al-Jawharah*, 75; *Tuḥfat*, 490.

269 There are three opinions on the order of superiority. See *Al-Jawharah*, 79; *Tuḥfat*, 505–508; *Nūr al-ẓalām*, 137.

وَأَفْضَلُ هَذَا الْقَرْنِ أَهْلُ الْحُدَيْبِيَةِ الَّذِيْنَ بَايَعُوْهُ بَيْعَةَ الرِّضْوَانِ، فَهُمْ أَلْفٌ وَأَرْبَعُمِائَةِ رَجُلٍ.

The best among this generation are the People of al-Ḥudaybiyyah who pledged allegiance at Bayʻat al-Riḍwān, comprising 1,400 men.[270]

وَأَفْضَلُهُمْ أَهْلُ أُحُدٍ، وَهُمْ سَبْعُمِائَةٍ مِنَ الْمُؤْمِنِينَ.

Superior among them are the People of Uḥud, comprising 700 believers.[271]

وَأَفْضَلُهُمْ أَهْلُ بَدْرٍ، وَهُمْ ثَلَاثُمِائَةٍ وَثَلَاثَةَ عَشَرَ رَجُلًا.

Superior among them are the People of Badr, comprising 313 men.[272]

وَأَفْضَلُهُمُ الْأَرْبَعُوْنَ أَهْلُ دَارِ الْخَيْزُرَانِ.

Superior among them are the forty People of Dār al-Khayzurān.

وَأَفْضَلُهُمُ الْعَشَرَةُ الَّذِيْنَ شَهِدَ لَهُمُ النَّبِيُّ ﷺ بِالْجَنَةِ وَهُمْ: أَبُوْ بَكْرٍ وَعُمَرُ وَعُثْمَانُ وَعَلِـيٌّ وَطَلْحَةُ وَالزُّبَيْرُ وَعَبْدُ الرَّحْمَنِ بْنُ عَوْفٍ وَسَعْدٌ وَسَعِيدٌ وَأَبُو عُبَيْدَةَ بْنُ الْجَرَّاحِ.

Superior among them are the ten to whom the Prophet (may Allah bless him and give him peace) testified that they would enter the Garden. They are: Abū Bakr, ʻUmar, ʻUthmān, ʻAlī, Ṭalḥah [bin ʻUbayd Allāh], al-Zubayr [bin al-ʻAwwām], ʻAbd al-Raḥmān bin ʻAwf, Saʻd [bin Abī Waqqāṣ], Saʻīd [bin Zayd], and Abū ʻUbaydah [ʻĀmir] bin al-Jarrāḥ.[273]

---

270 *Al-Jawharah*, 78; *Tuḥfat*, 503.
271 Cf. *Al-Jawharah*, 78; *Tuḥfat*, 502.
272 *Al-Jawharah*, 78; *Tuḥfat*, 497–8.
273 Cf. *Al-Jawharah*, 77; *Tuḥfat*, 496.

وَأَفْضَلُ هَؤُلَاءِ الْعَشَرَةِ الْخُلَفَاءُ الرَّاشِدُونَ الْأَرْبَعَةُ الْأَخْيَارِ، وَأَفْضَلُهُمْ عَلَى حَسَبِ تَرْتِيبِهِمْ فِي الْخِلَافَةِ - وَهِيَ النِّيَابَةُ عَنِ النَّبِيِّ ﷺ فِي عُمُومِ مَصَالِحِ الْمُؤْمِنِينَ - فَأَفْضَلُهُمْ أَبُو بَكْرٍ ثُمَّ عُمَرُ ثُمَّ عُثْمَانُ ثُمَّ عَلِيٌّ.

Superior among these ten are the Rightly Guided Caliphs: the four excellent ones.[274] Their superiority follows their chronological order in the caliphate (*khilāfah*), which refers to representing the Prophet (may Allah bless him and give him peace) in safeguarding the general interests of the believers.[275] Thus, the best of them is Abū Bakr, followed by 'Umar, then 'Uthmān, and then 'Alī.[276]

وَلِهَؤُلَاءِ الْأَرْبَعَةِ فِي مُدَّةِ الْخِلَافَةِ ثَلَاثُونَ سَنَةً، كَمَا قَالَ ﷺ: «الْخِلَافَةُ بَعْدِي ثَلَاثُونَ ثُمَّ تَصِيرُ مُلْكًا عَضُوضًا»، أَيْ: ذَا عِضٍّ وَتَضْيِيقٍ؛ لِأَنَّ الْمُلُوكَ يَضُرُّونَ بِالرَّعِيَّةِ، حَتَّى كَأَنَّهُمْ يَعْضُونَ عَضًا، فَالْمُرَادُ أَنَّهُ ذُو تَضْيِيقٍ وَمَشَقَّةٍ عَلَى الرَّعِيَّةِ، فَتَوَلَّى الْخِلَافَةَ بَعْدَ النَّبِيِّ ﷺ وَأَبُو بَكْرٍ رَضِيَ اللَّهُ عَنْهُ سَنَتَيْنِ وَثَلَاثَةَ أَشْهُرٍ وَعَشَرَةَ أَيَّامٍ، وَتَوَلَّاهَا عُمَرُ رَضِيَ اللَّهُ عَنْهُ عَشَرَةً، وَتَوَلَّاهَا عُثْمَانُ رَضِيَ اللَّهُ عَنْهُ اثْنَتَيْ عَشَرَةَ، وَتَوَلَّاهَا عَلِيٌّ رَضِيَ اللَّهُ عَنْهُ سِتًّا، وَقِيلَ: لَمْ تَكْمُلِ الْمُدَّةُ الَّتِي قَدَّرَهَا النَّبِيُّ ﷺ إِلَّا بِخِلَافَةِ الْحَسَنِ بْنِ عَلِيٍّ، ثُمَّ تَوَلَّاهَا مُعَاوِيَةُ بْنُ أَبِي سُفْيَانَ تِسْعَ عَشَرَةَ سَنَةً، وَقَالَ مُعَاوِيَةُ: أَنَا أَوَّلُ الْمُلُوكِ، وَخِلَافَتُهُ صَحِيحَةٌ بَعْدَ مَوْتِ عَلِيٍّ رَضِيَ اللَّهُ عَنْهُ، وَبَعْدَ خَلْعِ الْحَسَنِ بْنِ عَلِيٍّ نَفْسَهُ عَنِ الْخِلَافَةِ وَتَسْلِيمِهَا إِلَى مُعَاوِيَةَ، وَخِلَافَتُهُ مَذْكُورَةٌ فِي قَوْلِ النَّبِيِّ ﷺ وَهُوَ مَا رُوِيَ عَنِ النَّبِيِّ ﷺ أَنَّهُ قَالَ: «تَدُورُ رَحَى الْإِسْلَامِ خَمْسًا وَثَلَاثِينَ سَنَةً أَوْ سِتًّا وَثَلَاثِينَ أَوْ سَبْعَةً وَثَلَاثِينَ». وَالْمُرَادُ بِالرَّحَى فِي الْحَدِيثِ الْقُوَّةُ فِي الدِّينِ، وَالْخَمْسُ سِنِينَ الْفَاضِلَةُ مِنْ

---

274 Cf. *Al-Jawharah*, 76; *Tuḥfat*, 492.

275 *Al-Jawharah*, 76; *Tuḥfat*, 491.

276 Cf. *Al-Jawharah*, 76; *Tuḥfat*, 493.

الثَّلَاثِينَ فَهِيَ مِنْ جُمْلَةِ خِلَافَةِ مُعَاوِيَةَ إِلَى تَمَامِ تِسْعَ عَشَـرَةَ سَنَةً وَشُهُورٍ؛ لِأَنَّ الثَّلَاثِينَ كَمُلَتْ بِعَلِيٍّ رَضِيَ اللَّهُ عَنْهُ.

The duration of the caliphate for these four caliphs totals thirty years, as the Prophet (may Allah bless him and give him peace) said: "The caliphate after me will last thirty [years]. Then it will become a biting kingship,"[277] meaning a reign characterised by harshness and oppression, since kings typically cause harm to their subjects, as if biting into them. The intended meaning is that it will become oppressive and difficult for the people.[278]

Abū Bakr held the caliphate after the Prophet (may Allah bless him and give him peace) for two years, three months, and ten days; 'Umar for ten [years]; 'Uthmān for twelve; and 'Alī undertook it for six.[279]

However, it is said that the period specified by the Prophet (may Allah bless him and give him peace) only reaches completion with the inclusion of the caliphate of al-Ḥasan bin 'Alī.[280]

Afterwards, Mu'āwiyah bin Abī Sufyān held the caliphate for nineteen years. Mu'āwiyah said, "I am the first of the kings."[281] His caliphate is valid following the death of 'Alī (may Allah be pleased with him) and after al-Ḥasan bin 'Alī abdicated the caliphate, handing it over to Mu'āwiyah.[282]

Mu'āwiyah's caliphate is referenced indirectly in a statement of the Prophet (may Allah bless him and give him peace): "The millstone (raḥā) of Islam will turn for thirty-five years or thirty-six or thir-

---

277   Imām al-Suyūṭī's *Jāmi' al-aḥādīth* lists variations of this hadith under number 12202, sourced to al-Ṭayālisī, Aḥmad, Na'īm, and Abū Ya'lā, al-Baghawī, Ibn Ḥibbān, al-Tirmidhī (*ḥasan*), al-Ṭabarānī, Abū Dāwūd, Abū Nu'aym from Safīnah. Cf. Ibn Ḥajar, *Fatḥ al-Bārī*, 8:77, where he attributes it to Aḥmad, the authors of the *Sunan*, Ibn Ḥibbān (who judged it *ṣaḥīḥ*), and others.

278   *Al-Jawharah*, 76; *Tuḥfat*, 491.

279   *Al-Jawharah*, 76; *Tuḥfat*, 491.

280   *Al-Jawharah*, 76; *Tuḥfat*, 491.

281   Ibn Abī Shaybah, 35891, 30714... from "a shaykh from the people of Madīnah." *Al-Jawharah*, 76; *Tuḥfat*, 491.

282   For the hadith, see *Al-Jawharah*, 76; *Tuḥfat*, 492.

ty-seven."[283] Here, "millstone" (*raḥā*) in the hadith refers to strength and stability in religion. The additional five years beyond the original thirty [mentioned previously] are included within Muʿāwiyah's nineteen-year and some months caliphate, since the thirty-year duration concluded with ʿAlī (may Allah be pleased with him).[284]

HIS CHILDREN

(وَيَنْبَغِي) أَيْ: يُطْلَبُ (لِلشَّخْصِ أَنْ يَعْرِفَ أَوْلَادَهُ ﷺ) عِدًّا وَتَرْتِيبًا فِي الْوِلَادَةِ؛ لِأَنَّهُ يَنْبَغِي لِلشَّخْصِ أَنْ يَعْرِفَ سَادَاتِ الْأُمَّةِ (وَهُمْ) أَيْ: الْأَوْلَادُ (سَبْعَةٌ): ثَلَاثَةُ ذُكُورٍ وَأَرْبَعَةُ إِنَاثٍ (عَلَى الصَّحِيْحِ) وَهُوَ قَوْلُ أَكْثَرِ أَهْلِ النَّسَبِ، وَقَالَ الدَّارَقُطْنِيُّ: هُوَ الْأَثْبَتُ.

‹**It is appropriate**› meaning it is recommended ‹**for an individual to know the children of the Prophet (may Allah bless him and give him peace)**› their number and order of birth, because it is commendable to know the noble figures of this community‹.›[285]

‹**They**› meaning his children ‹**are seven**›: three males and four females ‹**according to the sound opinion**›, which is the view of genealogists‹.› Al-Dāraquṭnī said that it is the most established [opinion].

[They are:]

(سَـيِّدُنَا الْقَاسِمُ) وَكَانَ ﷺ مُشْـتَهِرًا بِأَبِي الْقَاسِمِ؛ لِأَنَّهُ أَوَّلُ أَوْلَادِهِ، وَقَدْ نَصَّ الْعُلَمَاءُ عَلَى أَنَّهُ يَحْرُمُ عَلَى غَيْرِهِ ﷺ التَّكَنِّي بِذَلِكَ سَـوَاءٌ مُدَّةَ حَيَاتِهِ ﷺ وَبَعْدَهَا عَلَى الصَّحِيْحِ، وَقَدْ عَاشَ سَيِّدُنَا الْقَاسِمُ سَبْعَةَ عَشَرَ شَهْرًا

---

283 Imām al-Suyūṭī's *Jāmiʿ al-aḥādīth* lists a variation under number 10681, sourced to Aḥmad and al-Ḥākim from Ibn Masʿūd.

284 *Al-Jawharah*, 76; *Tuḥfat*, 492.

285 al-Bājūrī, *Taḥqīq al-maqām*, 187–188; *Nūr al-ẓalām*, 121 – where he mentioned al-Faḍālī's *ʿAqīdat al-ʿawām* which is the base for al-Bājūrī's *Taḥqīq al-maqām*.

‹**Our master al-Qāsim**› He (may Allah bless him and give him peace) was famously known as "Abū al-Qāsim," as al-Qāsim was his firstborn child. The *'ulamā'* explicitly stated that it is prohibited for others besides him (may Allah bless him and give him peace) to adopt this *kunyā*,[286] both during his lifetime and afterward, according to the sound opinion.[287] Our master al-Qāsim lived for seventeen months.

(وَسَيِّدَتُنَا زَيْنَبُ) فَهِيَ بَعْدَ الْقَاسِمِ فِي الْوِلَادَةِ، أَدْرَكَتِ الْإِسْلَامَ وَهَاجَرَتْ، وَهِيَ أَكْبَرُ بَنَاتِهِ ﷺ عَلَى الْأَصَحِّ.

‹**Our lady Zaynab**› She was born after al-Qāsim, embraced Islam, emigrated [to Madīnah], and was the eldest of his daughters (may Allah bless him and give him peace) according to the soundest opinion.

(وَسِيِّدَتُنَا رُقَيَّةُ) كَانَتْ ذَاتَ جَمَالٍ، وَمَاتَتْ وَالنَّبِيُّ ﷺ فِي بَدْرٍ، وَلَمَّا عُزِّيَ بِهَا قَالَ [ﷺ]: «الْحَمْدُ لِلَّهِ، دَفْنُ الْبَنَاتِ مِنَ الْمَكْرُمَاتِ».

‹**Our lady Ruqayyah**› She was known for her beauty. She died while the Prophet (may Allah bless him and give him peace) was at Badr. When informed of her death, he [ﷺ] said, "Praise be to Allah. Burying daughters is an honourable act."[288]

(وَسَيِّدَتُنَا فَاطِمَةُ) وَسُمِّيَتْ فَاطِمَةُ لِأَنَّ اللَّهَ تَعَالَى قَدْ فَطَمَهَا وَذُرِّيَّتَهَا عَنِ النَّارِ يَوْمَ الْقِيَامَةِ، فَكَانَتْ أَحَبَّ أَهْلِهِ ﷺ إِلَيْهِ، وَكَانَ إِذَا أَرَادَ سَفَرًا يَكُونُ آخِرُ عَهْدِهِ بِهَا، وَإِذَا قَدِمَ كَانَتْ أَوَّلَ مَا يَدْخُلُ عَلَيْهَا، وَلَمْ يَكُنْ لَهُ ﷺ

---

286 A *kunyā* is "Abū…" or "Umm…", that is "Father of…" or "Mother of…".

287 Imām al-Shāfiʿī considered it unlawful categorically, i.e. during his lifetime and after his passing and whether or not the individual's name is "Muḥammad"; while the other three considered it unlawful during his lifetime but lawful after his passing. (May Allah bless him and give him peace.) *Al-Jawharah*, 81; *Tuḥfat*, 517; *Nūr al-ẓalām*, 138.

288 Imām al-Suyūṭī's *Jāmiʿ al-aḥādīth* lists variations of this hadith under numbers 11784 and 39096. The first is sourced to al-Ṭabarānī and Ibn ʿAsākir from Ibn ʿAbbās, and Ibn al-Jawzī in *Al-Mawḍūʿāt*. The second is sourced to al-ʿAskarī's *Al-Amthāl*.

عَقِبَ إِلَّا مِنْهَا، فَانْتَشَرَ نَسْلُهُ مِنْهَا مِنْ جِهَةِ السِّبْطَيْنِ الْحَسَنِ وَالْحُسَيْنِ رَضِيَ اللَّهُ عَنْهُمَا.

‹**Our lady Fāṭimah**› She was named "Fāṭimah"[289] because Allah (Exalted is He) has withheld her and her progeny from the Fire on the Day of Judgement. She was the most beloved of his household to him (may Allah bless him and give him peace). Whenever he intended to travel, she was the last person he saw, and upon returning, she was the first he visited. He (may Allah bless him and give him peace) had no descendants except through her. His lineage continued through her by way of the two grandsons al-Ḥasan and al-Ḥusayn. (May Allah be pleased with them both.)

(وَسَيِّدَتُنَا أُمُّ كَلْثُومٍ) إِنَّمَا تُعْرَفُ بِهَذِهِ الْكُنْيَةِ فَلَا يُعْرَفُ لَهَا اسْمٌ، وَمَاتَتْ سَنَةَ تِسْعٍ مِنَ الْهِجْرَةِا، وَرُوِيَ أَنَّهُ ﷺ جَلَسَ عَلَى الْقَبْرِ وَعَيْنَاهُ تَذْرِفَانِ وَقَالَ: «هَلْ فِيكُمْ مَنْ أَحَدٍ لَمْ يُجَامِعْ[290] اللَّيْلَةَ»، فَقَالَ أَبُو طَلْحَةَ: «أَنَا»، فَقَالَ: «انْزِلْ قَبْرَهَا» فَنَزَلَ.

‹**Our lady Umm Kulthūm**› She is known by this *kunyā*; no actual name is known for her. She died during the ninth year after the Hijra. It was narrated that the Prophet (may Allah bless him and give him peace) sat by her grave weeping, and said, "Did one of you not engage in marital relations last night?" Abū Ṭalḥah replied, "I did not." He (may Allah bless him and give him peace) said, "Descend into her grave," and Abū Ṭalḥah complied.[291]

(وَسَيِّدُنَا عَبْدُ اللَّهِ وَهُوَ الْمُلَقَّبُ بِـ «الطَّيِّبِ» وَ «الطَّاهِرِ») وَقِيلَ: هُمَا اسْمَانِ لِشَخْصَيْنِ بِإِسْقَاطِ عَبْدِ اللَّهِ فَجُمْلَةُ أَوْلَادِهِ ثَمَانِيَةٌ، وَقِيلَ: كَذَلِكَ مَعَ زِيَادَةِ عَبْدِ اللَّهِ فَهُمْ تِسْعَةٌ.

---

289 The word means to be weaned, disengaged, or withheld.
290 Al-Bukhārī has: (يُقَارِفْ).
291 With the variation noted above: al-Bukhārī, 1342.

‹**Our master ʿAbd Allāh (nicknamed "Al-Ṭayyib" and "Al-Ṭāhir")**›
It is said that they were two separate individuals excluding "ʿAbd Allāh," thus totalling eight children. Another view includes "ʿAbd Allāh" separately, making them nine.

(وَسَــيِّدُنَا إِبْرَاهِيْــمُ) رُوِيَ أَنَّــهُ ﷺ قَالَ لَيْلَةَ وِلَادَتِهِ: «وُلِــدَ لِي اللَّيْلَةَ غُلَامٌ سَــمَّيْتُهُ بِاسْــمِ أَبِي إِبْرَاهِيْمَ»، وَمِنْ ذَلِكَ يُؤْخَذُ مَشْرُوعِيَّةُ التَّسْمِيَةِ مِنْ حِيْنِ الْوِلَادَةِ، وَأَمَّا حَدِيْثُ الْأَمْرِ بِتَسْمِيَةِ الْمَوْلُودِ يَوْمَ السَّابِعِ فَالْمَقْصُوْدُ مِنْهَا أَنَّهَا لَا تُؤَخَّرُ عَنْـهُ، لَا أَنَّهَا لَا تَكُنْ إِلَّا فِيْهِ، بَلْ هِيَ مَشْرُوعَةٌ مِنْ حِيْنَ الْوِلَادَةِ إِلَيْهِ، وَعَاشَ سَبْعِيْنَ يَوْمًا.

‹**Our master Ibrāhīm**› It is narrated that on the night of his birth, he (may Allah bless him and give him peace) said, "A boy was born to me tonight, and I named him with the name of my father Ibrāhīm."[292] From this, the permissibility of naming from the time of birth is derived. As for the hadith commanding naming on the seventh day, it means naming is not delayed beyond it, not that it must occur on that day. Thus, naming is permissible from birth until the seventh day. Ibrāhīm lived seventy days.

(وَكُلُّهُــمْ مِــنْ سَــيِّدَتِنَا خَدِيجَةَ الْكُبْرَى) وَهِــيَ أَوَّلُ امْرَأَةٍ تَزَوَّجَ بِهَا رَسُــوْلُ اللَّهِ ﷺ، وَلَمْ يَتَزَوَّجْ غَيْرَهَا حَتَّى مَاتَتْ، وَهِيَ أَفْضَلُ نِسَــائِهِ ﷺ كَمَا قَالَ بَعْضُهُمْ مِنْ بَحْرِ الْبَسِيطِ:

فُضْلى النِّسا بِنْتُ عِمْرانَ فَفاطِمَةُ ۞ خَدِيجَةٌ ثُمَّ مَنْ قَدْ بَرَّأَ اللَّهُ

(إِلَّا إِبْرَاهِيْمَ فَمِنْ مَارِيَةَ الْقِبْطِيَّةِ) كَانَتْ سَرِيَّةً لَهُ ﷺ أَهْدَاهَا لَهُ الْمُقَوْقِسُ الْقِبْطِيُّ، وَأَهْــدَى مَعَهَا أُخْتَهَا سِيْرِيْنَ، وَخَصِيًّا يُقَالُ لَـهُ: «مَابُوْرٌ»، وَأَلْفُ مِثْقَالٍ مِنْ ذَهَبٍ، وَعِشْرِيْنَ ثَوْبَةً لَيِّنَةً، وَبَغْلَةً شَــهْبَاءَ - وَهِيَ «دُلْدُلُ» -،

---

292 With (فَسَمَّيْتُهُ): Imām al-Suyūṭī's *Jāmiʿ al-aḥādīth* lists variations of this hadith under number 25309, sourced to Aḥmad, al-Bukhārī, Muslim, Abū Dāwūd, and Ibn Ḥibbān from Anas.

وَحِمَارُ أَشْـهَبُ - وَهُوَ «عُفَيْرٌ»، وَيُقَالُ لَهُ: «يَعْفُورُ» -، وَعَسَلًا مِنْ عَسَلِ بِنْهَا، فَأَعْجَبَ الْعَسَـلُ النَّبِيَّ ﷺ وَدَعَا فِي عَسَـلِ بِنْهَا بِالْبَرَكَةِ. وَكَانَتْ سَرَارِيُهُ أَرْبَعَةً.

‹**All of them are from our lady Khadījah al-Kubrā.**› She was the first woman the Messenger of Allah (may Allah bless him and give him peace) married, and he married no other until after her death. She is considered the best of his wives (may Allah bless him and give him peace), as some have expressed poetically (in the metre of *al-basīṭ*):

> The best women are [Maryam] the daughter of ʿImrān, then
> Fāṭimah, Khadījah, then the one whom Allah declared
> innocent [ʿĀʾishah].[293]

‹**...except for our master Ibrāhīm, who was from Māriyah the Copt**›,[294] a concubine gifted to him (may Allah bless him and give him peace) by al-Muqawqis, the Coptic ruler. Also gifted with her were her sister Sīrīn, a eunuch named Mābūr, one-thousand *mithqāl*s of gold, twenty fine garments, a grey mule named Duldul, a grey donkey named ʿUfayr (or called Yaʿfūr), and some honey from [the village of] Binhā. The Prophet (may Allah bless him and give him peace) liked the honey and supplicated for the blessing of the honey of Binhā.

His concubines were four [in number].[295]

وَقَدْ نَظَمَ بَعْضُهُمْ أَوْلَادَهُ ﷺ عَلَى تَرْتِيبِ الْوِلَادَةِ مِنْ بَحْرِ الطَّوِيلِ فَقَالَ:

وَأَوَّلُ أَوْلَادِ النَّبِـيِّ قَاسِـمُ الرِّضَـى * بِكُنْيَتِـهِ الْمُخْتَارُ فَافْهَـمْ وَحَصِّـلَا

وَزَيْنَـبُ تَتْلُوهُ رُقَيَّـةُ بَعْدَهَـا * وَفَاطِمَةُ الزَّهْرَاءُ جَـاءَتْ عَلَى الْوَلَا

كَـذَا أُمُّ كُلْثُـومٍ تَعُـدُّو بَعْدَهَـا * فِي الْإِسْلَامِ عَبْدُ اللَّهِ جَاءَ مُكَمَّلَا

---

293 al-Bājūrī, *Taḥqīq al-maqām*, 190.

294 Concerning the mothers of his children: al-Bājūrī, *Taḥqīq al-maqām*, 190; *Nūr al-ẓalām*, 121.

295 Māriyah bint Shamʿūn, Rayḥānah bint Shamʿūn, a third given by Zaynab bint Jaḥsh, and a fourth as spoils of war. See al-Qasṭalānī, *Al-Mawāhib al-ladunni-yyah* (Cairo: Al-Maktabah al-Tawfīqiyyah, n.d.), 1:512.

وَكُلُّهُـمْ كَانُـوا لَـهُ مِـنْ خَدِيْجَـةٍ ۞ وَقَـدْ جَـاءَ إِبْرَاهِيْـمُ فِي طَيْبَـةٍ تَلَا

مِـنْ الْمَـرْأَةِ الْحَسْـنَاءِ مَارِبَـةٍ فَقُلْ ۞ عَلَيْهِـمْ سَلَامُ اللَّهِ مِسْكًا وَمَنْدَلَا

Some scholars arranged his children (may Allah bless him and give him peace) according to birth order, in a verse in the metre of *al-ṭawīl*:

> The first of the Prophet's children is Qāsim, the Content; By
>   his *kunya* the Chosen One is known – so understand and
>   grasp this.
> Zaynab followed him, then Ruqayyah after her; Then Fāṭimah
>   al-Zahrā' arrived next in succession.
> Likewise, Umm Kulthūm followed after her[296]; And, in Islam,
>   'Abd Allāh came, completing the number.
> All of them were from Khadījah And later Ibrāhīm came in
>   Ṭaybah (Madīnah),
> Born from the fine woman Māriyah – so say May Allah's peace
>   be upon them, fragranced with musk and sandalwood.[297]

(وَهَـذَا) أَيْ: قَوْلُهُ: «وَيَنْبَغِـي أَنْ يَعْرِفَ»، أَوْ قَوْلُهُ: «خَاتِمَةٌ» إِلَى الْآخَرِ (آخِرُ مَا يَسَّرَهُ اللَّهُ مِنْ فَضْلِهِ وَكَرَمِهِ، وَالْحَمْدُ لِلَّهِ رَبِّ الْعَالَمِيْنَ) أَتَى بِالْحَمْدَلَةِ اقْتِدَاءً بِأَهْلِ الْجَنَّةِ، فَإِنَّ ذَلِكَ آخِرُ دُعَائِهِمْ (وَصَلَّى اللَّهُ عَلَى سَيِّدِنَا مُحَمَّدٍ وَعَلَى آلِهِ وَصَحْبِهِ وَسَلَّمَ) إِنَّمَا عَبَّرَ بِالْمَاضِي إِشَـارَةً تَحَقَّقِ الصَّلَاةِ وَالسَّلَامِ الْمَطْلُوبَيْنِ، وَلَا بُدَّ.

‹This› meaning him saying "It is appropriate to know," or him saying, "Conclusion" until the end ‹is the last of what Allah has fa-

---

296 This hemistich and the prior one are swapped in every other source I have found.

297 The earliest mention I found is in al-Ṣāliḥī al-Shāmī (d. 942AH), *Subul al-hudā wa-l-rashād fī sīrat khayr al-ʿubād* (Beirūt: Dār al-Kutub al-ʿilmiyyah, 1414/1993), 11:17.

cilitated from His bounty and generosity. All praise belongs to Allah, Lord of the worlds.›

He [the author] concluded with praise of Allah following the example of the people of Paradise, whose last supplication is praise. ‹**May Allah bless our master Muḥammad, his family, and companions, and grant them peace.**› He expressed [this supplication] in the past tense, indicating certainty of the requested prayers and blessings being fulfilled, which is inevitable.

CLOSING REMARKS

[الخَاتِمَةُ]

وَهَذَا آخِرُ مَا يَسَّرَهُ اللَّهُ تَعَالَى عَلَى الرِّسَالَةِ اللَّطِيفَةِ الَّتِي لِقَاصِدِيهَا خَفِيفَةٌ، وَلِمُتَعَلِّمِيهَا نَافِعَةٌ، وَاللَّهَ أَسْأَلُ وَبِنَبِيِّهِ أَتَوَسَّـلُ أَنْ يَجْعَلَ هَذِهِ الْكِتَابَةَ خَالِصَةً لِوَجْهِـهِ الْكَرِيـمِ، وَأَنْ يَنْفَعَ بِهَا النَّفْعَ الْعَمِيمَ، وَالْمَرْجُوُّ مِمَّنْ أَطْلَعَ عَلَيْهَا أَنْ يَدْعُوَ لِي بِالْغُفْرَانِ لِلذُّنُوبِ وَالْعِصْيَانَ مِنَ الْمَوْلَى الرَّؤُوفِ الرَّحْمَنِ، وَصَلَّى اللَّهُ عَلَى سَيِّدِ وَلَدِ عَدْنَانَ فِي كُلِّ وَقْتٍ وَأَوَانٍ، وَالْحَمْدُ لِلَّهِ رَبِّ الْعَالَمِينَ، وَلَا حَوْلَ وَلَا قُوَّةَ إِلَّا بِاللَّهِ الْعَلِيِّ الْعَظِيمِ.

This is the conclusion of what Allah (Exalted is He) has facilitated concerning this concise treatise, which is light for those who seek it and beneficial for those who learn it. And I ask Allah, and I entreat through His Prophet, that He make this writing purely for His noble countenance, and that He grant it extensive benefit. Whoever reviews it is kindly requested to supplicate for me to the Compassionate and Merciful Lord for forgiveness from sins and disobedience. May Allah bless the Master of the descendants of ʿAdnān at every moment and time. All praise belongs to Allah, Lord of the Worlds. There is no power nor might except through Allah, the Most High, the Great.

قَالَ الْمُؤَلِّف: وَكَانَ الْفَرَاغُ مِنْ جَمْعِهَا فِي الْيَوْمِ السَّابِعِ مِنْ شَـهْرِ رَبِيعِ الْأَوَّلِ الْمُبَـارَكِ مِنْ شُـهُورِ سَنَةِ ١٢٩٧ مِـنْ الْهِجْرَةِ النَّبَوِيَّـةِ عَلَى صَاحِبِهَا أَفْضَلُ الصَّلَاةِ وَأَتَمُّ التَّحِيَّةَ، وَاللَّهُ أَعْلَمُ.

124

The author said: Its compilation was completed on the seventh day of the month of Rabīʿ al-Awwal of the months of the year 1297 of the prophetic Hijrah [1880 CE] – upon its master be the best prayers and most complete salutations – and Allah knows best. ﷺ

BIBLIOGRAPHY

[المَصادِرُ]

al-ʿAjlūnī, Ismāʿīl bin Muḥammad. *Kashf al-Khafāʾ*. Cairo: Maktabat al-Qudsī, 1351.

al-Anṣārī, Zakariyā. *Asnā al-maṭālib*. Beirut: Al-Maktab al-Islāmī, n.d..

al-Asfahānī, Abū Nuʿaym. *Ḥilyat al-awliyāʾ*. Cairo: Al-Saʿādah, 1974/1394.

al-Ashʿarī, Abū Ḥasan. *Maqālāt al-islāmiyyīn*. n.p.: Al-Maktabah al-ʿAṣriyyah, 1426/2005.

al-ʿAsqalānī, Ibn Ḥajar, and Muḥammad ibn Ismāʿīl al-Bukhārī. *Fatḥ al-Bārī bi sharḥ Ṣaḥīḥ al-Bukhārī*. Edited by Muḥammad Fuʾād ʿAbd al-Bāqī and Muḥibb al-Dīn al-Khaṭīb. Cairo: Maktabat al-Salafiyya, 1390/1970.

———. *Al-Talkhīṣ al-ḥabīr*. Egypt: Muʾassisah Quṭibah, 1995/1416.

Abū Dāwūd, Sulaymān bin al-Ashʿath al-Sajisānī. *Al-Sunan* (“Abū Dāwūd”). Edited by Muḥammad Muḥya al-Dīn ʿAbd al-Ḥamīd. Beirut: Dār al-Fikr, n.d.

Abū Yaʿlā al-Mawṣilī. *Musnad Abī Yaʿlā*. Edited by Ḥusayn Salīm Asad. Damascus: Dār al-Maʾmūn li-l-Turāth, 1984.

al-Bayhaqī, Abū Bakr. *Al-Biʿth wa al-nushūr*. Beirut: Markaz al-Khidamāt wa-l-Abḥāth, 1986/1406.

———. *Dalāʾil al-nabuwwah*. Beirut: Dār al-Kutub al-ʿIlmiyyah, 1405.

———. *Shuʿab al-īmān* (“al-Bayhaqī”). Edited by ʿAbd al-ʿAlī ʿAbd al-Ḥamīd Ḥāmid, et al. Riyadh: Maktabat al-Rushd, 2003/1423.

al-Bājūri, Ibrāhīm. *Tuḥfat al-murīd ʿalā Jawharat al-tawḥīd* (“*Jawharah*”). Edited by Ali Gomaa. Cairo: Dār al-Salām, 2002/1422.

———. *Taḥqīq al-maqām ʿalā Kifāyat al-ʿawāmm* ("*Taḥqīq al-maqām*"). Beirut: Dār al-Kutub al-ʿIlmiyyah, 2007.

al-Bukhārī, Muḥammad bin Ismāʿīl Abū ʿAbd Allāh. *Al-Jāmiʿ al-ṣaḥīḥ al-mukhtaṣar min umūr rasūli Llāh ﷺ wa sunanihi wa ayyāmihi* (*Ṣaḥīḥ al-Bukhārī*) ("al-Bukhārī"). Edited by Muḥammad Zuhayr bin Nāsir al-Nāṣir. n.a.: Dār Tawq al-Najāh, 1422AH.

al-Dhahabī, Shams al-Dīn. *Siyar aʿlām al-nubalāʾ*. Cairo: Dār al-Ḥadīth, 2006/1427.

al-Ghazālī, Abū Ḥāmid. *Iḥyāʾ ʿulūm al-dīn*. Dār al-Maʿrifah, n.d..

al-Ḥākim, Abū ʿAbd Allāh Muḥammad. *Al-Mustadrak ʿala al-Ṣaḥīḥayn* ("al-Ḥākim"). Edited by Muṣṭafā ʿAbd al-Qādir ʿAṭā. Beirut: Dār al-Kutub al-ʿIlmiyyah, 1990/1411.

Ibn ʿAsākir. *Tārīkh Demashq*. Beirut: Dār al-Fikr, 1995/1415.

Ibn Ḥanbal, Aḥmed. *Al-Musnad* ("Aḥmad"). Edited by Shuʿayb al-Arnāʾūṭ, ʿĀdil Murshid, et al. Beirut: Muʾassisah al-Risālah, 2001/1421.

Ibn Ḥibbān, Muḥammad al-Bustī and al-Amīr ʿAlāʾ al-Dīn ʿAlī bin Balbān al-Fārasī. *Al-Iḥsān fī taqrīb Ṣaḥīḥ Ibn Ḥibbān* ("Ibn Ḥibbān"). Edited by Shūʿayb al-Arnāʾūṭ. ʿAmmān: Muʾassisat al-Risālah, 1988/1408.

Ibn Mājah, Abū ʿAbd Allāh Muḥammad bin Yazīd al-Qizwīnī. *Sunan Ibn Mājah* ("Ibn Mājah"). Edited by Muḥammad Fūʾād ʿAbd al-Bāqī. Aleppo: Dār Iḥyāʾ al-Kutub alʿArabiyyah, n.d.

Ibn al-Mulaqqin. *Tuḥfat al-muḥtāj*. Beirut: Al-Maktabah al-Islāmiyyah, 1994.

al-ʿIrāqī, Zayn al-Dāin. *Takhrīj aḥādīth Iḥyāʾ ʿulūm al-dīn*. Beirut: Dār Ibn Ḥazm, 2005/1426.

al-Jāwī, Muḥammad Nawawī al-Jāwī al-Bantanī. *Al-Thimār al-yāniʿ*. Beirut: Dār al-Kutub al-ʿIlmiyyah, 2013/1434.

———. *Tījān al-darārī*. Printed within *Majmūʿ shams rasāʾil fī l-ʿaqāʾid*. Amman: Dār al-nūr al-mubīn, 2013.

Al-Mubārakfurī, ʿAbd al-Raḥmān. *Al-Tuḥfat al-aḥwadhī*. Beirut: Dār al-Kutub al-ʿIlmiyyah, 1353.

Muslim bin al-Ḥajjāj. *Al-Musnad al-ṣaḥīḥ al-mukhtaṣar bi-naql al-ʿadl ʿan al-ʿadl ilā rasūl Allāh* ﷺ ("Muslim"). Edited by Muḥammad Fuʾād ʿAbd al-Bāqī. Beirut: Dār Iḥyāʾ al-Turāth, n.d.

al-Nasāʾī, Abū ʿAbd al-Raḥmān Aḥmed bin Shuʿayb. *Al-Mujtabā* ("al-Nasāʾī"). Edited by ʿAbd al-Fattāḥ Abū Ghuddah, 2nd ed. Aleppo: Maktab al-Maṭbūʿāt al-Islāmiyyah, n.d.

———. *Al-Sunan al-kubrā.* Edited by ʿAbd al-Ghaffār Sulayman al-Bandārī. Beirut: Dār al-Kutub al-ʿIlmiyyah, n.d.

al-Nawawī, Ibrāhīm bin Sharaf. *Kitāb al-adhkār.* Dār Ibn Ḥazm, 2004/1425.

———. *Al-Minhāj sharḥ Ṣaḥīḥ Muslim bin al-Hajjāj.* Beirut: Dār Iḥyāʾ al-Turāth al-ʿArabī, 1392.

———. *Rawḍat al-ṭālibīn.* Beirut: Al-Maktab al-Islāmī, 1991/1412.

ʿAlī al-Qārī, Mullā ʿAlī. *Mirqāt al-mafātīḥ sharḥ Mishkāt al-maṣābīḥ.* Lebanon: Dar al-Fikr, 2002/1422.

al-Qurṭubī, Shams al-Dīn. *Al-Tadhkirah bi aḥwāl al-mawt.* Riyāḍ: Dār al-Minhāj, 1425.

al-Shaʿrānī, ʿAbd al-Wahhāb. *Al-Minaḥ al-saniyyah ʿalā Al-Waṣiyyah al-Maṭbūliyyah.*

al-Shirbīnī, al-Khaṭīb. *Al-Sirāj al-Munīr.* Cairo: Bulāq, 1285.

———. *Mughnī al-muḥtāj.* Beirut: Dār al-Kutub al-ʿIlmiyyah, 1994/1415.

al-Sulamī, Abū ʿAbd al-Raḥmān. *Ṭabaqāt al-ṣūfiyyah.* Beirut: Dār al-Kutub al-ʿIlmiyyah, 1997/1419.

al-Suyūṭī. *Jāmiʿ al-aḥādīth.* Cairo: n.p., 2002/1423.

———. *Jamʿ al-jawāmiʿ.* Cairo: al-Azhar al-Sharīf, 2005/1426.

———. *Al-Jāmiʿ al-ṣaghīr.* N.p: Al-Maktabah al-Shāmilah, n.d.

———. *Al-Tawshīḥ sharḥ Al-Jāmiʿ al-ṣaḥīḥ.* Riyāḍ: Maktabat al-Rusdh, 1998/1419.

al-Ṭabarānī, Sulaymān bin Aḥmed bin Ayyūb bin Muṭīr. *Al-Muʿjam al-kabīr.* Edited by Ḥamdī al-Salafī, 2nd ed. n.a.: Maktabat al-ʿUlūm wa-l-Ḥikam, n.d.

al-Tirmidhī, Muḥammad bin ʿĪsā bin Sawrah bin Mūsā. *Al-Sunan* ("al-Tirmidhī"). Edited by Aḥmed Muḥammad Shākir, et al,

2nd edition. Cairo: Sharikah Maktabah wa Maṭbaʿah Muṣṭafā
al-Bābī al-Ḥalabī, 1975/1395.
al-ʿUqaylī, Abū Jaf'ar. *Al-Ḍuʿafāʾ al-kabīr.* Beirut: Dār al-Kutub al-ʿIlmiyyah, 1984/1404.

DETAILED TABLE OF CONTENTS

المُحْتَوَيَاتُ المفصلة

Also from Islamosaic

Ark of Salvation

Connecting to the Quran

Etiquette with the Quran

Infamies of the Soul

Hadith Nomenclature Primers

Hanbali Acts of Worship

Ibn Juzay's Sufic Exegesis

Sharḥ Al-Waraqāt

Shaykh al-Sulamī's Waṣiyyah

The Accessible Conspectus

The Correct Approach to 'Unpacking The Select Creed'

The Encompassing Epistle

The Evident Memorandum

The Ladder to Success in Truly Loving Allah Paperback

The Ultimate Conspectus